C-4056

CAREER EXAMINATION SERIES

THIS IS YOUR **PASSBOOK**® FOR ...

SCHOOL BUS DRIVER

NLC®

NATIONAL LEARNING CORPORATION®

passbooks.com

NLC®

National Learning Corporation

212 Michael Drive, Syosset, NY 11791
(516) 921-8888 • www.passbooks.com
E-mail: info@passbooks.com

PUBLISHED IN THE UNITED STATES OF AMERICA

PASSBOOK® SERIES

THE *PASSBOOK® SERIES* has been created to prepare applicants and candidates for the ultimate academic battlefield – the examination room.

At some time in our lives, each and every one of us may be required to take an examination – for validation, matriculation, admission, qualification, registration, certification, or licensure.

Based on the assumption that every applicant or candidate has met the basic formal educational standards, has taken the required number of courses, and read the necessary texts, the *PASSBOOK® SERIES* furnishes the one special preparation which may assure passing with confidence, instead of failing with insecurity. Examination questions – together with answers – are furnished as the basic vehicle for study so that the mysteries of the examination and its compounding difficulties may be eliminated or diminished by a sure method.

This book is meant to help you pass your examination provided that you qualify and are serious in your objective.

The entire field is reviewed through the huge store of content information which is succinctly presented through a provocative and challenging approach – the question-and-answer method.

A climate of success is established by furnishing the correct answers at the end of each test.

You soon learn to recognize types of questions, forms of questions, and patterns of questioning. You may even begin to anticipate expected outcomes.

You perceive that many questions are repeated or adapted so that you can gain acute insights, which may enable you to score many sure points.

You learn how to confront new questions, or types of questions, and to attack them confidently and work out the correct answers.

You note objectives and emphases, and recognize pitfalls and dangers, so that you may make positive educational adjustments.

Moreover, you are kept fully informed in relation to new concepts, methods, practices, and directions in the field.

You discover that you arre actually taking the examination all the time: you are preparing for the examination by "taking" an examination, not by reading extraneous and/or supererogatory textbooks.

In short, this PASSBOOK®, used directedly, should be an important factor in helping you to pass your test.

SCHOOL BUS DRIVER

DUTIES

Drives a school bus in accordance with state law and rules and regulations of the school district. Cares for passengers' safety. Makes proper reports regarding accidents, inoperative or faulty equipment and unusual occurrences. Cares for and protects the assigned vehicle. Performs related duties.

SCOPE OF THE EXAMINATION

The written test will be of the multiple-choice type and may include questions on: awareness of proper work attitudes, courtesy, responsibilities in dealing with children and general responsibilities in handling school property; ability to read and interpret instructions and bulletins on transit operations and rules and regulations; awareness of safety and defensive driving concepts in transit operations; ability to read and interpret basic schedules; ability to read and interpret route maps and to select proper transfer points and best route; arithmetic; and other areas related to the transportation of children to and from school and activities.

HOW TO TAKE A TEST

I. YOU MUST PASS AN EXAMINATION

A. WHAT EVERY CANDIDATE SHOULD KNOW

Examination applicants often ask us for help in preparing for the written test. What can I study in advance? What kinds of questions will be asked? How will the test be given? How will the papers be graded?

As an applicant for a civil service examination, you may be wondering about some of these things. Our purpose here is to suggest effective methods of advance study and to describe civil service examinations.

Your chances for success on this examination can be increased if you know how to prepare. Those "pre-examination jitters" can be reduced if you know what to expect. You can even experience an adventure in good citizenship if you know why civil service exams are given.

B. WHY ARE CIVIL SERVICE EXAMINATIONS GIVEN?

Civil service examinations are important to you in two ways. As a citizen, you want public jobs filled by employees who know how to do their work. As a job seeker, you want a fair chance to compete for that job on an equal footing with other candidates. The best-known means of accomplishing this two-fold goal is the competitive examination.

Exams are widely publicized throughout the nation. They may be administered for jobs in federal, state, city, municipal, town or village governments or agencies.

Any citizen may apply, with some limitations, such as the age or residence of applicants. Your experience and education may be reviewed to see whether you meet the requirements for the particular examination. When these requirements exist, they are reasonable and applied consistently to all applicants. Thus, a competitive examination may cause you some uneasiness now, but it is your privilege and safeguard.

C. HOW ARE CIVIL SERVICE EXAMS DEVELOPED?

Examinations are carefully written by trained technicians who are specialists in the field known as "psychological measurement," in consultation with recognized authorities in the field of work that the test will cover. These experts recommend the subject matter areas or skills to be tested; only those knowledges or skills important to your success on the job are included. The most reliable books and source materials available are used as references. Together, the experts and technicians judge the difficulty level of the questions.

Test technicians know how to phrase questions so that the problem is clearly stated. Their ethics do not permit "trick" or "catch" questions. Questions may have been tried out on sample groups, or subjected to statistical analysis, to determine their usefulness.

Written tests are often used in combination with performance tests, ratings of training and experience, and oral interviews. All of these measures combine to form the best-known means of finding the right person for the right job.

II. HOW TO PASS THE WRITTEN TEST

A. NATURE OF THE EXAMINATION

To prepare intelligently for civil service examinations, you should know how they differ from school examinations you have taken. In school you were assigned certain definite pages to read or subjects to cover. The examination questions were quite detailed and usually emphasized memory. Civil service exams, on the other hand, try to discover your present ability to perform the duties of a position, plus your potentiality to learn these duties. In other words, a civil service exam attempts to predict how successful you will be. Questions cover such a broad area that they cannot be as minute and detailed as school exam questions.

In the public service similar kinds of work, or positions, are grouped together in one "class." This process is known as *position-classification*. All the positions in a class are paid according to the salary range for that class. One class title covers all of these positions, and they are all tested by the same examination.

B. FOUR BASIC STEPS

1) Study the announcement

How, then, can you know what subjects to study? Our best answer is: "Learn as much as possible about the class of positions for which you've applied." The exam will test the knowledge, skills and abilities needed to do the work.

Your most valuable source of information about the position you want is the official exam announcement. This announcement lists the training and experience qualifications. Check these standards and apply only if you come reasonably close to meeting them.

The brief description of the position in the examination announcement offers some clues to the subjects which will be tested. Think about the job itself. Review the duties in your mind. Can you perform them, or are there some in which you are rusty? Fill in the blank spots in your preparation.

Many jurisdictions preview the written test in the exam announcement by including a section called "Knowledge and Abilities Required," "Scope of the Examination," or some similar heading. Here you will find out specifically what fields will be tested.

2) Review your own background

Once you learn in general what the position is all about, and what you need to know to do the work, ask yourself which subjects you already know fairly well and which need improvement. You may wonder whether to concentrate on improving your strong areas or on building some background in your fields of weakness. When the announcement has specified "some knowledge" or "considerable knowledge," or has used adjectives like "beginning principles of..." or "advanced ... methods," you can get a clue as to the number and difficulty of questions to be asked in any given field. More questions, and hence broader coverage, would be included for those subjects which are more important in the work. Now weigh your strengths and weaknesses against the job requirements and prepare accordingly.

3) Determine the level of the position

Another way to tell how intensively you should prepare is to understand the level of the job for which you are applying. Is it the entering level? In other words, is this the position in which beginners in a field of work are hired? Or is it an intermediate or advanced level? Sometimes this is indicated by such words as "Junior" or "Senior" in the class title. Other jurisdictions use Roman numerals to designate the level – Clerk I, Clerk II, for example. The word "Supervisor" sometimes appears in the title. If the level is not indicated by the title, check the description of duties. Will you be working under very close supervision, or will you have responsibility for independent decisions in this work?

4) Choose appropriate study materials

Now that you know the subjects to be examined and the relative amount of each subject to be covered, you can choose suitable study materials. For beginning level jobs, or even advanced ones, if you have a pronounced weakness in some aspect of your training, read a modern, standard textbook in that field. Be sure it is up to date and has general coverage. Such books are normally available at your library, and the librarian will be glad to help you locate one. For entry-level positions, questions of appropriate difficulty are chosen – neither highly advanced questions, nor those too simple. Such questions require careful thought but not advanced training.

If the position for which you are applying is technical or advanced, you will read more advanced, specialized material. If you are already familiar with the basic principles of your field, elementary textbooks would waste your time. Concentrate on advanced textbooks and technical periodicals. Think through the concepts and review difficult problems in your field.

These are all general sources. You can get more ideas on your own initiative, following these leads. For example, training manuals and publications of the government agency which employs workers in your field can be useful, particularly for technical and professional positions. A letter or visit to the government department involved may result in more specific study suggestions, and certainly will provide you with a more definite idea of the exact nature of the position you are seeking.

III. KINDS OF TESTS

Tests are used for purposes other than measuring knowledge and ability to perform specified duties. For some positions, it is equally important to test ability to make adjustments to new situations or to profit from training. In others, basic mental abilities not dependent on information are essential. Questions which test these things may not appear as pertinent to the duties of the position as those which test for knowledge and information. Yet they are often highly important parts of a fair examination. For very general questions, it is almost impossible to help you direct your study efforts. What we can do is to point out some of the more common of these general abilities needed in public service positions and describe some typical questions.

1) General information

Broad, general information has been found useful for predicting job success in some kinds of work. This is tested in a variety of ways, from vocabulary lists to questions about current events. Basic background in some field of work, such as sociology or economics, may be sampled in a group of questions. Often these are principles which have become familiar to most persons through exposure rather than through formal training. It is difficult to advise you how to study for these questions; being alert to the world around you is our best suggestion.

2) Verbal ability

An example of an ability needed in many positions is verbal or language ability. Verbal ability is, in brief, the ability to use and understand words. Vocabulary and grammar tests are typical measures of this ability. Reading comprehension or paragraph interpretation questions are common in many kinds of civil service tests. You are given a paragraph of written material and asked to find its central meaning.

3) Numerical ability

Number skills can be tested by the familiar arithmetic problem, by checking paired lists of numbers to see which are alike and which are different, or by interpreting charts and graphs. In the latter test, a graph may be printed in the test booklet which you are asked to use as the basis for answering questions.

4) Observation

A popular test for law-enforcement positions is the observation test. A picture is shown to you for several minutes, then taken away. Questions about the picture test your ability to observe both details and larger elements.

5) Following directions

In many positions in the public service, the employee must be able to carry out written instructions dependably and accurately. You may be given a chart with several columns, each column listing a variety of information. The questions require you to carry out directions involving the information given in the chart.

6) Skills and aptitudes

Performance tests effectively measure some manual skills and aptitudes. When the skill is one in which you are trained, such as typing or shorthand, you can practice. These tests are often very much like those given in business school or high school courses. For many of the other skills and aptitudes, however, no short-time preparation can be made. Skills and abilities natural to you or that you have developed throughout your lifetime are being tested.

Many of the general questions just described provide all the data needed to answer the questions and ask you to use your reasoning ability to find the answers. Your best preparation for these tests, as well as for tests of facts and ideas, is to be at your physical and mental best. You, no doubt, have your own methods of getting into an exam-taking mood and keeping "in shape." The next section lists some ideas on this subject.

IV. KINDS OF QUESTIONS

Only rarely is the "essay" question, which you answer in narrative form, used in civil service tests. Civil service tests are usually of the short-answer type. Full instructions for answering these questions will be given to you at the examination. But in case this is your first experience with short-answer questions and separate answer sheets, here is what you need to know:

1) Multiple-choice Questions

Most popular of the short-answer questions is the "multiple choice" or "best answer" question. It can be used, for example, to test for factual knowledge, ability to solve problems or judgment in meeting situations found at work.

A multiple-choice question is normally one of three types—

- It can begin with an incomplete statement followed by several possible endings. You are to find the one ending which *best* completes the statement, although some of the others may not be entirely wrong.
- It can also be a complete statement in the form of a question which is answered by choosing one of the statements listed.
- It can be in the form of a problem – again you select the best answer.

Here is an example of a multiple-choice question with a discussion which should give you some clues as to the method for choosing the right answer:

When an employee has a complaint about his assignment, the action which will *best* help him overcome his difficulty is to

A. discuss his difficulty with his coworkers
B. take the problem to the head of the organization
C. take the problem to the person who gave him the assignment
D. say nothing to anyone about his complaint

In answering this question, you should study each of the choices to find which is best. Consider choice "A" – Certainly an employee may discuss his complaint with fellow employees, but no change or improvement can result, and the complaint remains unresolved. Choice "B" is a poor choice since the head of the organization probably does not know what assignment you have been given, and taking your problem to him is known as "going over the head" of the supervisor. The supervisor, or person who made the assignment, is the person who can clarify it or correct any injustice. Choice "C" is, therefore, correct. To say nothing, as in choice "D," is unwise. Supervisors have and interest in knowing the problems employees are facing, and the employee is seeking a solution to his problem.

2) True/False Questions

The "true/false" or "right/wrong" form of question is sometimes used. Here a complete statement is given. Your job is to decide whether the statement is right or wrong.

SAMPLE: A roaming cell-phone call to a nearby city costs less than a non-roaming call to a distant city.

This statement is wrong, or false, since roaming calls are more expensive.

This is not a complete list of all possible question forms, although most of the others are variations of these common types. You will always get complete directions for answering questions. Be sure you understand *how* to mark your answers – ask questions until you do.

V. RECORDING YOUR ANSWERS

Computer terminals are used more and more today for many different kinds of exams.

For an examination with very few applicants, you may be told to record your answers in the test booklet itself. Separate answer sheets are much more common. If this separate answer sheet is to be scored by machine – and this is often the case – it is highly important that you mark your answers correctly in order to get credit.

An electronic scoring machine is often used in civil service offices because of the speed with which papers can be scored. Machine-scored answer sheets must be marked with a pencil, which will be given to you. This pencil has a high graphite content which responds to the electronic scoring machine. As a matter of fact, stray dots may register as answers, so do not let your pencil rest on the answer sheet while you are pondering the correct answer. Also, if your pencil lead breaks or is otherwise defective, ask for another.

Since the answer sheet will be dropped in a slot in the scoring machine, be careful not to bend the corners or get the paper crumpled.

The answer sheet normally has five vertical columns of numbers, with 30 numbers to a column. These numbers correspond to the question numbers in your test booklet. After each number, going across the page are four or five pairs of dotted lines. These short dotted lines have small letters or numbers above them. The first two pairs may also have a "T" or "F" above the letters. This indicates that the first two pairs only are to be used if the questions are of the true-false type. If the questions are multiple choice, disregard the "T" and "F" and pay attention only to the small letters or numbers.

Answer your questions in the manner of the sample that follows:

32. The largest city in the United States is
    - A. Washington, D.C.
    - B. New York City
    - C. Chicago
    - D. Detroit
    - E. San Francisco

1) Choose the answer you think is best. (New York City is the largest, so "B" is correct.)
2) Find the row of dotted lines numbered the same as the question you are answering. (Find row number 32)
3) Find the pair of dotted lines corresponding to the answer. (Find the pair of lines under the mark "B.")
4) Make a solid black mark between the dotted lines.

VI. BEFORE THE TEST

Common sense will help you find procedures to follow to get ready for an examination. Too many of us, however, overlook these sensible measures. Indeed, nervousness and fatigue have been found to be the most serious reasons why applicants fail to do their best on civil service tests. Here is a list of reminders:

- Begin your preparation early – Don't wait until the last minute to go scurrying around for books and materials or to find out what the position is all about.
- Prepare continuously – An hour a night for a week is better than an all-night cram session. This has been definitely established. What is more, a night a week for a month will return better dividends than crowding your study into a shorter period of time.
- Locate the place of the exam – You have been sent a notice telling you when and where to report for the examination. If the location is in a different town or otherwise unfamiliar to you, it would be well to inquire the best route and learn something about the building.
- Relax the night before the test – Allow your mind to rest. Do not study at all that night. Plan some mild recreation or diversion; then go to bed early and get a good night's sleep.
- Get up early enough to make a leisurely trip to the place for the test – This way unforeseen events, traffic snarls, unfamiliar buildings, etc. will not upset you.
- Dress comfortably – A written test is not a fashion show. You will be known by number and not by name, so wear something comfortable.
- Leave excess paraphernalia at home – Shopping bags and odd bundles will get in your way. You need bring only the items mentioned in the official notice you received; usually everything you need is provided. Do not bring reference books to the exam. They will only confuse those last minutes and be taken away from you when in the test room.
- Arrive somewhat ahead of time – If because of transportation schedules you must get there very early, bring a newspaper or magazine to take your mind off yourself while waiting.
- Locate the examination room – When you have found the proper room, you will be directed to the seat or part of the room where you will sit. Sometimes you are given a sheet of instructions to read while you are waiting. Do not fill out any forms until you are told to do so; just read them and be prepared.
- Relax and prepare to listen to the instructions
- If you have any physical problem that may keep you from doing your best, be sure to tell the test administrator. If you are sick or in poor health, you really cannot do your best on the exam. You can come back and take the test some other time.

VII. AT THE TEST

The day of the test is here and you have the test booklet in your hand. The temptation to get going is very strong. Caution! There is more to success than knowing the right answers. You must know how to identify your papers and understand variations in the type of short-answer question used in this particular examination. Follow these suggestions for maximum results from your efforts:

1) Cooperate with the monitor

The test administrator has a duty to create a situation in which you can be as much at ease as possible. He will give instructions, tell you when to begin, check to see that you are marking your answer sheet correctly, and so on. He is not there to guard you, although he will see that your competitors do not take unfair advantage. He wants to help you do your best.

2) Listen to all instructions

Don't jump the gun! Wait until you understand all directions. In most civil service tests you get more time than you need to answer the questions. So don't be in a hurry. Read each word of instructions until you clearly understand the meaning. Study the examples, listen to all announcements and follow directions. Ask questions if you do not understand what to do.

3) Identify your papers

Civil service exams are usually identified by number only. You will be assigned a number; you must not put your name on your test papers. Be sure to copy your number correctly. Since more than one exam may be given, copy your exact examination title.

4) Plan your time

Unless you are told that a test is a "speed" or "rate of work" test, speed itself is usually not important. Time enough to answer all the questions will be provided, but this does not mean that you have all day. An overall time limit has been set. Divide the total time (in minutes) by the number of questions to determine the approximate time you have for each question.

5) Do not linger over difficult questions

If you come across a difficult question, mark it with a paper clip (useful to have along) and come back to it when you have been through the booklet. One caution if you do this – be sure to skip a number on your answer sheet as well. Check often to be sure that you have not lost your place and that you are marking in the row numbered the same as the question you are answering.

6) Read the questions

Be sure you know what the question asks! Many capable people are unsuccessful because they failed to *read* the questions correctly.

7) Answer all questions

Unless you have been instructed that a penalty will be deducted for incorrect answers, it is better to guess than to omit a question.

8) Speed tests

It is often better NOT to guess on speed tests. It has been found that on timed tests people are tempted to spend the last few seconds before time is called in marking answers at random – without even reading them – in the hope of picking up a few extra points. To discourage this practice, the instructions may warn you that your score will be "corrected" for guessing. That is, a penalty will be applied. The incorrect answers will be deducted from the correct ones, or some other penalty formula will be used.

9) Review your answers

If you finish before time is called, go back to the questions you guessed or omitted to give them further thought. Review other answers if you have time.

10) Return your test materials

If you are ready to leave before others have finished or time is called, take ALL your materials to the monitor and leave quietly. Never take any test material with you. The monitor can discover whose papers are not complete, and taking a test booklet may be grounds for disqualification.

VIII. EXAMINATION TECHNIQUES

1) Read the general instructions carefully. These are usually printed on the first page of the exam booklet. As a rule, these instructions refer to the timing of the examination; the fact that you should not start work until the signal and must stop work at a signal, etc. If there are any *special* instructions, such as a choice of questions to be answered, make sure that you note this instruction carefully.

2) When you are ready to start work on the examination, that is as soon as the signal has been given, read the instructions to each question booklet, underline any key words or phrases, such as *least*, *best*, *outline*, *describe* and the like. In this way you will tend to answer as requested rather than discover on reviewing your paper that you *listed without describing*, that you selected the *worst* choice rather than the *best* choice, etc.

3) If the examination is of the objective or multiple-choice type – that is, each question will also give a series of possible answers: A, B, C or D, and you are called upon to select the best answer and write the letter next to that answer on your answer paper – it is advisable to start answering each question in turn. There may be anywhere from 50 to 100 such questions in the three or four hours allotted and you can see how much time would be taken if you read through all the questions before beginning to answer any. Furthermore, if you come across a question or group of questions which you know would be difficult to answer, it would undoubtedly affect your handling of all the other questions.

4) If the examination is of the essay type and contains but a few questions, it is a moot point as to whether you should read all the questions before starting to answer any one. Of course, if you are given a choice – say five out of seven and the like – then it is essential to read all the questions so you can eliminate the two that are most difficult. If, however, you are asked to answer all the questions, there may be danger in trying to answer the easiest one first because you may find that you will spend too much time on it. The best technique is to answer the first question, then proceed to the second, etc.

5) Time your answers. Before the exam begins, write down the time it started, then add the time allowed for the examination and write down the time it must be completed, then divide the time available somewhat as follows:

- If 3-1/2 hours are allowed, that would be 210 minutes. If you have 80 objective-type questions, that would be an average of 2-1/2 minutes per question. Allow yourself no more than 2 minutes per question, or a total of 160 minutes, which will permit about 50 minutes to review.
- If for the time allotment of 210 minutes there are 7 essay questions to answer, that would average about 30 minutes a question. Give yourself only 25 minutes per question so that you have about 35 minutes to review.

6) The most important instruction is to *read each question* and make sure you know what is wanted. The second most important instruction is to *time yourself properly* so that you answer every question. The third most important instruction is to *answer every question*. Guess if you have to but include something for each question. Remember that you will receive no credit for a blank and will probably receive some credit if you write something in answer to an essay question. If you guess a letter – say "B" for a multiple-choice question – you may have guessed right. If you leave a blank as an answer to a multiple-choice question, the examiners may respect your feelings but it will not add a point to your score. Some exams may penalize you for wrong answers, so in such cases *only*, you may not want to guess unless you have some basis for your answer.

7) Suggestions
   a. Objective-type questions
      1. Examine the question booklet for proper sequence of pages and questions
      2. Read all instructions carefully
      3. Skip any question which seems too difficult; return to it after all other questions have been answered
      4. Apportion your time properly; do not spend too much time on any single question or group of questions
      5. Note and underline key words – *all, most, fewest, least, best, worst, same, opposite,* etc.
      6. Pay particular attention to negatives
      7. Note unusual option, e.g., unduly long, short, complex, different or similar in content to the body of the question
      8. Observe the use of "hedging" words – *probably, may, most likely,* etc.
      9. Make sure that your answer is put next to the same number as the question
      10. Do not second-guess unless you have good reason to believe the second answer is definitely more correct
      11. Cross out original answer if you decide another answer is more accurate; do not erase until you are ready to hand your paper in
      12. Answer all questions; guess unless instructed otherwise
      13. Leave time for review

   b. Essay questions
      1. Read each question carefully
      2. Determine exactly what is wanted. Underline key words or phrases.
      3. Decide on outline or paragraph answer

4. Include many different points and elements unless asked to develop any one or two points or elements
5. Show impartiality by giving pros and cons unless directed to select one side only
6. Make and write down any assumptions you find necessary to answer the questions
7. Watch your English, grammar, punctuation and choice of words
8. Time your answers; don't crowd material

8) Answering the essay question

Most essay questions can be answered by framing the specific response around several key words or ideas. Here are a few such key words or ideas:

M's: manpower, materials, methods, money, management
P's: purpose, program, policy, plan, procedure, practice, problems, pitfalls, personnel, public relations

a. Six basic steps in handling problems:
   1. Preliminary plan and background development
   2. Collect information, data and facts
   3. Analyze and interpret information, data and facts
   4. Analyze and develop solutions as well as make recommendations
   5. Prepare report and sell recommendations
   6. Install recommendations and follow up effectiveness

b. Pitfalls to avoid
   1. *Taking things for granted* – A statement of the situation does not necessarily imply that each of the elements is necessarily true; for example, a complaint may be invalid and biased so that all that can be taken for granted is that a complaint has been registered
   2. *Considering only one side of a situation* – Wherever possible, indicate several alternatives and then point out the reasons you selected the best one
   3. *Failing to indicate follow up* – Whenever your answer indicates action on your part, make certain that you will take proper follow-up action to see how successful your recommendations, procedures or actions turn out to be
   4. *Taking too long in answering any single question* – Remember to time your answers properly

IX. AFTER THE TEST

Scoring procedures differ in detail among civil service jurisdictions although the general principles are the same. Whether the papers are hand-scored or graded by machine we have described, they are nearly always graded by number. That is, the person who marks the paper knows only the number – never the name – of the applicant. Not until all the papers have been graded will they be matched with names. If other tests, such as training and experience or oral interview ratings have been given, scores will be combined. Different parts of the examination usually have different weights. For example, the written test might count 60 percent of the final grade, and a rating of training and experience 40 percent. In many jurisdictions, veterans will have a certain number of points added to their grades.

After the final grade has been determined, the names are placed in grade order and an eligible list is established. There are various methods for resolving ties between those who get the same final grade – probably the most common is to place first the name of the person whose application was received first. Job offers are made from the eligible list in the order the names appear on it. You will be notified of your grade and your rank as soon as all these computations have been made. This will be done as rapidly as possible.

People who are found to meet the requirements in the announcement are called "eligibles." Their names are put on a list of eligible candidates. An eligible's chances of getting a job depend on how high he stands on this list and how fast agencies are filling jobs from the list.

When a job is to be filled from a list of eligibles, the agency asks for the names of people on the list of eligibles for that job. When the civil service commission receives this request, it sends to the agency the names of the three people highest on this list. Or, if the job to be filled has specialized requirements, the office sends the agency the names of the top three persons who meet these requirements from the general list.

The appointing officer makes a choice from among the three people whose names were sent to him. If the selected person accepts the appointment, the names of the others are put back on the list to be considered for future openings.

That is the rule in hiring from all kinds of eligible lists, whether they are for typist, carpenter, chemist, or something else. For every vacancy, the appointing officer has his choice of any one of the top three eligibles on the list. This explains why the person whose name is on top of the list sometimes does not get an appointment when some of the persons lower on the list do. If the appointing officer chooses the second or third eligible, the No. 1 eligible does not get a job at once, but stays on the list until he is appointed or the list is terminated.

X. HOW TO PASS THE INTERVIEW TEST

The examination for which you applied requires an oral interview test. You have already taken the written test and you are now being called for the interview test – the final part of the formal examination.

You may think that it is not possible to prepare for an interview test and that there are no procedures to follow during an interview. Our purpose is to point out some things you can do in advance that will help you and some good rules to follow and pitfalls to avoid while you are being interviewed.

What is an interview supposed to test?

The written examination is designed to test the technical knowledge and competence of the candidate; the oral is designed to evaluate intangible qualities, not readily measured otherwise, and to establish a list showing the relative fitness of each candidate – as measured against his competitors – for the position sought. Scoring is not on the basis of "right" and "wrong," but on a sliding scale of values ranging from "not passable" to "outstanding." As a matter of fact, it is possible to achieve a relatively low score without a single "incorrect" answer because of evident weakness in the qualities being measured.

Occasionally, an examination may consist entirely of an oral test – either an individual or a group oral. In such cases, information is sought concerning the technical knowledges and abilities of the candidate, since there has been no written examination for this purpose. More commonly, however, an oral test is used to supplement a written examination.

Who conducts interviews?

The composition of oral boards varies among different jurisdictions. In nearly all, a representative of the personnel department serves as chairman. One of the members of the board may be a representative of the department in which the candidate would work. In some cases, "outside experts" are used, and, frequently, a businessman or some other representative of the general public is asked to serve. Labor and management or other special groups may be represented. The aim is to secure the services of experts in the appropriate field.

However the board is composed, it is a good idea (and not at all improper or unethical) to ascertain in advance of the interview who the members are and what groups they represent. When you are introduced to them, you will have some idea of their backgrounds and interests, and at least you will not stutter and stammer over their names.

What should be done before the interview?

While knowledge about the board members is useful and takes some of the surprise element out of the interview, there is other preparation which is more substantive. It *is* possible to prepare for an oral interview – in several ways:

1) Keep a copy of your application and review it carefully before the interview

This may be the only document before the oral board, and the starting point of the interview. Know what education and experience you have listed there, and the sequence and dates of all of it. Sometimes the board will ask you to review the highlights of your experience for them; you should not have to hem and haw doing it.

2) Study the class specification and the examination announcement

Usually, the oral board has one or both of these to guide them. The qualities, characteristics or knowledges required by the position sought are stated in these documents. They offer valuable clues as to the nature of the oral interview. For example, if the job involves supervisory responsibilities, the announcement will usually indicate that knowledge of modern supervisory methods and the qualifications of the candidate as a supervisor will be tested. If so, you can expect such questions, frequently in the form of a hypothetical situation which you are expected to solve. NEVER go into an oral without knowledge of the duties and responsibilities of the job you seek.

3) Think through each qualification required

Try to visualize the kind of questions you would ask if you were a board member. How well could you answer them? Try especially to appraise your own knowledge and background in each area, *measured against the job sought*, and identify any areas in which you are weak. Be critical and realistic – do not flatter yourself.

4) Do some general reading in areas in which you feel you may be weak

For example, if the job involves supervision and your past experience has NOT, some general reading in supervisory methods and practices, particularly in the field of human relations, might be useful. Do NOT study agency procedures or detailed manuals. The oral board will be testing your understanding and capacity, not your memory.

5) Get a good night's sleep and watch your general health and mental attitude

You will want a clear head at the interview. Take care of a cold or any other minor ailment, and of course, no hangovers.

What should be done on the day of the interview?

Now comes the day of the interview itself. Give yourself plenty of time to get there. Plan to arrive somewhat ahead of the scheduled time, particularly if your appointment is in the fore part of the day. If a previous candidate fails to appear, the board might be ready for you a bit early. By early afternoon an oral board is almost invariably behind schedule if there are many candidates, and you may have to wait. Take along a book or magazine to read, or your application to review, but leave any extraneous material in the waiting room when you go in for your interview. In any event, relax and compose yourself.

The matter of dress is important. The board is forming impressions about you – from your experience, your manners, your attitude, and your appearance. Give your personal appearance careful attention. Dress your best, but not your flashiest. Choose conservative, appropriate clothing, and be sure it is immaculate. This is a business interview, and your appearance should indicate that you regard it as such. Besides, being well groomed and properly dressed will help boost your confidence.

Sooner or later, someone will call your name and escort you into the interview room. *This is it.* From here on you are on your own. It is too late for any more preparation. But remember, you asked for this opportunity to prove your fitness, and you are here because your request was granted.

What happens when you go in?

The usual sequence of events will be as follows: The clerk (who is often the board stenographer) will introduce you to the chairman of the oral board, who will introduce you to the other members of the board. Acknowledge the introductions before you sit down. Do not be surprised if you find a microphone facing you or a stenotypist sitting by. Oral interviews are usually recorded in the event of an appeal or other review.

Usually the chairman of the board will open the interview by reviewing the highlights of your education and work experience from your application – primarily for the benefit of the other members of the board, as well as to get the material into the record. Do not interrupt or comment unless there is an error or significant misinterpretation; if that is the case, do not hesitate. But do not quibble about insignificant matters. Also, he will usually ask you some question about your education, experience or your present job – partly to get you to start talking and to establish the interviewing "rapport." He may start the actual questioning, or turn it over to one of the other members. Frequently, each member undertakes the questioning on a particular area, one in which he is perhaps most competent, so you can expect each member to participate in the examination. Because time is limited, you may also expect some rather abrupt switches in the direction the questioning takes, so do not be upset by it. Normally, a board member will not pursue a single line of questioning unless he discovers a particular strength or weakness.

After each member has participated, the chairman will usually ask whether any member has any further questions, then will ask you if you have anything you wish to add. Unless you are expecting this question, it may floor you. Worse, it may start you off on an extended, extemporaneous speech. The board is not usually seeking more information. The question is principally to offer you a last opportunity to present further qualifications or to indicate that you have nothing to add. So, if you feel that a significant qualification or characteristic has been overlooked, it is proper to point it out in a sentence or so. Do not compliment the board on the thoroughness of their examination – they have been sketchy, and you know it. If you wish, merely say, "No thank you, I have nothing further to add." This is a point where you can "talk yourself out" of a good impression or fail to present an important bit of information. Remember, *you close the interview yourself.*

The chairman will then say, "That is all, Mr. ______, thank you." Do not be startled; the interview is over, and quicker than you think. Thank him, gather your belongings and take your leave. Save your sigh of relief for the other side of the door.

How to put your best foot forward

Throughout this entire process, you may feel that the board individually and collectively is trying to pierce your defenses, seek out your hidden weaknesses and embarrass and confuse you. Actually, this is not true. They are obliged to make an appraisal of your qualifications for the job you are seeking, and they want to see you in your best light. Remember, they must interview all candidates and a non-cooperative candidate may become a failure in spite of their best efforts to bring out his qualifications. Here are 15 suggestions that will help you:

1) Be natural – Keep your attitude confident, not cocky

If you are not confident that you can do the job, do not expect the board to be. Do not apologize for your weaknesses, try to bring out your strong points. The board is interested in a positive, not negative, presentation. Cockiness will antagonize any board member and make him wonder if you are covering up a weakness by a false show of strength.

2) Get comfortable, but don't lounge or sprawl

Sit erectly but not stiffly. A careless posture may lead the board to conclude that you are careless in other things, or at least that you are not impressed by the importance of the occasion. Either conclusion is natural, even if incorrect. Do not fuss with your clothing, a pencil or an ashtray. Your hands may occasionally be useful to emphasize a point; do not let them become a point of distraction.

3) Do not wisecrack or make small talk

This is a serious situation, and your attitude should show that you consider it as such. Further, the time of the board is limited – they do not want to waste it, and neither should you.

4) Do not exaggerate your experience or abilities

In the first place, from information in the application or other interviews and sources, the board may know more about you than you think. Secondly, you probably will not get away with it. An experienced board is rather adept at spotting such a situation, so do not take the chance.

5) If you know a board member, do not make a point of it, yet do not hide it

Certainly you are not fooling him, and probably not the other members of the board. Do not try to take advantage of your acquaintanceship – it will probably do you little good.

6) Do not dominate the interview

Let the board do that. They will give you the clues – do not assume that you have to do all the talking. Realize that the board has a number of questions to ask you, and do not try to take up all the interview time by showing off your extensive knowledge of the answer to the first one.

7) Be attentive

You only have 20 minutes or so, and you should keep your attention at its sharpest throughout. When a member is addressing a problem or question to you, give him your undivided attention. Address your reply principally to him, but do not exclude the other board members.

8) Do not interrupt

A board member may be stating a problem for you to analyze. He will ask you a question when the time comes. Let him state the problem, and wait for the question.

9) Make sure you understand the question

Do not try to answer until you are sure what the question is. If it is not clear, restate it in your own words or ask the board member to clarify it for you. However, do not haggle about minor elements.

10) Reply promptly but not hastily

A common entry on oral board rating sheets is "candidate responded readily," or "candidate hesitated in replies." Respond as promptly and quickly as you can, but do not jump to a hasty, ill-considered answer.

11) Do not be peremptory in your answers

A brief answer is proper – but do not fire your answer back. That is a losing game from your point of view. The board member can probably ask questions much faster than you can answer them.

12) Do not try to create the answer you think the board member wants

He is interested in what kind of mind you have and how it works – not in playing games. Furthermore, he can usually spot this practice and will actually grade you down on it.

13) Do not switch sides in your reply merely to agree with a board member

Frequently, a member will take a contrary position merely to draw you out and to see if you are willing and able to defend your point of view. Do not start a debate, yet do not surrender a good position. If a position is worth taking, it is worth defending.

14) Do not be afraid to admit an error in judgment if you are shown to be wrong

The board knows that you are forced to reply without any opportunity for careful consideration. Your answer may be demonstrably wrong. If so, admit it and get on with the interview.

15) Do not dwell at length on your present job

The opening question may relate to your present assignment. Answer the question but do not go into an extended discussion. You are being examined for a *new* job, not your present one. As a matter of fact, try to phrase ALL your answers in terms of the job for which you are being examined.

Basis of Rating

Probably you will forget most of these "do's" and "don'ts" when you walk into the oral interview room. Even remembering them all will not ensure you a passing grade. Perhaps you did not have the qualifications in the first place. But remembering them will help you to put your best foot forward, without treading on the toes of the board members.

Rumor and popular opinion to the contrary notwithstanding, an oral board wants you to make the best appearance possible. They know you are under pressure – but they also want to see how you respond to it as a guide to what your reaction would be under the pressures of the job you seek. They will be influenced by the degree of poise you display, the personal traits you show and the manner in which you respond.

ABOUT THIS BOOK

This book contains tests divided into Examination Sections. Go through each test, answering every question in the margin. At the end of each test look at the answer key and check your answers. On the ones you got wrong, look at the right answer choice and learn. Do not fill in the answers first. Do not memorize the questions and answers, but understand the answer and principles involved. On your test, the questions will likely be different from the samples. Questions are changed and new ones added. If you understand these past questions you should have success with any changes that arise. Tests may consist of several types of questions. We have additional books on each subject should more study be advisable or necessary for you. Finally, the more you study, the better prepared you will be. This book is intended to be the last thing you study before you walk into the examination room. Prior study of relevant texts is also recommended. NLC publishes some of these in our Fundamental Series. Knowledge and good sense are important factors in passing your exam. Good luck also helps. So now study this Passbook, absorb the material contained within and take that knowledge into the examination. Then do your best to pass that exam.

EXAMINATION SECTION

EXAMINATION SECTION
TEST 1

DIRECTIONS: Each question or incomplete statement is followed by several suggested answers or completions. Select the one that BEST answers the question or completes the statement. *PRINT THE LETTER OF THE CORRECT ANSWER IN THE SPACE AT THE RIGHT.*

1. What is the BEST reason for not driving fast when there is a thin layer of water on the roadway? 1.____

   A. The water on the roadway is more slippery than wet pavement
   B. Your tires will tend to ride on top of the water
   C. Spray from other cars will make it hard to see clearly
   D. The spray may cause the engine to stop

2. You are driving down an icy residential street with some dry patches. Suddenly there is trouble a block ahead and you have to stop. You are going 20 mph. What should you do? 2.____

   A. Take foot off accelerator and allow engine to slow the bus
   B. Apply the brakes and wait until you hit dry pavement
   C. Pump the brake hard several times
   D. Shift into low gear

3. On a cold, wet day, the road is generally the most slippery 3.____

   A. on a curve
   B. on a hill
   C. in a tunnel
   D. on a bridge

4. A little loose sand or gravel on dry pavement 4.____

   A. gives you better traction
   B. may lead to a skid
   C. is particularly dangerous when the road is wet
   D. means there is construction ahead

5. If you suddenly lose your hydraulic brakes, going 35 mph, you should first pump your brakes, sound horn and flash your lights. Then: 5.____

   A. activate red flashing warning lamps
   B. drive off the road
   C. immediately downshift to 2nd gear
   D. try to shift to a lower gear

6. The rear of your bus has skidded to the right. You have turned your wheel to the right and the bus is beginning to fishtail to the left. To get back on course, you should 6.____

   A. straighten the wheel
   B. brake
   C. counter-steer left
   D. counter-steer right

7. You have just been forced to pull onto a firm shoulder to avoid an oncoming car. After the car passes, you see a highway sign directly in your path. You are going 30 mph. If you cannot stop in time, you should make sure the road is now clear and 7.____

A. turn sharply back onto the roadway
B. turn gradually back onto the roadway
C. brake gently and turn sharply back onto the roadway
D. brake gently and turn slowly back onto the roadway

8. As you come over the top of a hill at 40 mph, you see a car stalled in your lane right in front of you. You cannot stop in time. In the oncoming lane is a pickup truck. The shoulder is clear and wide enough for the bus. What should you do? 8.____

A. Hit the brake hard and if you still cannot stop, take foot off brake and try to steer onto the shoulder
B. Apply steady hard pressure to the brake and try to steer around the right of the car and onto the shoulder
C. Pump the brake and try to steer left between the car and truck
D. Leave your foot off the brake and try to steer right around the car onto the shoulder

9. You are driving at a high speed. Suddenly you hear a loud "pow" and the front of your bus begins to shake. You should 9.____

A. brake hard
B. brake gradually
C. keep your foot off the brake
D. turn off the road quickly

10. You are in the passing lane of a four-lane road with traffic on both sides. Suddenly an oncoming car crosses the centerline and heads right for you. You first try to get that driver's attention with horn, etc. Then: 10.____

A. hit the brake and brace yourself for a head-on collision
B. brake and steer right
C. brake and steer left
D. dodge oncoming car by crossing centerline, then steering back to your lane

11. Treating for shock, you should: 11.____

A. place a coat, jacket, etc. under the victim
B. put coat, jacket, etc. under and over sparingly according to temperature
C. put coat, jacket, etc. under and over and apply external heat
D. none of these

12. If a car hits a power pole, what would you check for first? 12.____

A. Hot wires
B. Injuries
C. Victims to be removed
D. None of these

13. If a victim is not breathing, you should: 13.____

A. call a doctor and wait
B. check airway, give artificial respiration
C. take victim to hospital
D. none of these

14. If a victim has possible chest injuries and is not breathing, what method would you use? 14.____

A. Back-pressure arm-lift
B. Mouth-to-mouth
C. Rush to hospital
D. None of these

15. When driving on a field trip, you may be expected to drive a(n) ______ route. 15.____

A. hazardous
B. longer than usual
C. unfamiliar
D. all of the above

16. It may be your responsibility to prepare a trip______ report. 16.____

A. accident
B. evaluation
C. chaperone
D. authorization

17. If band instruments or other large items are to be transported on a field trip, they should be 17.____

A. stored in a storage space under the bus
B. kept behind stanchion bars if carried in passenger compartment
C. kept out of the aisles and away from the emergency door(s)
D. any of the above

18. You should check that no students board the bus at any time during the field trip unless authorized by you or by a(n) 18.____

A. chaperone
B. parent
C. another bus driver
D. none of the above

19. The final authority over student conduct while on the bus going on a field trip rests with 19.____

A. parents
B. you
C. chaperones
D. your supervisor

20. Students who are unfamiliar with the bus' rules of conduct may have to be given special 20.____

A. consideration
B. instructions
C. privileges
D. badges

21. The best way to learn an unfamiliar route is to 21.____

A. use a map
B. play it "by ear"
C. travel the route in your car prior to field trip
D. all of the above

22. A field trip to a destination which takes over an hour to reach may also have 22.____

A. sightseeing
B. overnight lodging requirements
C. rest stops
D. both b and c

23. Which of the following student behavior must NOT be permitted on a field trip? 23.____

A. Leaning out windows
B. Rocking the bus
C. Both a and b
D. Singing/cheering

24. Excesses in student behavior must be restrained because 24.____

A. they're getting graded
B. you must concentrate on your driving
C. chaperones can't help with discipline
D. all of the above

25. Accident fatalities and rear-end collisions can be expected to be high in ______ areas as a result of the increase of pedestrian and motor vehicle traffic. 25.____

A. expressway
B. rural
C. urban
D. all of the above

26. To detect hazards, you must be able to distinguish______ within a complex, changing traffic situation. 26.____

A. clues
B. taillights
C. accidents
D. rules

27. You should develop a(n)______ of the clues associated with each hazard. 27.____

A. avoidance pattern
B. "mental image"
C. peripheral vision
D. distraction habit

28. You should focus your eyes at farther distances ahead on the roadway as your speed 28.____

A. decreases
B. stabilizes
C. increases
D. none of the above

29. Many collisions occur at intersections where______ is obstructed or limited by buildings, vegetation or parked cars. 29.____

A. hearing
B. stopping
C. path
D. vision

30. The more intently you fix your central vision on a particular object, the ______ aware you will be of clues from your larger field of indirect vision. 30.____

A. less
B. more
C. better
D. more directly

31. Driving alongside parked vehicles is potentially hazardous because your view is limited and hazards can appear when there is little time or space for 31.____

A. accelerating quickly
B. evasive action
C. parking maneuvers
D. both a and c

32. An example of a single vehicle hazard is 32.____

A. an army convoy
B. traffic at turnpike toll booths
C. a slow moving tractor
D. a car passing you when there is a vehicle in the oncoming lane

33. Multiple vehicle hazards include 33.____

A. vehicles tailgating the bus
B. a driver on an on-ramp entering the flow of traffic on a freeway
C. vehicles that limit another vehicle's visibility
D. all of the above

34. Any point in the roadway at which drivers are confronted with decisions are potential 34.____

A. single vehicle hazards
B. combination vehicle/roadway hazards
C. off-road hazards
D. none of the above

35. You should______ the movement of other vehicles on and approaching the roadway so you can react safely. 35.____

A. separate
B. observe
C. compete with
D. avoid

36. You use the horn and directional signals to make sure that you are ______ by other drivers. 36.____

A. not crowded
B. overtaken
C. being observed
D. yielded to

37. Maintaining adequate separation means keeping a______ between your bus and other vehicles. 37.____

A. margin of safety
B. margin of space
C. extra space cushion
D. all of the above

38. In addition to manipulative skills, you use your______ skills in estimating the required space around the bus. 38.____

A. psycho-motor
B. driving
C. perceptual
D. unconscious

39. At night, the primary perceptual clue for judging your closing rate on the vehicle ahead is 39.____

A. the distance between the lead vehicle's taillights
B. the size of the lead vehicle's taillights
C. the brightness of the lead vehicle's taillights
D. none of the above

40. You use your______ vision to observe vehicles not in your direct path of vision. 40.____

A. depth
B. night
C. central
D. peripheral

41. You should develop the habit of______ 360 degrees around the bus. 41.____

A. scanning
B. screening
C. driving
D. separating

42. Which of the following circumstances call for a greater than normal following distance? When you are: 42.____

A. behind an ambulance
B. behind a motorcycle
C. fatigued
D. all of the above

43. You should maintain appropriate lateral separation when 43.____

A. being passed
B. being tailgated
C. approaching a car stopped at a stop sign
D. all of the above

44. Which of the following clues aid in maintaining longitudinal separation? 44.____

A. Animals in the roadway
B. Noise from traffic in cross streets
C. Level of your gas gauge
D. Your speedometer reading
E. None of the above

45. Which of the following conditions would you treat first? 45.____

A. No breathing
B. Unconscious
C. Bleeding heavily
D. Dizzy

KEY (CORRECT ANSWERS)

1. B	11. B	21. C	31. B	41. A
2. A	12. A	22. D	32. C	42. D
3. D	13. B	23. C	33. D	43. A
4. B	14. B	24. B	34. B	44. D
5. D	15. D	25. C	35. B	45. C
6. C	16. D	26. A	36. C	
7. B	17. D	27. B	37. D	
8. A	18. A	28. C	38. C	
9. C	19. B	29. D	39. A	
10. B	20. B	30. A	40. D	

TEST 2

DIRECTIONS: Each question or incomplete statement is followed by several suggested answers or completions. Select the one that BEST answers the question or completes the statement. *PRINT THE LETTER OF THE CORRECT ANSWER IN THE SPACE AT THE RIGHT.*

Questions 1-10

Read each situation listed 1 through 10 and write the letter of the ACTION listed below (A-J) that you would take in the space at the right:

1. You are at the bottom of a snow-covered hill and you see cars stopped upon the hill 1.____
2. You notice wet leaves all across the street 2.____
3. You see a snowdrift in your lane (4-lane divided highway) 3.____
4. You are following another bus and the road begins to be icy 4.____
5. You are following another bus and the road begins to be icy 5.____
6. You are approaching a long, snow-covered hill 6.____
7. You are on a highway in the rain, and your bus begins to hydroplane 7.____
8. You turn on your windshield washers and an ice glaze forms on your windshield, making it impossible to see 8.____
9. You are approaching a city intersection where you want to turn – it has just started to rain 9.____
10. You are on packed snow and an accident happens just ahead 10.____

A. Drive slower

B. Start up slowly

C. Speed up a little

D. Stop the bus

E. Increase following distance

F. Pump brakes rapidly

G. Pump brakes rapidly

H. Turn more slowly

I. Ease up on the accelerator

J. Look out side windows to keep sight of road; gradually brake and pull off

Questions 11 - 20

Read each statement numbered 11 through 20 and, in the space at the right, print the letter of the answer from the list below that best completes the statement:

11. A child whose actual age is 12 years old but whose mental age is 8 is classified as _____ 11.____

12. A child who must use a wheelchair is _____ 12.____

13. A child with neurologically based processing problems is said to be _____ 13.____

14. _____ patterns of each exceptional child are individual problems and should be handled accordingly 14.____

15. _____ are responsible for having the exceptional child ready to be transported to school each morning 15.____

16. Many buses used to transport exceptional children are equipped with _____ for the restraint and safety of the passengers 16.____

17. You must be able to operate the _____ on the bus during the loading and unloading procedure 17.____

18. Developmentally disabled and learning disabled students are likely to have a short _____ 18.____

19. Exceptional students are likely to be upset by disturbances in the normal_____ 19.____

20. Parents and doctors of exceptional children should provide you with information on any type of_____ the child may be taking 20.____

A. Bus attendants
B. Medication
C. Behavior
D. Seatbelts
E. Wheelchairs
F. Developmentally disabled
G. Attention span
H. Learning disabled
I. Parents
J. Ramp
K. Accident
L. Physically handicapped
M. Routine
N. Bus driver

21. Before you can set priorities for treatment, you must evaluate: 21.____

    A. the scene for dangerous conditions
    B. types of injuries
    C. need for immediate treatment
    D. all of the above

22. Two types of injuries that require prompt treatment are: 22.____

    A. severe bleeding and blocked airways
    B. blocked airways and headache
    C. sprained ankle and leg cramps
    D. lightheadedness and nausea

23. When might you have to move an injured person BEFORE you administer first aid? 23.____

 A. When the injured person is not completely comfortable
 B. When the victim is in a spot that is not suitably lit for first aid administration
 C. When dangerous conditions (ex. fire) exist at the scene
 D. When the victim requests to be moved despite injuries

24. With any serious injury, you should also treat the person for 24.____

 A. dizziness
 B. neck injuries
 C. shock
 D. blood loss

Questions 25-50

Read statements 25 through 50 and, in the space at the right, mark "T" if the statement is true and "F" if it is false:

25. To minimize the effects of shock, keep the victim lying down and make him comfortable 25.____

26. The tourniquet should be used only for severe life-threatening hemorrhage that cannot be controlled by other means 26.____

27. Whenever possible, a person should be treated where he is found 27.____

28. If blood soaks through a dressing, remove dressing and apply another dressing 28.____

29. If you do not have a bus attendant, you must carry or guide each child onto the bus and fasten his seatbelt, if one is provided 29.____

30. Physically handicapped students have a lower mental age than non-handicapped students 30.____

31. If a child has a seizure, you should give him artificial respiration 31.____

32. When one child displays disruptive behavior, you must also be concerned about how the other passengers are affected 32.____

33. You should insist that no students soil themselves on your bus 33.____

34. Any point at which the roadway is compressed (e.g., a four-lane road narrows into two lanes) represents a conflict point 34.____

35. Lack of communication by other drivers on the road is not a hazard to your safe driving 35.____

36. A driver frequently changing lanes is a potential hazard 36.____

37. Drivers who do not signal prior to a maneuver are potentially hazardous 37.____

38. There are certain locations on any route where you can anticipate that other vehicles will decelerate 38.____

39. The condition of the shoulder of the road shouldn't concern you if you don't intend to pull off the roadway 39.____

40. In urban areas, you have to be more alert for traffic lights because of neon lights and other lights on the street 40.____

41. The primary hazard around playgrounds, residential areas and schools is that other drivers tend to tailgate 41.____

42. You should depend on other drivers to signal their intentions as you do 42.____

43. You can use usual and unusual clues to assess how bad a hazard is before you take action 43.____

44. You should always swerve to avoid animals or pedestrians in the roadway 44.____

45. To maintain the appropriate lateral separation distance when changing lanes, you should position the bus in the center of the new lane 45.____

46. In general, pass on the right on a four-lane roadway 46.____

47. A "panic stop" is always better than no stop at all 47.____

48. When approaching a vehicle that is taking up two lanes, you should maintain longitudinal separation 48.____

49. When approaching an intersection with a car coming from the left cross street signaling his intention to turn right, it is all right to proceed into the intersection after the car has begun to turn 49.____

50. Since you drive a school bus, you have the right of way on a narrow bridge 50.____

KEY (CORRECT ANSWERS)

1. D	11. F	21. D	31. F	41. F
2. A	12. L	22. A	32. T	42. F
3. F	13. H	23. C	33. F	43. T
4. E	14. C	24. C	34. T	44. F
5. B	15. I	25. T	35. F	45. T
6. C	16. D	26. T	36. T	46. F
7. I	17. J	27. T	37. T	47. F
8. J	18. G	28. F	38. T	48. T
9. H	19. M	29. T	39. F	49. T
10. G	20. B	30. F	40. T	50. F

TEST 3

DIRECTIONS: Each question or incomplete statement is followed by several suggested answers or completions. Select the one that BEST answers the question or completes the statement. *PRINT THE LETTER OF THE CORRECT ANSWER IN THE SPACE AT THE RIGHT.*

Questions 1 -44

Read statements 1 through 44 and, in the space at the right, mark "T" if the statement is true and "F" if it is false:

1. Two seconds is the minimum time interval to maintain behind a vehicle you are following 1.____
2. Drivers tend to underestimate bus lengths and distance measured in feet 2.____
3. You must know the approximate size of your bus so you can estimate whether your bus can safely clear structures with restricted lateral and overhead space 3.____
4. When driving on poor roads, a considerable part of your attention should be devoted to getting through with the greatest degree of comfort to the passengers and without damaging the bus 4.____
5. Probably the greatest danger on rural roads which are not hard-surfaced is the questionable condition of the outer edges of the grade 5.____
6. If your wheels run off the paved surface on a narrow road, you should slow down and turn your wheels gradually to cut back onto the pavement 6.____
7. Blind and uncontrolled intersections are often found on rural roads 7.____
8. One of the most common faults of school bus drivers in urban areas is that they do not stay in the proper lane of traffic 8.____
9. It's better to drive much slower than other urban traffic rather than much faster 9.____
10. You have more help in controlling the position of your bus at an intersection in an urban area than you do in any residential or rural intersection because at an urban intersection there are traffic lights, traffic officers, safety islands, etc. 10.____
11. Driving at twilight is more dangerous than driving during daylight 11.____
12. Distance and speed estimation for oncoming, standard-size vehicles at night is almost equal to that of daytime driving 12.____
13. If it's unexpectedly necessary to pull the bus off onto the shoulder of the road at night, you should activate the red flashing warning lights 13.____
14. A basic rule for driving in adverse weather is to shift to a lower gear 14.____
15. To avoid getting stuck or spinning the wheels when driving on ice, you should try to keep the bus moving slowly and steadily forward in gear 15.____

16. Accidents blamed on skidding or bad weather conditions are classed as preventable 16.____

17. When driving in snow and ice, you brake while negotiating turns 17.____

18. The problems of reduced visibility due to poor weather are similar to the reduced visibility due to darkness 18.____

19. When driving on an expressway, you should drive within a 25 percent range of the speed of traffic 19.____

20. When entering an expressway, you should stay in the acceleration lane until you are up to the speed of the traffic flow 20.____

21. If your wheels go off the pavement on an expressway, brake quickly to avoid collision 21.____

22. When you want to exit from an expressway, you should not activate your turn signal until you pull into the deceleration lane 22.____

23. You should enter the expressway by merging sharply into the flow of traffic, provided an acceptable gap of at least 8 seconds is permitted 23.____

24. You should not drive with your foot resting on the brake pedal 24.____

25. You should race the engine to warm it up because it's hard on the engine to drive it while it's cold 25.____

26. If you "lug" the engine when you go up hills (try to go up in too high a gear) you'll wear out the brake shoes 26.____

27. You should not drive the bus if oil pressure is low 27.____

28. You should *usually* avoid skipping gears when you upshift and downshift 28.____

29. Springs and shock absorbers are part of the suspension component 29.____

30. "Slipping the clutch" is the driving habit that wears out a clutch most quickly 30.____

31. The condition of the road (potholes, bumps) has the worst effect on the electrical system 31.____

32. If the ammeter indicates discharge, you should have your brakes checked immediately 32.____

33. Preventive maintenance consists of correctly diagnosing symptoms of component malfunctions 33.____

34. If your temperature gauge rises higher than normal, you should report it 34.____

35. If your bus swerves when you apply the brakes, it could mean that one or more wheels are not braking evenly 35.____

36. If your bus slips out of gear, you should shut off the engine immediately 36.____

37. If you hear a squealing sound when you depress the clutch pedal, it usually means your brake linings are worn 37.____

38. If the steering on your bus becomes very difficult, your wheels could be improperly aligned 38.____

39. If smoke appears around wires or switches, you should disconnect the battery immediately 39.____

40. If your lights are dim, you should go ahead and drive 40.____

41. If your bus bounces or rolls from side to side easily, you are just driving too fast for conditions 41.____

42. If you notice exhaust fumes, it is nothing to worry about unless your muffler is also excessively loud 42.____

43. If your engine "misses" at high speeds, you should shut off the engine immediately 43.____

44. A driver who frequently changes lanes should not be considered a potential hazard 44.____

45. What is your responsibility to parents when you know the bus will be late on the afternoon run due to a bad storm? 45.____

    A. Have the children call their parents and alert them of the situation
    B. Notify them of the delay and provide an estimated arrival time
    C. None; the parents should find out on their own
    D. Contact the school and have someone get the information out to all parents

46. What should you do if no one is home to receive the child in the afternoon? 46.____

    A. Let the child go to a friend's house
    B. Do not leave until a parent or guardian returns home, then continue with your run
    C. Take him to an alternate person (friend, neighbor, etc.) if someone else is designated on the child's information card
    D. Return the child to the school to wait for a parent or guardian

47. Who should you report to if you observe a child having an adverse reaction to medication? 47.____

    A. Parent
    B. Teacher
    C. Child's doctor
    D. All of the above

48. How would you explain to your passengers and their parents that the bus route is being changed to pick up a new student? 48.____

    A. New pick-up time should be specified, and passengers assured that the route will be different but nothing to worry about
    B. Apologize for the new student and continue without additional explanation
    C. Inform them of the new pick-up time only
    D. Provide information about the new student to all parents this way they can review the new situation themselves

49. Why must each exceptional child be treated individually? 49.____

A. Their problems vary widely
B. Each has their own level of comprehension, tolerance, adaptability, etc.
C. Both A and B
D. Neither A nor B

50. Suppose a child behaves in ways that aren't typical for him and that violently upset other bus passengers. What would you NOT do to try to resolve the problem? 50.____

A. Pull off the road and stop the bus
B. Try to eliminate the cause of the problem, if it is known
C. Radio for help or stop a passing motorist if it gets beyond your control
D. Yell at the child or children until they are no longer a distraction

---

KEY (CORRECT ANSWERS)

1.	F	11.	T	21.	F	31.	F	41.	F
2.	T	12.	T	22.	F	32.	F	42.	F
3.	T	13.	F	23.	F	33.	F	43.	F
4.	T	14.	T	24.	T	34.	T	44.	F
5.	T	15.	T	25.	F	35.	T	45.	B
6.	T	16.	T	26.	F	36.	F	46.	C
7.	T	17.	F	27.	T	37.	F	47.	D
8.	T	18.	T	28.	T	38.	T	48.	A
9.	F	19.	T	29.	T	39.	T	49.	C
10.	F	20.	T	30.	T	40.	F	50.	D

EXAMINATION SECTION
TEST 1

DIRECTIONS: Each question or incomplete statement is fol'lowed by several suggested answers or completions. Select the one that BEST answers the question or completes the statement. *PRINT THE LETTER OF THE CORRECT ANSWER IN THE SPACE AT THE RIGHT.*

1. A successful school transportation operation depends MOST upon the high quality of dedication and performance by the 1.____

   A. school administrator
   B. driver
   C. transportation director
   D. supervisor
   E. vehicle maintenance personnel

2. It is NOT the driver's responsibility to 2.____

   A. conduct pre- and post-trip checks on the vehicle
   B. maintain orderly conduct of passengers
   C. communicate effectively with the public
   D. enforce wearing of seatbelts
   E. complete reports

3. The training program for maintenance and service personnel does NOT have to include 3.____

   A. procedure for recognizing cause and effect relationship between driving habits and vehicle maintenance
   B. recovery procedures for vehicles involved in accident or breakdown
   C. preparation of maintenance records
   D. establishment of parts inventory control procedures
   E. repair procedures for each type of vehicle in the fleet

4. A student's riding privileges may be suspended when 4.____

   A. drugs or controlled substances are used on the bus
   B. classroom conduct is not observed on the bus
   C. hazardous materials are brought on the bus
   D. rights of others are jeopardized
   E. safe operation of the bus is jeopardized

5. It is recommended that school officials provide 5.____

   A. clearly marked walkways through the school bus zones
   B. controlled traffic flow through the school bus zones
   C. clearly marked parking patterns through the school bus zones
   D. adequate space for backing of transportation equipment
   E. all of the above

6. What distinguishes a Circular Route? It 6.____

A. is the most economical
B. enables the first student who boards the bus in the morning to be the first to disembark in the evening
C. eliminates the need for students to cross the roadway
D. holds the number of miles a student must ride to a minimum
E. permits one bus to transport more than one load of students

7. Which method for dissemination of information is BEST for informing the public about procedures the schools will follow in cases of severe weather conditions? 7.____

A. Radio
B. Telephone calls
C. Public address system
D. Public press
E. Bulletins

8. What is the BEST method for communicating with students regarding all forms of safety? 8.____

A. Meetings
B. Public address system
C. Bulletins
D. Conference
E. Television

9. Insurance agents should be contacted to determine if additional coverage is necessary when the activity trip is scheduled to 9.____

A. another town
B. another county
C. another state
D. any distance greater than fifty miles
E. any location beyond the school district's boundaries

10. What is the LEAST important factor to be considered in selecting a bus for a trip? 10.____

A. Climate conditions
B. Parking requirements
C. Age group of students
D. Driver familiarity with the route
E. Miles to be traveled

11. Transportation for handicapped students requires an assessment of their ______ capacities. 11.____

A. physical
B. social
C. emotional
D. intellectual
E. all of the above

12. Which of the following is NOT a characteristic of a student with a learning disability? 12.____

A. Average or higher intellectual ability
B. Disorganized in solving problems
C. Demonstrates extreme emotional behaviors
D. Friendly and affectionate
E. Hyperactivity

13. Arrangements for special education students' transportation should be communicated to 13.____

A. parents
B. school personnel
C. other students on the bus
D. the driver
E. all of the above

14. What must be considered to effect behavior modification? 14.____

    A. Ages of the students
    B. Nature of the reward
    C. Clear definition of what constitutes acceptable behavior
    D. All of the above
    E. None of the above

15. What is the driver's PRIME responsibility when a handicapped student has a seizure? To 15.____

    A. administer the student's medication
    B. place something in the student's mouth to prevent tongue injury
    C. restrain the student's limbs to avoid broken bones
    D. see that the student rests comfortably afterward
    E. all of the above

16. What is the MOST important preparation for special education student management in an emergency? 16.____

    A. Appointing a student to take over
    B. Notifying school and parents
    C. Reassuring the students
    D. Teaching pupils what to expect
    E. Preplanning students' needs

17. Suspension of special education students from the bus is usually MOST appropriate when 17.____

    A. there is clear evidence of lack of respect for authority
    B. the safety of other students is threatened
    C. the misbehavior is repeated
    D. behavior is drug or alcohol related
    E. there is alternate transportation available to the student

18. Which of the following is NOT in the best interest for behavior control? 18.____

    A. Rearranging seating positions
    B. Relaxing classroom behavioral expectations
    C. Suspension of bus privileges
    D. Allowing students to suggest and enforce rules
    E. Referral to school psychologist

19. Comfort is a HIGH priority when the student has a(n) 19.____

    A. visual impairment
    B. orthopedic handicap
    C. hearing impairment
    D. intellectual impairment
    E. emotional impairment

20. Facial expression and body language are important aspects in communicating with 20.____

    A. the emotionally disturbed
    B. the visually handicapped
    C. learning disabled students

D. developmentally disabled students
E. hearing impaired students

21. A dry run prior to a scheduled trip date is MOST recommended when 21.____

A. night driving may be involved
B. terrain or road difficulties may be encountered
C. destination parking is other than students' destination
D. bridges or tunnels may be encountered
E. specialized equipment may be used

22. What is the PRIMARY role of the driver transporting handicapped students? To 22.____

A. accommodate student's needs
B. promote successful student management
C. assess and anticipate the needs of individual problems
D. give personal attention to each student
E. drive the bus

23. Who has the FINAL responsibility on an activity bus? 23.____

A. Chaperone
B. Teacher
C. Parent supervisor
D. Senior chaperone
E. Bus driver

24. The Bureau of Motor Carrier Safety Manual recommends which maximum limit for the driver of an activity bus? 24.____

A. ten hours of duty of which eight are driving time
B. ten hours of continuous off-duty prior to a long trip
C. no more than forty hours driving per week
D. no more than sixty hours driving per week
E. twelve hours continuous off-duty prior to a long trip

25. Which of the following is NOT an objective of a planned maintenance program? 25.____

A. Preventing road failures
B. Enhancing appearance of the school bus
C. Improving the handling and performance characteristics
D. Conserving fuel
E. Extending the bus' useful life

KEY (CORRECT ANSWERS)

1. B
2. D
3. A
4. E
5. A
6. B
7. A
8. B
9. C
10. B
11. E
12. D
13. E
14. D
15. D
16. E
17. B
18. B
19. B
20. E
21. B
22. E
23. E
24. D
25. C

TEST 2

DIRECTIONS: Each question or incomplete statement is followed by several suggested answers or completions. Select the one that BEST answers the question or completes the statement. *PRINT THE LETTER OF THE CORRECT ANSWER IN THE SPACE AT THE RIGHT.*

1. Employee personnel records usually do NOT include 1.____

   A. causes of absences
   B. criminal records
   C. marital status
   D. confirmed work history
   E. psychological evaluation

2. When are alternately flashing red lights used? 2.____

   A. When poor visibility conditions exist
   B. When bus is crossing railroad tracks
   C. When bus is stopping to take on or discharge passengers
   D. When bus is stopped to take on or discharge passengers
   E. All of the above

3. Which of the following policies are determined by state statute and/or state regulations? 3.____

   A. Policy with regard to transportation of non-public school students
   B. Policy relative to supervision of students while loading and unloading at school sites and enroute
   C. Procedure for determining eligibility for student transportation service
   D. Use of special lighting and signaling equipment on the bus
   E. Policy with regard to standees, length of time in transit, and type of supervision required

4. Which of the following is NOT a qualification of the director of student transportation? 4.____

   A. A record free of criminal convictions
   B. An undergraduate degree or equivalent experience
   C. Ability to work effectively with a broad range of individuals
   D. Ability to provide comprehensive bus driver training program
   E. Ability to manage personnel and resources

5. The driver training program SHOULD include instruction in 5.____

   A. repair procedures
   B. recovery procedures for vehicles involved in an accident
   C. procedures for performing pre- and post-trip inspections
   D. preparation of maintenance records
   E. all of the above

6. All of the following are bus regulations regarding student demeanors EXCEPT: 6.____

   A. Students are to remain seated
   B. Students are to place school-related objects in aisles
   C. Students are prohibited from eating on the bus

D. Students are prohibited from leaving or boarding the bus at locations other than assigned home or school stop
E. Students are permitted to pass objects on, from, or into buses

7. Students should be instructed on 7.____

A. proper storage of material that cannot be held on their laps
B. safe eating and drinking procedures on the bus
C. entering and leaving the bus
D. passing objects on, from, or into the bus
E. all of the above

8. Which type route eliminates the need for the student to cross the roadway? 8.____

A. Shoestring route
B. Retracing route
C. Double routing
D. Emergency route
E. Circular route

9. A systemic inspection of the bus before each trip is the responsibility of the 9.____

A. bus garage personnel
B. school administration
C. transportation supervisor
D. driver
E. service and maintenance personnel

10. What is the BEST way to inform parents of all school and state regulations? 10.____

A. Conferences
B. Telephone calls
C. Letters
D. Meetings
E. Radio

11. Safety criteria for evaluating the transportation system usually does NOT include 11.____

A. property damage accidents
B. moving traffic violations
C. complaints
D. route and routing procedures
E. road failures

12. How many days in advance of a trip date should driver assignment take place? ______ day(s). 12.____

A. 7 B. 1 C. 3 D. 2 E. 5

13. Which of the following is NOT a consideration for selecting drivers for trip assignments? 13.____

A. License held
B. Seniority
C. Skill
D. Familiarity with trip vehicle
E. Familiarity with area to be traveled

14. Which group of students does NOT represent any unusual behavior problems? 14.____

 A. Developmentally disabled students
 B. Learning disabled students
 C. Hearing disabled students
 D. All of the above
 E. None of the above

15. A lack of stability from day to day in desirable behavior is characteristic of ______ students. 15.____

 A. emotionally disturbed
 B. learning disabled
 C. developmentally disabled
 D. visually handicapped
 E. hearing impaired

16. What type of student is MOST likely to have few self-care skills? ______ students. 16.____

 A. Learning disabled
 B. Developmentally disabled
 C. Emotionally disturbed
 D. Orthopedically handicapped
 E. Visually handicapped

17. What is the BEST approach to special education students? 17.____

 A. Promptly correct any unsuitable behavior
 B. Tell rather than show pupils what you want them to do
 C. Define rules clearly and enforce them firmly
 D. Allow some latitude because of students' handicaps
 E. Do not expect students to accept responsibility for their own actions

18. Behavior modification when applied to special education students requires 18.____

 A. giving a reward after demonstration of appropriate behavior
 B. long-term behavioral goals
 C. liberal amounts of praise to encourage acceptable behavior
 D. establishing rules that can be easily followed
 E. taking appropriate disciplinary action for each rule infraction

19. Which of the following confidential information should the aide on a bus transporting handicapped students have? 19.____

 A. Nature of student's handicap
 B. Emergency health care information
 C. Name and phone number of student's parents
 D. All of the above
 E. None of the above

20. It is BEST to seat a young and hyperactive special education student 20.____

 A. with a very young student
 B. at the front of the bus
 C. at the rear of the bus
 D. with an older, well-behaved student
 E. with a fragile student

21. All medically-related incidents involving special education students require 21.____

A. summoning professional medical attention
B. the driver to give medication or medical assistance
C. reporting to school and parents at earliest possible moment
D. all of the above
E. none of the above

22. Visually handicapped students respond BEST when 22.____

A. they are given independence
B. they are consistently reminded what is expected of them
C. angry outbursts and punishment is avoided
D. they are addressed by name
E. body language is used to reinforce speech

23. What is the LAST consideration in planning for the transportation of special education students? 23.____
The

A. group of students on the vehicle
B. design of the car seats
C. type of supports needed
D. type of vehicle required
E. class placement of students

24. The driver of handicapped children needs to be more 24.____

A. controlled B. alert C. flexible
D. lenient E. rigid

25. Which of the following is USUALLY necessary when a special trip is planned? 25.____

A. Bus is equipped with radio
B. Public address system is installed
C. Driver is provided with cash
D. Driver is provided with a uniform
E. Seats are equipped with seatbelts

KEY (CORRECT ANSWERS)

1. E
2. D
3. A
4. D
5. C

6. B
7. C
8. B
9. D
10. C

11. D
12. C
13. A
14. C
15. A

16. B
17. C
18. A
19. D
20. D

21. C
22. D
23. A
24. C
25. C

EXAMINATION SECTION
TEST 1

DIRECTIONS: Each question or incomplete statement is followed by several suggested answers or completions. Select the one that BEST answers the question or completes the statement. *PRINT THE LETTER OF THE CORRECT ANSWER IN THE SPACE AT THE RIGHT.*

Questions 1-3.

DIRECTIONS: Questions 1 through 3 are to be answered on the basis of the following schedule for running time. Running Time is the scheduled time for a bus to travel from one stop to the next. The arrow indicates the direction in which the bus travels. For example, the running time from Main St. to School St., eastbound, is 5 minutes during the hours from 10:00 P.M. to 6:00 A.M., and 9 minutes from 6:00 A.M. to 10:00 P.M. If you want to know when a bus that leaves School St. at 11:00 P.M. should arrive at Pearl St., you should add the 14 minutes running time to 11:00 P.M. to obtain 11:14 P.M.

<u>RUNNING TIME</u>

	10:00 PM to 6:00 AM				6:00 AM to 10:00 PM			
Bus Stop	Eastbound		Westbound		Eastbound		Westbound	
Main St. to School St.	5	↓	6	↑	9	↓	11	↑
School St. to Bank St.	4		5		7		I 8	
Bank St. to Market St.	5		6		10		12	
Market St. to Pearl St.	5		6		9		11	
Pearl St. to State St.	4		5		7		8	
Totals	23		28		42		50	

1. An eastbound bus leaves School St. at 1:30 P.M. At what time will it arrive at Market St.? ______ P.M. 1.____

   A. 1:39 B. 1:41 C. 1:47 D. 1:50

2. If a passenger boarding a westbound bus at State St. wishes to be at Bank St. by 3:00 P.M., the last bus he should take is one that leaves no later than ______ P.M. 2.____

   A. 2:21 B. 2:29 C. 2:34 D. 2:43

3. A westbound bus leaves Pearl St. at 11 P.M. but has an 18 minute delay because of a sick passenger at Market St. The bus is delayed for another 4 minutes due to a broken traffic light at School St. What time will the bus arrive at Main St.? 3.____

   A. 11:45 P.M. B. 11:50 P.M.
   C. 12:07 AM. D. 12:15 AM.

4. To help prevent passenger accidents inside a bus, which of the following starting and stopping procedures should a bus operator follow? 4.____
______ acceleration when starting and ______ when stopping.

A. Gradual; gradual slowing down
B. Rapid; rapid braking
C. Gradual; rapid braking
D. Rapid; gradual slowing down

5. When a bus operator is driving a bus, a flashing yellow light at an intersection means that he should 5.____

A. stop
B. stop, then proceed slowly
C. proceed with caution
D. maintain his speed through the intersection

Questions 6-8.

DIRECTIONS: Questions 6 through 8 are to be answered on the basis of the following schedule for Headway. Headway is the scheduled time between one bus and the next bus, and this varies according to the time of day. For example, from 12 Noon to 4 P.M., the time between buses is 10 minutes, and from 5:00 A.M. to 9:00 A.M., it is 5 minutes.

HEADWAY

				Minutes
5:00 A.M	...... to	9:00 A.M	......	5
9:00 A.M	...... to	12:00 Noon	.....	8
12:00 Noon	...... to	4:00 P. M	......	10
4:00 P. M	...... to	7:00 P. M	......	5
7:00 P. M	...... to	11:00 P. M	......	15
11:00 P.M	...... to	5:00 A.M	......	30

6. At 7:00 A.M., a man just misses a bus. 6.____
About how many minutes will he have to wait for the next bus?

A. 5 B. 8 C. 9 D. 11

7. At 8:33 P.M., a woman arrives at a bus stop. The last bus left her stop on schedule 3 minutes ago. The next scheduled bus has been cancelled due to faulty equipment. The bus following the cancelled bus is running three minutes late because of heavy traffic. 7.____
At what time should another bus arrive at the woman's stop?

A. 8:40 A.M. B. 8:57 P.M. C. 9:03 P.M. D. 9:06 P.M.

8. What is the difference between the headway times at 11:50 A.M. and 11:20 P.M.? 8.____
______ minutes

A. 15 B. 20 C. 22 D. 25

9. In heavy traffic, which of the following turn situations is potentially MOST hazardous? 9.____

   A. Right turn from one two-way street onto another two-way street
   B. Left turn from a one-way street onto a two-way street
   C. Right turn from a two-way street onto a one-way street
   D. Left turn from one two-way street onto another two-way street

10. As you approach an intersection in your bus, you note that the traffic light is red and you hear the wailing noise of an ambulance siren. A police officer at the intersection motions for you to go through the light. Under the circumstances, you should 10.____

    A. stop until you can determine the location of the ambulance
    B. stop until the light turns green, then proceed
    C. proceed to the middle of the intersection and stop so that you can better determine the location of the ambulance
    D. proceed through the intersection

11. Which of the following actions should a bus operator take if he notices a boy climbing on the back of his bus? 11.____

    A. Reduce speed and continue on his route
    B. Make sudden stops and starts to shake the boy off
    C. Stop the bus, inform his passengers why he is stopping, and then order the boy off the bus
    D. Ignore the boy and continue his trip at a normal speed

Questions 12-15.

DIRECTIONS: Questions 12 through 15 are to be answered on the basis of the following schedule. Running time is the scheduled time for a bus to travel from one stop to the next. The arrow indicates the direction in which the bus travels. For example, the running time from the Railroad Station to Main & Oak is 5 minutes. Lay-over time is the time spent at the terminal before leaving on the next trip.

Bus Stop	<u>Southbound</u> Running Time (Minutes)		<u>Northbound</u> Running Time (Minutes)	
Railroad Station	(leaves)	↓	5	↑
Main & Oak	5		4	
Main & Elm	4		6	
Main & Ash	6		3	
Main & Pine	3		5	
Main & Birch	5		4	
Farmer's Market	4		8	
Plum & State	8		7	
Apple & State	7		7	
Pear & State	7		6	
Peach & State	6		5	
Court House	5		(leaves)	

Note: Layover time at each of the terminals, *Railroad Station Terminal* and *Court House Terminal,* is 5 minutes.

12. What is the running time, in minutes, from Peach & State northbound to Main & Ash? 12.____

A. 37 B. 40 C. 42 D. 45

13. If a bus leaves the Railroad Station at 8:10 A.M., at what time should it arrive at the Court House? 13.____
______ A.M.

A. 9:05 B. 9:08 C. 9:10 D. 9:12

14. If a bus leaves the Court House at 9:05 A.M., at what time should it arrive at Farmer's Market? 14.____
______ A.M.

A. 9:30 B. 9:35 C. 9:38 D. 9:43

15. How much time will it take a bus leaving Main & Pine southbound to arrive back at Main & Pine on the return trip? 15.____
1 hour, ______ minutes

A. 17 B. 19 C. 29 D. 33

Questions 16-20.

DIRECTIONS: Questions 16 through 20 are to be answered SOLELY on the basis of the BUS OPERATOR'S DAILY TRIP SHEET shown below. At each terminal, at the end of a trip, the operator takes the readings on the cash counter and fare card counter which are part of the fare box and enters them on the BUS OPERATOR'S DAILY TRIP SHEET. The part of the BUS OPERATOR'S DAILY TRIP SHEET shown below is a record of the fare box readings for a specific working day for Bus Operator Birch. Note that a trip covers the distance from one terminal to the other. When Operator Birch left the Rowland Street terminal for the first trip of his working day, the cash counter registered $677.25 from a previous operator's run, and the fare card counter registered 113 fares. Birch left Rowland Terminal at 12:51 P.M. and completed his first trip over the route and arrived at the Tully Street Terminal at 1:28 P.M. Assume that at each terminal arriving and leaving times are identical. For the remainder of his working day, he rode back and forth along his route, arriving at the Rowland and Tully terminals at the times indicated on the BUS OPERATOR'S DAILY TRIP SHEET. His fare box readings were taken and entered on the trip sheet shown below immediately upon arrival at the terminals. When answering these questions, assume the fare is $2.25 and that all passengers are required to pay the full fare. Also assume that the card fares collected are worth $2.25 each.

BUS OPERATOR'S DAILY TRIP SHEET

		FARE BOX READINGS AT THE END OF EACH TRIP	
POINT LEAVING FROM	TIME	CASH	CARDS
Rowland Street Terminal	12:51 PM	677.25	113
Tully Street Terminal	1:28 PM	756.00	117
Rowland Street Terminal	2:08 PM	810.00	122
Tully Street Terminal	2:45 PM	893.25	131
Rowland Street Terminal	3:25 PM	987.75	133
Tully Street Terminal	4:04 PM	1,102.50	144
Rowland Street Terminal	4:38 PM	1,212.75	147
Tully Street Terminal	5:18 PM	1,233.00	148

16. How much cash was collected between 1:28 P.M. and 3:25 P.M.? 16.____

A. $198.75 B. $228.75 C. $231.75 D. $326.25

17. How many fares were collected between 2:45 P.M. and 4:38 P.M.? 17.____

A. 16 B. 17 C. 25 D. 147

18. What is the value of the card fares collected from 12:51 P.M. to 5:18 P.M.? 18.____

A. $74.25 B. $78.75 C. $81.00 D. $83.25

19. How many passengers got on the bus between 2:08 P.M. and 4:04 P.M.? 19.____

A. 144 B. 152 C. 157 D. 176

20. What was the total number of passengers carried during the entire run from 12:51 P.M. to 5:18 P.M.? 20.____

A. 245 B. 269 C. 282 D. 583

Questions 21-27.

DIRECTIONS: Questions 21 through 27 are to be answered SOLELY on the basis of the description of the accident and the ACCIDENT REPORT shown below and on the following page. The ACCIDENT REPORT contains 38 numbered spaces. Read the description and look at the ACCIDENT REPORT before answering these questions.

Description of Accident: At 1:15 P.M., on July 20, 2011, an auto with license plate# 51VOMNY, driven by Martha Ryan, license number R21692-33739 295897-41, and owned by George Ryan, traveling east on Fulton Street, crashed into the right front wheel of a moving Flxible bus, T.A. Vehicle No. 7026, license plate no. 10346-K, at the inter-section of Jay Street and Fulton Street. The bus was covering Run 12 on Route B67. The auto was a green 2004 Chevrolet Malibu. The bus with 15 passengers was traveling south on Jay Street. The bus had a green traffic light in its favor at the Jay St. - Fulton St. intersection. The bus driver was Art Simmons, Badge No. 5712, license number S 24368 35274 263 745-42.

Two passengers in the bus fell onto the floor. An elderly woman (age 65) bruised her left knee. A male (age 25) bruised the palm of his right hand. The auto driver's daughter, Mary (age 19), who was in the right front seat, bumped her head on the windshield. The police and an ambulance were summoned. The three injured persons were taken to Cumberland Hospital by Attendant John Hawkins. Police Officer Thomas Brown, Badge No. 2354, from the 68th Precinct, took statements from witnesses to the accident.

ACCIDENT REPORT
TO BE FILLED IN BY BUS OPERATOR

Route 1 Run 2 T.A. Vehicle Type: Bus Truck Auto Other Vehicle 3 T.A. Vehicle No. 4 T.A. License Plate No. 5 Make 6 Date of Accident 7 Hour 8 Street Lights On 9
Place of Accident 10
Direction of T.A. Vehicle 11 Direction of Other Vehicle 12
State if operating on one- or two-way street: T.A. Vehicle 13 way
Other Vehicle 14 way
Did accident occur in bus stop area? 15
JNumoer 01 passengers in T.A. Vehicle 16
JNumber of persons in other vehicle 17
Trallic lights involved 18 Color of same when leaving near corner 19 Was ambulance called? 20 Persons taken to what hospital? 21
Was police officer present? 22 Officer's No. 23 Precinct 24
Name of owner of other vehicle 25
License No. of other vehicle 26
Address of owner of other vehicle 27
color ol other vehicle 28 Model of other vehicle 29
Year of other vehicle 30 Make of other vehicle 31
Name of driver of other vehicle 32
Address of driver of other vehicle 33
License JNo. of driver of other vehicle 34
Uther driver male or female 35
BUS OPERATOR IDENTIFYING INFORMATION: PASS # 36; BADGE # 37;
LICENSE # 38

21. Which of the following should be entered in Space 4? 21.____

A. B67 B. 12 C. 7026 D. 10346K

22. Which of the following should be entered in Space 12? 22.____

A. North B. South C. East D. West

23. Which of the following should be entered in Space 16? 23.____

A. 10 B. 12 C. 15 D. 67

24. Which of the following should be entered in Space 24? 24.____

A. 62 B. 67 C. 68 D. 2354

25. Which of the following should be entered in Space 28? 25.____

A. Red B. Blue C. Yellow D. Green

26. Which of the following should be entered in Space 32? 26.____

A. Martha Ryan
B. Mary Ryan
C. George Ryan
D. John Hawkins

27. Which of the following should be entered in Space 37? 27.____

A. 2354 B. 5712 C. 51 VOM-NY D. 5127

28. An angry passenger scolds Bus Operator George Smith for not stopping at a bus stop. Smith did not hear the passenger signal, but there was a lot of traffic noise and he realizes the passenger might have signalled. 28.____
Of the following, the BEST action for the bus operator to take is to

A. keep driving, say nothing, and stop at the next bus stop for which he hears a signal
B. stop the bus immediately and let the passenger off
C. tell the passenger in no uncertain terms to signal clearly in the future and, as a lesson to the passenger, skip the next stop as well
D. explain that he did not hear a signal and let the passenger off at the next stop

29. As a bus approaches a crowded bus stop, an elderly passenger sitting with a cane near the front of the bus rings the bell to get off. 29.____
Which of the following is the BEST action for the bus operator to take?

A. Stop short of the bus stop, let the elderly passenger out the front door, then pull into the bus stop.
B. Pull into the bus stop, open the front and rear doors, and tell the elderly passenger to walk to the rear door to get off.
C. Pull into the bus stop, open the doors, and tell the crowd, *Please let this passenger off.*
D. Pull into the bus stop, let the crowd on first, then permit the elderly passenger to get out the front door.

30. At an intersection with no traffic control device, which of the following has the right-of-way over the others? 30.____
A

A. pedestrian in a crosswalk
B. vehicle making a right turn
C. vehicle approaching the intersection
D. bus crossing the intersection

Questions 31-35.

DIRECTIONS: Questions 31 through 35 are to be answered SOLELY on the basis of the EXCLUSIVE LANE RULES printed below.

EXCLUSIVE LANE RULES

Bus Operators using the exclusive bus and taxi lane westbound to the Howard Tunnel in the eastbound roadway of the Porter Express-way should be guided by the following rules:

1. Headlights must be turned on just before entering the bus lane .
2. Speed must not exceed 35 miles per hour. Police will enforce this limit.
3. At least a 200-foot spacing must be maintained behind the vehicle ahead.
4. If a traffic cone is in the lane, drive over it. Do not attempt to go around it and do not stop your bus.
5. Lane hours are only from 7:00 A.M. to 10:00 A.M. Do not enter at any other time or if the lane is closed.
6. Do not leave the lane at any time, not even to pass a disabled vehicle, except under police direction.

7. Do not open doors or discharge passengers from a disabled bus until police assistance has arrived.
8. Any Transit Authority bus in the exclusive lane able to accommodate discharged passengers from a disabled bus of any company will do so without requiring payment of additional fare.

31. Transit Authority Bus Operator James Hanzelik is operating his bus in the exclusive bus and taxi lane. He is carrying 25 passengers and has room for about 40 more. Hanzelik comes upon an Antelope Bus Company bus which has broken down in front of him in his lane. The Antelope bus has 20 passengers in it. Hanzelik stops his bus. A short time later, a police officer arrives on the scene. 31.____
Bus Operator Hanzelik should pass the disabled bus under the direction of the police officer after first

A. taking on the passengers from the disabled bus without charge
B. taking on the passengers of the disabled bus and charging each of them the difference between the Transit Authority fare and the Antelope Bus Company fare
C. politely declining to take on the passengers of the disabled bus because it is not a Transit Authority bus
D. taking on the passengers of the disabled bus and charging each of them the regular Transit Authority fare

32. You are driving a bus in the exclusive bus and taxi lane. If you observe a traffic cone in the middle of your lane, you should 32.____

A. stop your bus and place the traffic cone where it belongs
B. go around the traffic cone to avoid destroying it
C. drive over the traffic cone
D. call for the police to move the traffic cone

33. Bus Operator Peter Globe is traveling in the exclusive bus and taxi lane when his bus becomes disabled. He stops his bus in the lane and phones for police assistance. While he is waiting for the police to arrive, another bus in the same lane pulls up behind him. The second bus has enough room to accommodate his passengers. After consulting with the other bus operator, he transfers his passengers to the second bus without charging an additional fare. 33.____
Bus Operator Globe's action was

A. *proper;* because the other bus had sufficient room to accommodate his passengers
B. *improper;* because he transferred the passengers without police assistance
C. *proper;* because both buses stayed in the exclusive lane
D. *improper;* because he did not charge his passengers an additional fare

34. A bus operator driving his bus legally in the exclusive bus and taxi lane should have his headlights on 34.____

A. only when he is passing another vehicle
B. only when the driver ahead is driving too slowly
C. if his speed exceeds 35 miles per hour
D. at all times

35. Bus Operator Hector Gonzalez is driving his bus in the exclusive bus lane when he has to stop because of a disabled auto blocking his way. The auto had been traveling eastbound in the next lane but got a flat tire and came to a stop in the exclusive lane. Gonzalez waits until the police arrive to guide him around the disabled auto. After the police guide Gonzalez around the disabled auto, they leave. In order to reach the Howard Tunnel before 10:00 A.M., Bus Operator Gonzalez drives at 40 miles an hour and keeps a distance of 250 feet behind a taxi. He arrives at the Howard Tunnel without incident. His action was 35.____

A. *proper;* because the lane hours are from 7:00 A.M. to 10:00 A.M.
B. *improper;* because his speed exceeded 35 miles per hour
C. *proper;* because he made up for lost time in maintaining his schedule
D. *improper;* because he should not have waited for the police to guide him

---

KEY (CORRECT ANSWERS)

1. C
2. B
3. A
4. A
5. C

6. A
7. C
8. C
9. D
10. D

11. C
12. B
13. C
14. C
15. C

16. C
17. A
18. B
19. B
20. C

21. C
22. C
23. C
24. C
25. D

26. A
27. B
28. D
29. C
30. A

31. A
32. C
33. B
34. D
35. B

TEST 2

DIRECTIONS: Each question or incomplete statement is followed by several suggested answers or completions. Select the one that BEST answers the question or completes the statement. *PRINT THE LETTER OF THE CORRECT ANSWER IN THE SPACE AT THE RIGHT.*

Questions 1-2.

DIRECTIONS: Questions 1 and 2 are to be answered SOLELY on the basis of the information contained in the following two rules.

1. Bus operators must be relieved only at designated relief points and at the time specified in schedules, unless otherwise instructed by the proper authority. They must never leave their bus until properly relieved, and must not, under any circumstance, surrender the bus to another employee apparently unfit for duty.

2. If a passenger becomes disorderly, annoying, or dangerous, this passenger must be asked to leave the bus at the next designated bus stop.

1. Bus Operator Herbert Bacon is worried about his teenaged daughter who underwent a serious operation. He wants to phone his wife at the hospital to find out how his daughter is feeling. At a designated bus stop, he parks the bus and goes into a tobacco store to use the public telephone. 1.____
   His action was

   A. *proper;* because he parked in a designated bus stop
   B. *improper;* because he left the bus with no bus operator in charge
   C. *proper;* because the nature of the situation justified the phone call
   D. *improper;* because he could have used a telephone in the street

2. Bus Operator Wendy Green notices that a passenger who is obviously drunk is annoying the other passengers with his loud and embarrassing remarks. She asks him several times to be quiet, but he continues to bother the passengers. 2.____
   Bus Operator Green should stop the bus ______ and ask the drunken passenger to get off.

   A. immediately
   B. at the next dispatcher's station
   C: at the next red light
   D. at the next designated bus stop

3. Oak Street is one-way northbound and is intersected by Elm Street, which is one-way eastbound. 3.____
   If there are no traffic control devices at the intersection, and if traffic allows, it should be permissible to make a

   A. right turn from Elm Street into Oak Street
   B. right turn from Oak Street into Elm Street
   C. left turn from Oak Street into Elm Street
   D. four corner U-turn at the intersection

Questions 4-11.

DIRECTIONS: Questions 4 through 11 are to be answered by consulting the Bus Map on the following page. Notice that the left edge of the map is divided into spaces with letters, and the bottom edge of the map is divided into spaces with numbers. The lines for a space with a letter and the lines for a space with a number if extended across the map would meet and form a quadrant (or area). As an example, look at the sketch below which represents part of the map and note that the quadrant formed by an extension of the lines which are the boundaries of the F space and of the 2 space meet to form the F2 quadrant. In this quadrant on your map, you can find Lutheran Medical Center. The locations referred to in the questions below can be found within the quadrants shown in parentheses.

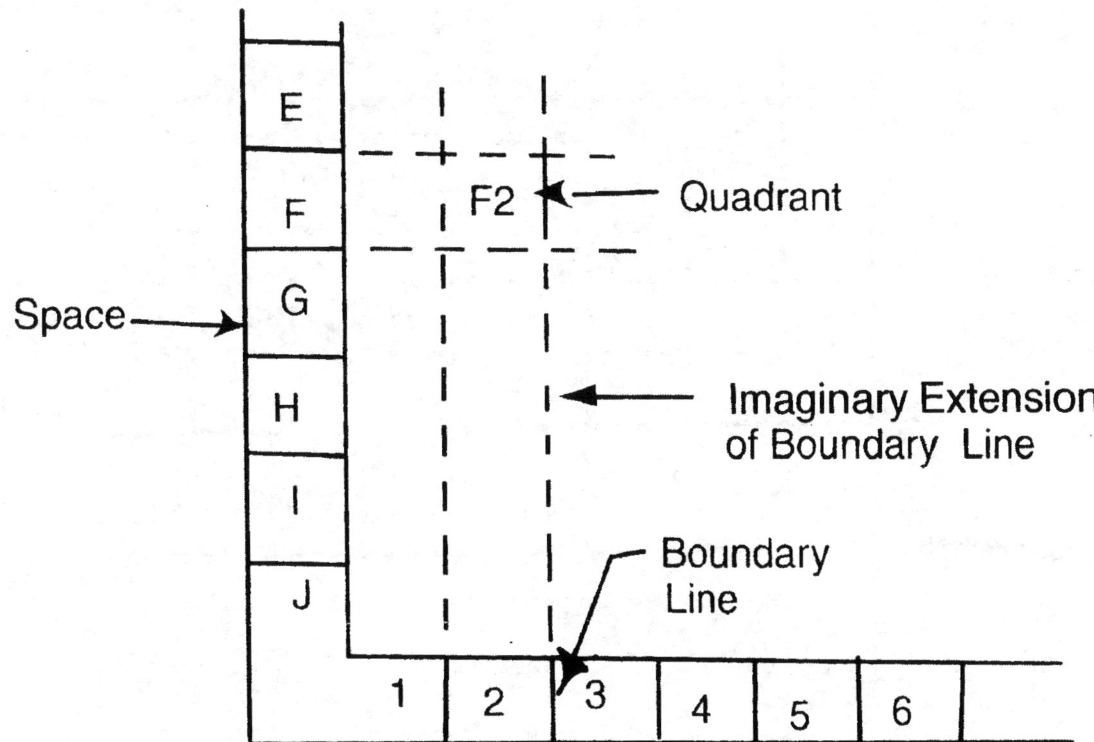

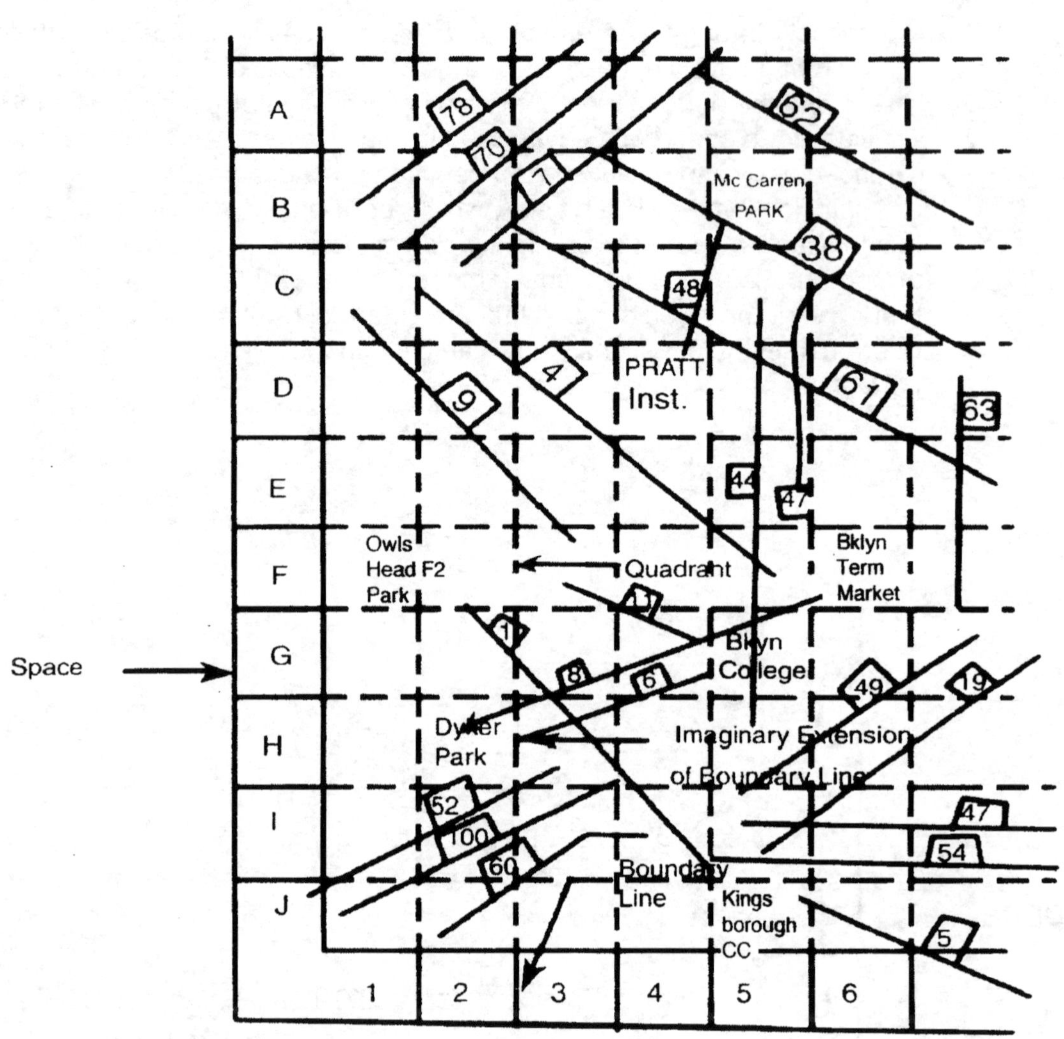

4. Which bus route goes from Brooklyn Terminal Market (quadrant F6) to Dyker Beach Park (quadrant H2)? 4.___

A. 78 B. 8 C. 70 D. 7

5. Which bus route goes from Pratt Institute (quadrant D4) to McCarren Park (quadrant B5)? 5.___

A. 62 B. 38 C. 48 D. 61

6. Which bus should you take to go from Kingsborough Community College (quadrant J5) to Owls Head Park (quadrants F1 and F2)? 6.___

A. 1 B. 4 C. 9 D. 49

7. Which bus route goes from Brooklyn College (quadrant G5) to the intersection of 49th Street and 8th Avenue (quadrant F3)? 7.___

A. 6 B. 11 C. 44 D. 70

8. Which bus route goes from the intersection of 79th Street and Kings Highway (quadrant H3) to Brooklyn College (quadrant G5)? 8.____

A. 6 B. 14 C. 38 D. 52

9. Which bus route goes from the intersection of Flushing Avenue and Nostrand Avenue (quadrant C5) to the inter-section of Nostrand Avenue and Quentin Road (quadrant H5)? 9.____

A. 100 B. 62 C. 48 D. 44

10. Which bus route goes from the intersection of Empire Blvd. and Rogers Avenue (quadrant E5) to the intersection of Myrtle Avenue and Throop Avenue (quadrant C5)? 10.____

A. 44 B. 47 C. 49 D. 54

11. Which bus route goes from the intersection of Ovington Avenue and Fifth Avenue (quadrant G2) to the intersection of 86th Street and Bay Parkway (quadrant H3)? 11.____

A. 1 B. 6 C. 5 D. 63

Questions 12-14.

DIRECTIONS: Questions 12 through 14 are to be answered SOLELY on the basis of the following SCHOOL BUS BULLETIN.

SCHOOL BUS BULLETIN

Anywhere in the state, including the city, when the red lights of a school bus flash, you must stop your vehicle before reaching the bus. This is the law, whether you are approaching the bus from the front, or overtaking it from the rear. In fact, you must stop even if the school bus is on the far side of a four-lane divided highway. Children might cross the road after getting off or before getting on the school bus, and they don't always stop to check in both directions before crossing. They depend on you, the motorist, to stop as the law requires. If the red lights of a school bus are flashing, you may pass it only if the school bus driver clearly signals you to do so, or you are directed to do so by a police officer.

12. It is evening rush hour during a very hot day. The bus you are operating is 15 minutes behind schedule because of very heavy traffic. The air conditioning system in your bus has broken down, and your passengers are uncomfortable, annoyed, and anxious to get home. You are on a wide, two-way street, and you approach a school bus which is parked with its red lights flashing on the other side of the street. The school bus driver is at the wheel, but you see no children in the bus or anywhere on the street.
Under the circumstances, you should ______ the school bus. 12.____

A. proceed with caution past
B. proceed with normal speed past
C. stop your bus before reaching
D. radio for a police officer to direct you past

13. You are a bus operator on a two-lane, one-way main street. You are in the left lane stopped in back of an automobile at a red light. In the lane to your right and in front of you is a school bus which is also waiting for the red light to change. There is no police officer at the corner. When the light changes to green, the car in front of you moves through the 13.____

intersection, but the school bus stalls and will not start. It does not flash its red lights. Under the circumstances, you may

A. pass the school bus because its red lights are not flashing
B. not pass the school bus because there may be children in it
C. pass the school bus only if the school bus driver signals for you to do so
D. not pass the school bus because there is no police officer on the scene

14. You are operating a Transit Authority bus on a one-way street. You approach a school bus from the rear. It is parked at the right curb with its red lights flashing. The school bus is almost filled with children, although a few more are waiting on the sidewalk to get on. After you stop your bus, the school bus driver, who is seated at the wheel of his bus, signals you to pass on the left. Under the circumstances, it would be 14.___

A. *proper* for you to pass the school bus because its driver signalled for you to do so
B. *improper* for you to pass the school bus because children were still boarding
C. *proper* for you to pass the school bus because most of the children were already inside the bus
D. *improper* for you to pass the school bus because its red lights were flashing

Questions 15-17.

DIRECTIONS: Questions 15 through 17 are to be answered SOLELY on the basis of the BULLETIN shown below.

COLORS OF MONTHLY ELEMENTARY AND REDUCED
FARE SCHOOL TICKETS - SUMMER 2011

For the summer of 2011, the colors of the tickets for the School Fare Program for school children will be as follows:

Monthly Elementary School Tickets

Elementary pass FREE - no payment of fare required.
July - Blue with Blue Date
August - Rose with Blue Date

High School Eligibility Cards

Students will pay 50 cents going to school in the A.M. and 50 cents on the return trip from school in the P.M. the entire Summer Session.
July - Beige (Green *S*)
August - Yellow (Green *S*)

Type #2 (r) & #3 (c) Rapid Transit Surface Extension

High school students presenting reduced fare passes for all Rapid Transit Surface Extension Routes - B/42, B/54, B/35, BX/55, and Q/49, will be required to pay $1 in the A.M. on the way to school for the entire Summer Session, July 6, 2011 through August 14, 2011.

15. Joe is a second year high school student attending the Summer Session. If he boards a bus on Wednesday, July 23, he 15.___

A. can ride free if he has a valid Blue ticket with Blue Date
B. must pay 50 cents and show a Beige (Green *S*) card

C. must pay 50 cents and show a Blue (Green *S*) card
D. must pay 50 cents and show a Yellow (Green *S*) card

16. Mary is a senior in high school attending the Summer Session. When she boards the Surface Extension Route B/54 on her way to taking the train to school, she must show her reduced fare pass and pay 16.____

A. no fare B. 50¢ C. $1 D. $7.50

17. George, a junior in high school, and his brother, Tyrone, in 5th grade, are both attending the Summer Session. If they board a bus on Tuesday, August 4th, the bus operator should look for a ______ ticket and a ______ card. 17.____

A. rose; yellow
B. blue; beige
C. blue; blue
D. rose; beige

18. You are a bus operator driving your bus at normal route speed. Suddenly, a man in a sportscar cuts sharply in front of you and continues to speed away from you. Which of the following actions would it be BEST for you to take now? 18.____

A. Accelerate to catch up to the sportscar, then cut it off.
B. Get the license number of the sportscar and radio a report to the police.
C. Slow down until the sportscar is at least a quarter mile ahead of you.
D. Continue along your route at normal speed.

Questions 19-21.

DIRECTIONS: Questions 19 through 21 are to be answered SOLELY on the basis of the REVERSE BUS MOVEMENT PROCEDURE shown below.

REVERSE BUS MOVEMENT PROCEDURE

Bus Operators may operate a bus in reverse only if they determine that no other turn or movement is possible. When operating in reverse, Bus Operators must follow all of the following steps in this procedure.

1. The movement in reverse must not be made until the bus operator has walked around to the back of the bus and made a visual inspection of the area behind the bus.
2. The bus operator must be guided by a responsible person, such as a police officer or another bus driver.
3. The person guiding the bus operator must station himself near the left rear of the bus.
4. When the bus operator has determined that it is safe to back up, he will signal by giving three toots of the horn immediately before starting the reverse movement.

19. Bus Operator Charles Waters has stopped directly behind a disabled bus and cannot move around the bus without backing up. Waters remains in his seat and asks a police officer to stand at the left rear of the bus to direct him. Waters toots his horn three times and slowly backs up just enough to go around the disabled bus. Bus Operator Water's actions in backing up the bus were IMPROPER because Waters 19.____

A. was not guided back by a responsible person
B. should have gotten permission from a supervisor before backing up

C. tooted his horn just before backing up
D. did not inspect the area behind the bus before backing up

20. Bus Operator Elaine Strollin determines that it is necessary to operate her bus in reverse. She inspects the area to the rear of her bus and determines that it is safe to back up. She toots her horn three times to attract the attention of a police officer to assist her in backing up the bus. The police officer goes to the proper position to direct Operator Strollin. With the passengers still in her bus, Operator Strollin is directed by the police officer and backs up her bus without incident .
Operator Strollin's actions in backing up the bus were 20.____

A. *proper* because she had followed the complete procedure for a reverse bus movement
B. *improper* because she did not discharge her passengers before backing up
C. *proper* because with a police officer present, the complete procedure for a reverse bus movement need not be followed
D. *improper* because she did not toot her horn three times just before backing up

21. A bus operator has decided that he must back up his bus. The operator has asked a responsible person to guide his bus back.
Where should he ask that person to stand? 21.____

A. In front of the bus
B. On the right side of the bus near the front door
C. At the left rear of the bus
D. At the right rear of the bus

22. A careful driver should allow 20 feet of stopping room for each ten miles an hour of speed. When driving at night, you should be able to stop within the roadway distance illuminated by your headlights.
If your headlights illuminate the roadway approximately 90 feet before you, your speed at night should NOT exceed about ______ miles per hour. 22.____

A. 25 B. 35 C. 45 D. 55

Questions 23-24.

DIRECTIONS: Questions 23 and 24 are to be answered on the basis of the following bulletin.

The Culture Bus Loops operate on Saturdays, Sundays, and some holidays. The buses on Culture Bus Loop I (M41) run on the loop through midtown and uptown Manhattan every 30 minutes during the winter and every 20 minutes during the summer, from 10:00 A.M. to 6:00 P.M., and make 22 stops. You may get off at any one of the stops, take in the sights, and then catch a later bus, or you can simply stay on the bus for the entire loop. Culture Bus Loop II (B88) provides another view of New York City, one that includes midtown and lower Manhattan, and some of Brooklyn as well. The buses on this loop run every 30 minutes, from 9:00 A.M. to 6:00 P.M. Running time is approximately 2 hours and 25 minutes. Tickets for the Culture Buses may be bought only on the buses. Since the driver cannot make change, and since our fare boxes will not accept paper currency, please have your $2.50 fare in any combination of silver or tokens and silver. The Culture Bus Loop I ticket is valid for certain transfer privileges to crosstown buses. By using the crosstown buses, you may tailor your day's itinerary. The Culture Bus Loop I ticket is also valid as an extension to and from the Cloisters on the M4 bus from Stop 10.

23. The Culture Loop II bus (B88) goes into which borough or boroughs? 23.____

A. Brooklyn and Manhattan
B. Brooklyn and Queens
C. Manhattan *only*
D. Manhattan and the Bronx

24. The Culture Bus Loop I ticket is also valid on the M4 bus as an extension to and from 24.____

A. Brooklyn Heights
B. the Cloisters
C. Greenwich Village
D. Staten Island

25. A bus that is traveling at 22 MPH with 30 passengers has a green light as it approaches an intersection. Just as the bus enters the intersection, the light changes from green to yellow. 25.____
Which of the following is the BEST action for the bus operator to take?

A. Stop short, back his bus out of the intersection, wait for the light to turn green again, then drive through the intersection.
B. Stop quickly, wait in the intersection for the light to turn green again, then drive through the inter-section .
C. Continue through the intersection at 22 MPH.
D. Speed up to get through the intersection before the light turns red.

26. You are driving your bus down a one-way street during the rush hour, and you are already 5 minutes behind schedule. You find that you must stop your bus because the street is blocked by a parcel delivery truck which is double-parked, and the driver is not in sight. 26.____
Which of the following is the FIRST action you should take?

A. Try to attract the attention of the truck driver by blowing your horn.
B. Back the bus out of the street.
C. Radio the police for a tow truck to come and haul away the parcel delivery truck.
D. Jump out of the bus and knock on the door of the house nearest to the parked truck.

27. A bus operator is behind schedule. He has closed his doors and is about to pull out of a bus stop and cross an intersection. The green light is about to change. 27.____
An elderly man raps on the door of the bus. The operator realizes that if he opens the door for the man to board, he will miss the light and get even further behind schedule.
Which of the following is the BEST action for the bus operator to take?

A. Pull away from the bus stop and continue on his route.
B. Go through the intersection before the light changes, then wait for the elderly man to cross the street and board his bus.
C. Open the door and let the man board the bus.
D. Open the door, let the man onto the bus, and tell the man he should have waited for the next bus.

Questions 28-29.

DIRECTIONS: Questions 28 and 29 are to be answered SOLELY on the basis of the information contained in the bulletin shown below on AIR POLLUTION.

AIR POLLUTION

No bus operator should permit the gasoline or diesel engine of his bus to discharge air-polluting gases while the bus is stationary at a route terminal. Operators must shut off bus engines, unless otherwise directed, immediately upon completing arrival at the terminal stop. All operators and supervisors should remain constantly alert for any Transit Authority vehicles emitting excessive fumes while in motion. They should report such vehicles immediately on their bus radios to Surface Control by bus number, together with any further available identifying information.

28. Nathan Pearl, a bus operator, is driving his bus along Flatbush Avenue when he notices black smoke being discharged from the exhaust of a bus coming in the opposite direction. 28.____
Of the following, what should Bus Operator Pearl do?

   A. Let the bus operator of the other bus take care of it.
   B. Tell the other operator about the pollution when he sees him in the garage after they have completed their runs.
   C. Call Surface Control to report the bus which is emitting black smoke.
   D. Write a report on the bus emitting black smoke when he completes his run, giving the bus number and other identifying information.

29. To avoid air pollution, bus operators are ordered to do which of the following? 29.____

   A. Drive no more than 12 miles an hour.
   B. Shut off the engine at bus stops where a large number of passengers are boarding and alighting.
   C. Shut off the engine at terminal stops.
   D. Close all windows of the bus so that passengers will not breathe in smoke or fumes being emitted by the bus.

30. A bus operator notices a wallet on the floor next to the driver's seat. While waiting at the next red light, he examines the contents of the wallet. It has $30 worth of bills and various cards identifying the owner as Charles Bergen. 30.____
Of the following, it would be MOST appropriate for the bus operator to

   A. hold onto the wallet during the run and return it if a passenger tells him he has lost his wallet and identifies himself as Charles Bergen
   B. ask passengers if anyone has lost a wallet, and then return the wallet if a person who identifies himself as Charles Bergen claims to have lost the wallet and can identify its contents
   C. pocket the money and inconspicuously place the wallet back on the floor. Anyone careless enough to drop his wallet deserves no sympathy.
   D. ask if anyone on the bus has lost a wallet with $30 in cash and return it if someone claims to have lost it

31. You are a bus operator. While you are stopped at a red light, a woman on board your bus, speaking English with a heavy foreign accent, asks you for directions. You do not understand her question. 31.____
Of the following, you should

   A. ask the woman to repeat her question more slowly
   B. ask one of the other passengers to give directions to the woman

C. hand the woman a bus map of the borough you are in
D. give the woman the phone number of the Transit Authority Travel Information Bureau

32. As you are driving your bus, you notice that traffic is close behind you. On a sidewalk about 150 feet ahead of you, some children are playing with a small rubber ball. Suddenly, the ball rolls into the street in the path of your bus. 32.____
Which of the following actions should you take?

A. Brake lightly, honk your horn, and be prepared to stop short if a child races after the ball.
B. Honk your horn and stop short in anticipation that one of the children might run after the ball.
C. Honk your horn and continue at normal speed, but be prepared to brake quickly.
D. Honk your horn, then speed up so as to get past the children as quickly as possible.

33. Your bus is 15 minutes behind schedule. The bus scheduled to follow yours has gotten ahead of you and is in the next bus stop. You wish to pass this bus. As you approach the bus stop, you notice that this bus is starting to pull out. 33.____
You should

A. honk your horn and pass the bus quickly
B. pull behind the bus and allow it to continue ahead
C. pull alongside the bus and tell the driver that you would appreciate it if he did not pass you again
D. make a turn to a lightly traveled parallel street going in your direction, then drive non-stop for several blocks to both pass the bus in front of you and get back on schedule

34. You are carrying 20 passengers in your bus on a one-way two-lane street. You notice that the car ahead of you is weaving erratically in and out of its lane. 34.____
Of the following, your MOST appropriate course of action is to

A. keep a big enough distance between the car and your bus to eliminate any possibility of contact
B. stay close behind the car and keep honking your horn until the driver of the car either pulls over to a curb or turns down a side street
C. stay as close behind the car as you can and be prepared to signal the first police officer you see
D. pass the car and speed away from it

35. Your bus is approaching an intersection with the green light in your favor. From the street on your right, a man on a bicycle is approaching the intersection. The man has sufficient time to stop at the intersection. 35.____
Of the following, the BEST action for you to take is to

A. exercise your right of way and cross the intersection at normal speed
B. stop and wait until you see what the cyclist does
C. proceed with caution, ready to apply brakes if necessary
D. accelerate through the light before the cyclist reaches the intersection

---

KEY (CORRECT ANSWERS)

1. B
2. D
3. B
4. B
5. C

6. A
7. B
8. A
9. D
10. B

11. A
12. C
13. A
14. A
15. B

16. C
17. A
18. D
19. D
20. D

21. C
22. C
23. A
24. B
25. C

26. A/C
27. C
28. C
29. C
30. B

31. A
32. A
33. B
34. A
35. C

EXAMINATION SECTION
TEST 1

DIRECTIONS: Each question or incomplete statement is followed by several suggested answers or completions. Select the one that BEST answers the question or completes the statement. *PRINT THE LETTER OF THE CORRECT ANSWER IN THE SPACE AT THE RIGHT.*

1. Present traffic procedure is to have one lane on many wide one-way streets marked out in yellow paint. 1.____
   This line is to be
   A. used by regular vehicles when a siren is heard
   B. cleared for vehicles about to make a left turn
   C. used exclusively by emergency vehicles
   D. cleared for emergency vehicles when a siren is heard

2. It is CORRECT to say that a(the) 2.____
   A. vehicle may be legally parked 15 feet from a fire hydrant
   B. legal speed limit in the city is 45 miles per hour
   C. distance required to stop at 10 m.p.h. is just half that required at 20 m.p.h.
   D. flashing yellow light means stop and then go

3. To stop a motor vehicle on an icy street with the LEAST chance of skidding, the operator should 3.____
   A. apply the brakes normally
   B. step on the accelerator lightly after releasing it
   C. make a number of light foot-brake applications
   D. apply the hand brake *only*

4. Transit employees are urged to be courteous to passengers MAINLY to 4.____
   A. assure safety
   B. maintain bus schedules
   C. win prizes
   D. maintain good public relations

5. Improper use of the horn of a motor vehicle is not permitted. 5.____
   It would be clearly IMPROPER for a bus operator to sound
   A. several short blasts to warn pedestrian stragglers in front of his bus at an intersection
   B. several short blasts to warn a motorist about to pull away from the curb in front of a moving bus
   C. three short blasts as a warning before he backs up
   D. two short blasts as he is passing another bus going in the opposite direction

6. A recognized principle in good urban transportation is that the interval between buses at any particular time of day should be uniform. 6.____
   The MOST likely consequence of an unusually long time gap between buses resulting from traffic conditions is

A. heavy riding on some buses
B. confusion of passengers
C. crossing accidents
D. loss of regular patronage

7. It is an indication of a safe driver if the operator 7.____

A. *seldom* yields the right-of-way
B. *seldom* runs ahead of schedule
C. *frequently* yields the right-of-way
D. *frequently* runs behind schedule

8. A person who has been a rider on buses can reason that the failure which would LEAST likely be the cause for a bus being taken out of service is a ______ door stuck ______ 8.____

A. rear; closed
B. front; closed
C. rear; open
D. front; open

Questions 9-18.

DIRECTIONS: Questions 9 through 18 are to be answered on the basis of the following description of an incident. Read the description carefully before answering these questions.

DESCRIPTION OF INCIDENT

On Tuesday, October 8, at about 4:00 P.M., Bus Operator Sam Bell, Badge No. 3871, whose accident record was perfect, was operating his half-filled bus, No. 4392Y, northbound, and on schedule along Dean Street. At this time, a male passenger who was apparently intoxicated started to yell and to use loud and profane language. The bus driver told this passenger to be quiet or to get off the bus. The passenger said that he would not be quiet but indicated that he wanted to get off the bus by moving toward the front door exit. When he reached the front of the bus, which at the time was in motion, the intoxicated passenger slapped the bus operator on the back and pulled the steering wheel sharply. This action caused the bus to sideswipe a passenger automobile coming from the opposite direction before the operator could stop the bus. The sideswiped car was a red 2004 Pontiac 2-door convertible, License 6416-KN, driven by Albert Holt. The bus driver kept the doors of his bus closed and blew the horn vigorously. The horn blowing was quickly answered as Sergeant Henry Burns, Badge No. 1208, and Patrolman Joe Cross, Badge No. 24643, happened to be following a few cars behind the bus in police car No. 736. The intoxicated passenger, who gave his name as John Doe, was placed under arrest, and Patrolman Cross took the names of witnesses while Sergeant Burns recorded the necessary vehicular information. Investigation showed that no one was injured in the accident and that the entire damage to the automobile was having its side slightly pushed in.

9. From the information given, it can be reasoned that 9.____

A. it was just beginning to rain
B. Dean Street is a two-way street
C. there were mostly women shoppers on the bus
D. most seats in the bus were filled

10. The name of the policeman who was riding in the police car with the sergeant was 10.____

A. Cross B. Bell C. Holt D. Burns

11. From the description, it is evident that the passenger automobile was traveling 11.____

A. north B. south C. east D. west

12. It is logical to conclude that the passenger automobile was damaged on its 12.____

A. front end B. rear end
C. right side D. left side

13. A fact concerning the intoxicated passenger that is clearly stated in the above description is that he 13.____

A. was intoxicated when he got on the bus
B. hit a fellow passenger
C. pulled the steering wheel sharply
D. was not arrested

14. The bus operator called the attention of the police by 14.____

A. sideswiping an oncoming car
B. yelling and using profane language
C. blowing his horn vigorously
D. stopping a police car coming from the opposite direction

15. A reasonable conclusion that can be drawn from the above description is that 15.____

A. the name John Doe was fictitious
B. the sideswiped automobile was from out of town
C. some of the passengers on the bus were injured
D. the bus operator tried to put the intoxicated passenger off the bus

16. The number of the police car involved in the incident was 16.____

A. 4392Y B. 6416-KN C. 1208 D. 736

17. From the facts stated, it is obvious that the bus operator was 17.____

A. behind schedule
B. driving too close to the center of the street
C. discourteous to the intoxicated passenger
D. a good driver

18. It is clearly stated that the 18.____

A. sideswiped automobile was a blue sedan
B. bus driver kept the bus doors closed until the police came
C. incident happened on a Thursday
D. police sergeant took down the names of witnesses

19. At terminals in residential areas where a bus remains for more than 3 minutes, operators are required to turn off their engines. 19.____
The LEAST important reason for stopping the engines is to

A. reduce noise
B. conserve fuel
C. reduce air pollution
D. minimize engine wear

20. Statistics show that automobile accidents occur MOST frequently 20.____

A. in the morning rush hours
B. around noon
C. soon after sunset
D. near midnight

21. A bus operator is liable under the law to receive a traffic ticket for 21.____

A. double standing when a bus stop is occupied by a car
B. not taking on all people waiting at a stop
C. passing a preceding bus on a grade
D. discharging a passenger at other than a bus stop

22. A bus operator approaching a green light sees a pedestrian crossing his path against the light. 22.____
If the pedestrian is two or three bus lengths away, the operator

A. is required to make a complete stop
B. should swing his bus closer to the curb
C. is required to report the pedestrian to the nearest police officer
D. should reduce his speed and blow his horn

23. The power to revoke a license to drive a motor vehicle is in the hands of the 23.____

A. Police Commissioner
B. Traffic Commissioner
C. Commissioner of Motor Vehicles
D. Mayor

24. When passing a playground, park or other area where children are playing or walking, 24.____

A. stop and then proceed with caution
B. slow down and proceed with caution
C. blow horn and make sure they see you
D. blow horn, stop, and then proceed with caution

Questions 25-34.

DIRECTIONS: Questions 25 through 34 are to be answered on the basis of the following sketch showing the routes of the Grand Avenue (solid line) and the Elm St. (dotted line) buses. Refer to this sketch when answering these questions.

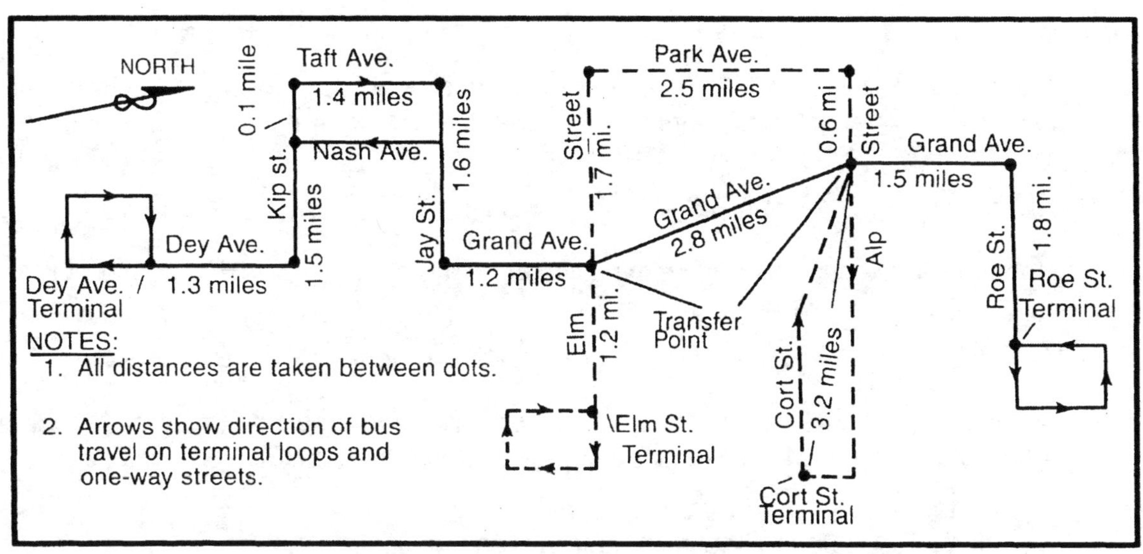

25. A bus on Alp St. going to the Cort St. terminal is moving 25.____

A. north B. east C. south D. west

26. If the distance around a terminal loop is one-half mile, the total distance that a bus must travel in one round trip between the Dey Ave. and Roe St. terminals, including both terminal loops, is NEAREST to ______ miles. 26.____

A. 26.2 B. 26.7 C. 27.2 D. 28.4

27. One street used by buses operating in both directions is 27.____

A. Taft Avenue
B. Roe Street
C. Cort Street
D. Nash Avenue

28. The bus route distance between the Elm St. and Cort St. terminals is ______ miles. 28.____

A. 8.6 B. 9.2 C. 9.7 D. 18.9

29. A passenger must transfer if he is going from Dey Ave. terminal to 29.____

A. Taft Ave.
B. Elm St.
C. Cort St.
D. Park Ave.

30. Buses are NOT required to make even one left turn at the terminal at 30.____

A. Cort St.
B. Dey Ave.
C. Elm St.
D. Roe St.

31. After discharging all passengers at the Dey Ave. terminal before going around the loop, the number of left turns a bus must make to reach Elm St. is 31.____

A. 1 B. 2 C. 3 D. 4

32. From the Cort St. terminal to Elm St., a bus travels a total distance of ______ miles. 32.____

A. 5.7 B. 6.0 C. 6.3 D. 7.2

33. If the common rule for estimating distance of 20 blocks to the mile is adhered to, then the number of blocks a bus travels on Grand Ave. is 33.____

A. 56 B. 80 C. 110 D. 136

34. If the timetable calls for a bus to cover the distance along Dey Ave. from the terminal to Kip St. in 12 minutes, the average speed of the bus on this stretch must be ______ miles per hour. 34.____

A. 1.1 B. 6.5 C. 10 D. 15.5

35. In the Civilian Defense air raid warning system a three minute warbling sound of the sirens is the ______ signal. 35.____

A. alert B. test C. all clear D. take cover

36. If a person should ask you, while on duty in your bus, for directions on how to reach a particular location to which you do not know the answer, your BEST course of action is to 36.____

A. tell the person you do not know
B. give the person the best directions you can think of
C. tell the person to buy a directory
D. explain to the person that the rules prohibit talking to an operator while he is on duty

37. The rules of the Transit Authority state that employees should not make any statements concerning transit accidents except to proper officials of the Transit Authority upon inquiry. 37.____
The PROBABLE reason for this rule is to

A. conceal facts that may be damaging
B. avoid conflicting testimony
C. prevent lawsuits
D. prevent unofficial statements from being accepted as official

38. As a potential bus operator, you should know that when you are about to back a bus, it is NEVER necessary for you to 38.____

A. check that there is sufficient room behind the bus
B. signal your intention
C. turn on back-up lights
D. check the brake air pressure

39. A flashing red traffic signal indicates that a driver 39.____

A. must stop and wait until the light stops flashing
B. must stop and then proceed when the way is clear
C. may make a right turn without stopping
D. must yield the right-of-way but does not have to stop

40. Operators should be instructed that collision accidents at street intersections protected by traffic lights can USUALLY be avoided if they will remember that 40.____

A. traffic lights are often out of order
B. a car coming from the right has the right-of-way
C. they can depend on the other drive obeying the lights
D. there is no substitute for an alert driver

Questions 41-50.

DIRECTIONS: Questions 41 through 50 are to be answered on the basis of the portion of a bus timetable shown below. Refer to this timetable in answering these questions.

TIME TABLE – LAKESIDE LINE – WEEKDAYS

SOUTH BOUND | NORTH BOUND

Bus No.	Mack St. Lv.	High St. Lv.	Ace St. Lv.	Burr St. Arr.	Burr St. Lv.	Ace St. Lv.	High St. Lv.	Mark St. Arr.
10	6:06	6:14	6:32	6:46	6:55	7:09	7:27	7:35
11	6:21	6:29	6:47	7:01	7:10	7:24	7:42	7:50
12	6:36	6:44	7:02	7:16	7:25	7:39	7:57	6:05
13	6:51	6:59	7:17	7:31	7:40	7:54	8:12	8:20
14	7:03	7:11	7:29	7:43	7:55	8:09	8:27	8:35
15	7:15	7:23	7:41	7:55	8:10	8:24	8:42	8:50
16	7:28	7:36	7:54	8:08	8:25	8:39	8:57	9:05
17	7:41	7:49	8:07	8:21L	-	-	-	-
10	7:51	7:59	8:17	8:31	8:40	8:54	9:12	9:20
18	P8:01	8:09	8:27	8:41	8:55	9:09	9:27	9:35
11	8:09	8:17	8:35	8 :49L	-	-	-	-
19	P8:17	8:25	8:43	8:57	9:10	9:24	9:42	9:50
12	8:25	8:33	8:51	9:05L	-	-	-	-
20	P8:33	8:41	8:59	9:13	9:25	9:39	9:57	10:05
13	8:43	8:51	9:09	9:23L	-	-	-	-
14	8:58	9:06	9:24	9:38	9:40	9:54	10:12	10:20

Notes:
1. The time interval between buses at a given point is called the headway.
2. The time interval between the arrival and departure of a bus at a terminal is called its layover.
3. P indicates that a bus not already in passenger senice is placed in service at the time and place shown.
4. L indicates that a bus is taken out of passenger service at the time and place shown and is sent to the garage.
5. Lv. means "leave," and Arr. means "arrive."

41. The MINIMUM headway shown between buses leaving Mack St. is ______ minutes. 41.____

A. 8 B. 10 C. 12 D. 15

42. The ACTUAL scheduled running time from Burr St. to High St. is ______ minutes. 42.____

A. 14 B. 32 C. 40 D. 64

43. The layover time for Bus No. 16 at Burr St. is ______ minutes. 43.____

A. 9 B. 12 C. 15 D. 17

44. Bus No. 11 is scheduled to 44.____

A. follow Bus No. 12 from Burr St. to Mack St., northbound
B. leave Ace St. exactly 20 minutes after it leaves Mack St., southbound
C. leave Burr St. for the garage after 8:49
D. be placed in service to begin its day's run at Mack St. at 8:09

45. The time shown in the timetable for any bus to make the run from Mack St. to Burr St. and return is ______ minutes ______ the layover time at Burr St. 45.____

A. 40; plus B. 40; minus
C. 80; minus D. 80; plus

46. The TOTAL number of northbound buses passing High St. between 8:00 and 8:45 is 46.____

A. 2 B. 3 C. 4 D. 5

47. The TOTAL number of buses which is scheduled to leave Mack St. between 7:45 and 8:45 and is also scheduled to return to Mack St. is 47.____

A. 4 B. 5 C. 6 D. 7

48. The MOST northerly street on this line is ______ St. 48.____

A. Ace B. Mack C. High D. Burr

49. A passenger boarding a bus at Burr St. and wishing to get to High St. as close as possible to 9:30 should board the bus which leaves at 49.____

A. 8:51 B. 8:55 C. 9:06 D. 9:10

50. The number of buses which is shown in the timetable as making two complete round trips is 50.____

A. 2 B. 3 C. 5 D. 6

KEY (CORRECT ANSWERS)

1.	D	11.	B	21.	D	31.	C	41.	A
2.	A	12.	D	22.	D	32.	C	42.	B
3.	C	13.	C	23.	C	33.	C	43.	D
4.	D	14.	C	24.	B	34.	B	44.	C
5.	D	15.	A	25.	B	35.	D	45.	D
6.	A	16.	D	26.	C	36.	A	46.	B
7.	C	17.	D	27.	B	37.	D	47.	A
8.	A	18.	B	28.	B	38.	C	48.	B
9.	B	19.	D	29.	D	39.	B	49.	B
10.	A	20.	C	30.	A	40.	D	50.	A

TEST 2

DIRECTIONS: Each question or incomplete statement is followed by several suggested answers or completions. Select the one that BEST answers the question or completes the statement. *PRINT THE LETTER OF THE CORRECT ANSWER IN THE SPACE AT THE RIGHT.*

1. The two rear wheels of a bus can turn at different speeds when necessary by means of the 1.____

   A. overdrive
   B. torque converter
   C. universal joint
   D. differential

2. To properly perform his duties, it is LEAST important for a bus driver to 2.____

   A. know the schedule of working conditions
   B. know the Transit Authority's operating rules
   C. be able to judge speed and distance
   D. know the times he is scheduled to be at various points

3. Manuals on driving stress the importance of allowing ample braking distance to the car ahead, the most common rule of thumb being to allow a car length for each ten miles per hour of speed. 3.____
   If the overall length of a car is 210 inches, the proper braking distance to allow at a speed of 40 miles per hour is NEAREST to ______ feet.

   A. 700
   B. 500
   C. 70
   D. 50

4. The safe speed on any road regardless of weather conditions is primarily a function of the ability of the vehicle operator to compensate for roadway and traffic conditions. This statement means MOST NEARLY that it is 4.____

   A. always safe to drive well below the posted or allowable speed
   B. permitted to drive a bus faster than the posted or allowable speed to compensate for traffic delays
   C. not safe to drive at the maximum posted or allowable speed under any weather conditions
   D. necessary for a bus operator to use his judgment to determine the safe operating speed

5. If your watch gains 20 minutes per day and you set it to the correct time at 7:00 A.M., the correct time, to the NEAREST minute, when the watch indicates 1:00 P.M. is 5.____

   A. 12:50
   B. 12:55
   C. 1:05
   D. 1:10

6. The law requires that cars having four-wheel brakes must be able to stop in 30 feet from a speed of 20 miles per hour, and in 120 feet from 40 miles per hour. 6.____
   From these requirements and your own knowledge of auto-mobiles in motion, it is MOST logical to conclude that

   A. the law is more lenient in regard to fast cars than slow cars
   B. when speed is doubled, the needed braking distance is multiplied by four
   C. drivers' reactions slow down greatly as speed increases
   D. any 20 mile per hour increase in speed will require 90 feet more of braking distance

Questions 7-16.

DIRECTIONS: Questions 7 through 16 are to be answered on the basis of the sketch shown below. Refer to this sketch when answering these questions. The sketch shows the situation shortly after the traffic lights have changed to green for north-south traffic and red for east-west traffic.

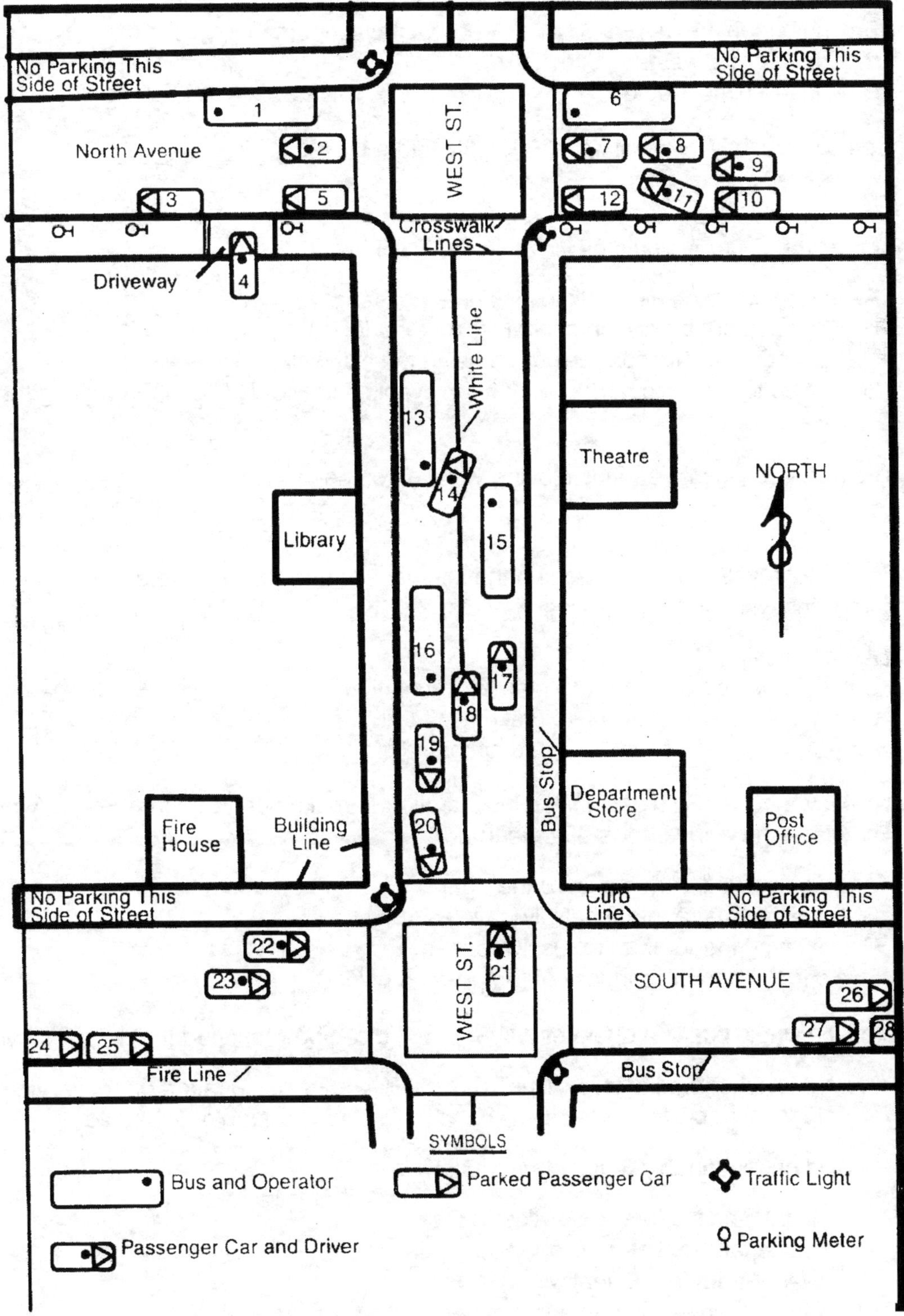

7. Of the following stopped cars, the one which is in the generally approved position to start to enter a parking space is the one numbered 7.____

A. 7 B. 8 C. 9 D. 11

8. It is clearly seen that the operator of Bus 1 is 8.____

A. in error in taking up the entire bus stop
B. not stopping, as Bus 6 will pick up the passengers
C. driving in a westerly direction
D. ahead of schedule

9. One car which is unquestionably illegally parked is No. 9.____

A. 3 B. 10 C. 12 D. 25

10. The driver of Car 4 would be violating the law if he 10.____

A. stopped at the sidewalk to pick up a passenger
B. failed to put on his directional signal for a left turn
C. did not blow his horn before crossing the sidewalk
D. failed to yield the right-of-way to any vehicle on North Ave. approaching the driveway

11. The car which is in a serious moving violation of the law is No. 11.____

A. 2 B. 4 C. 17 D. 19

12. If Cars 22 and 23 are approaching the intersection and the operators of both cars are complying with the law, it is clear that Car 22 12.____

A. is passing Car 23
B. cannot stop before reaching the intersection
C. is in the better position to make a left turn
D. will continue across the intersection

13. The driver of Car 20 has signaled his intention to make a left turn into South Avenue. The diagram clearly shows that the turn 13.____

A. was started from too far to the right
B. is being made into a heavily traveled street
C. is being made at an excessive speed
D. can be made regardless of the position of Car 21

14. If only a single bus line operates on West St., it can be reasoned that MOST likely Bus 14.____

A. 13 is scheduled to follow Bus 16
B. 16 is being taken out of service
C. 13 is more crowded than Bus 16
D. 16 is ahead of schedule

15. It would be reasonable to infer that MOST likely 15.____

A. no parking is allowed on West Street
B. the department store is open for business
C. West Street is 100 feet wide
D. the area shown is primarily residential

16. An example of a double-parked car is No. 16.____

A. 9 B. 10 C. 26 D. 27

17. Of the following, the GREATEST number of bus riders will be on the day after 17.____

A. New Year's B. July 4th C. Thanksgiving D. Christmas

18. The first aid procedure of not moving a person unless absolutely necessary is MOST important in the case of a person who has 18.____

A. broken a finger
B. fainted
C. collapsed from the heat
D. fractured his leg

19. A bus driver making change should be on the alert for counterfeit bills. 19.____
The BEST publicized means of detecting a counterfeit bill is to pay particular attention to the

A. feel of the paper
B. clarity of the portrait
C. width of the margin
D. size of the bill

20. The TOTAL value of 11 half-dollars, 27 quarters, 193 dimes, 108 nickels, 75 pennies is 20.____

A. \$27.70 B. \$30.40 C. \$37.70 D. \$43.20

21. A bus operator need NOT pull over to the curb and come to a stop 21.____

A. when signaled to do so by a policeman
B. at a bus stop where passengers are waiting
C. at the sound of a fire engine siren
D. when he hears the horn of the car behind

22. The Transit Authority's reduced fare cards, which are issued to children by the school, are printed in a different color for each school month. 22.____
If the cards used during one month were salmon color, this color would BEST be described as being

A. pink B. green C. blue D. gray

23. Bus operators have been instructed to confiscate reduced fare cards for any one of the following acts on the part of a student: (1) misbehavior, (2) vandalism, (3) passing card to another student, and (4) using card during unauthorized hours. 23.____
On this basis, a student caught cutting the seats of a bus with a penknife would have his card lifted for reason number

A. 1 B. 2 C. 3 D. 4

24. It is a rule that bus operators must not operate through or within established fire or police lines or over any unprotected hose of a fire department when laid down on any street unless allowed by proper authority. 24.____
This means that a bus operator may operate his bus

A. on the side of a street opposite a fire
B. over a fire hose if given permission by a fireman
C. past a traffic officer as soon as the light turns green
D. across the route of a parade whenever there is a break in the parade line

25. The Transit Authority permits the posting of advertisements in buses PRIMARILY because 25.___

A. passengers like to read the ads
B. advertisers pay for this privilege
C. it promotes safety
D. it improves the interior appearances of the buses

26. Safety rules are MOST useful because they 26.___

A. are a guide to avoid common dangers
B. prevent carelessness
C. fix responsibility for accidents
D. make it unnecessary to think

27. During rush hours, passengers are requested to have the correct fare ready when boarding a bus MAINLY because this 27.___

A. assures collection of all fares
B. permits a fuller bus load
C. results in less change being carried by the operator
D. helps to maintain the schedule

28. Traffic regulations forbid *dangerous* or *reckless* driving. In the absence of special signs, an example of such *dangerous* or *reckless* driving is 28.___

A. parking a car within 15 feet of a fire hydrant
B. driving on a hospital street at 25 miles per hour
C. passing a public school at noontime on a weekday at 10 miles per hour
D. frequently changing lanes in heavy traffic moving at 45 miles per hour on a parkway

29. If a passenger called a bus operator improper names but took no other action, the bus operator would show good judgment by 29.___

A. telling the passenger to keep his mouth shut
B. acting as if the passenger were not there
C. calling the passenger names in return
D. driving to the nearest policeman and preferring charges

30. It is a rule that, when street obstructions leave scant clearance for buses to pass, operators must stop before passing the obstruction and never proceed until certain that clearance is sufficient and that it is safe to do so. This means that 30.___

A. it is never safe to pass street obstructions
B. every bus must stop before passing an open manhole with a fence around it
C. the operator must stop if he must use the single narrow traffic lane between a parked truck and an open manhole
D. the operator may always pass an obstruction as long as he stops first

31. After a passenger has tendered the bus operator a dollar bill, has paid his fare, and received change, he goes some distance toward the back of the bus and then returns to the front, stating that he was shortchanged a quarter. The BEST action for a bus operator to take is to 31.____

A. give him the quarter if he is sufficiently argumentative
B. tell him to send a letter of complaint to the Mayor's complaint box
C. inform him that change must be counted when received
D. tell him that he must have dropped it in the bus

32. It is a rule that bus operators must not approach within 100 feet of a line of children during a school fire drill, nor interfere with, hinder, obstruct, or impede in any way whatsoever any such fire drill. 32.____
A bus operator, observing a school fire drill in progress in the next street ahead, could BEST comply with this rule by

A. making a right turn at the corner and going around the school
B. pulling up slowly to the person in charge of the drill
C. stopping at the corner until the fire drill is over
D. proceeding slowly along the opposite side of the street

33. A rule of the Transit Authority is that buses must never be moved except by operators certified as qualified, and by authorized student operators while supervised by a qualified operator. 33.____
This rule permits a bus to be moved at any time by any person

A. who is an approved operator
B. certified as a student operator
C. with a chauffeur's license
D. who knows how to operate a bus

34. When driving on a two-lane road at night, you see cars approaching from the opposite direction. 34.____
You should

A. increase your speed slightly
B. ride partly on the shoulder of the road
C. switch your headlights to low beam
D. blow your horn

35. If you are the driver of a car involved in an accident in which some one is injured, you are required by law to file a report of the accident within two 35.____

A. hours B. days C. weeks D. months

36. If the rear of a car starts to skid toward the right, it is usually possible to break out of the skid by 36.____

A. pumping the brake
B. cutting off the ignition
C. shifting to low gear
D. steering toward the right

37. According to the notice for this examination, a candidate must be acceptable for bonding. The MOST probable reason for this requirement is 37.____

A. to encourage honesty among operators
B. because operators handle money
C. because it saves the cost of making an investigation
D. to protect the city against lawsuits

38. It is MOST important for a bus driver to see that no vehicle is directly behind his bus when he is about to 38.____

A. pull out from a bus stop
B. pass another vehicle
C. back up
D. turn right

39. A vehicle is not permitted to pass a stopped school bus with red lights flashing because the flashing lights PROBABLY indicate that 39.____

A. the school bus is about to start
B. the school bus operator is in need of assistance
C. an emergency vehicle is coming from the opposite direction
D. children are crossing the road

40. The approved way to warm up a cold automobile engine is to 40.____

A. let the engine idle before driving off
B. add anti-freeze
C. drive at the speed limit for a few minutes
D. rock the car by shifting between reverse and low twice

41. In preparing to make a right turn, it is NOT necessary for you to 41.____

A. move to the extreme right-hand lane
B. slow down
C. give a hand or mechanical turn signal
D. come to a full stop

42. The one of the following days this year on which bus lines in the city can expect the GREATEST number of passengers is 42.____

A. May 30
B. June 5
C. July 4
D. December 25

43. According to the information given on the printed instructions in subway cars, a passenger wishing to recover an article believed lost in the subway should check with the 43.____

A. change booth where he got on
B. conductor on his train
C. lost property office
D. transit police office

Questions 44-50.

DIRECTIONS: Questions 44 through 50 are to be answered on the basis of the following paragraph. Refer to this paragraph in answering these questions.

DRINKING AND DRIVING

In fatal traffic accidents, a drinking driver is involved more than 30% of the time; on holiday weekends, more than 50% of the fatal accidents involve drinking drivers. Drinking to any extent reduces the judgment, self-control, and driving ability of any driver. Social drinkers, especially those who think they drive better after a drink, are a greater menace than commonly believed, and they outnumber the obviously intoxicated. Two cocktails may reduce visual acuity as much as wearing dark glasses at night. Alcohol is not a stimulant; it is classified medically as a depressant. Coffee or other stimulants will not offset the effects of alcohol; only time can eliminate alcohol from the bloodstream. It takes at least three hours to eliminate one ounce of pure alcohol from the bloodstream.

44. Alcohol is classified by doctors as a 44.____

A. stimulant B. sedative
C. depressant D. medicine

45. Social drinkers 45.____

A. never become obviously intoxicated
B. always drink in large groups
C. drive better after two cocktails
D. are a greater menace than commonly believed

46. Alcohol will BEST be eliminated from the bloodstream by 46.____

A. fresh air B. a stimulant
C. coffee D. time

47. More than half of the fatal accidents on holiday weekends involve ______ drivers. 47.____

A. inexperienced B. drinking
C. fast D. slow

48. Drinking to any extent does NOT 48.____

A. impair judgment
B. decrease visual acuity
C. reduce accident potential
D. affect driving ability

49. In traffic accidents resulting in death, a drinking driver is involved 49.____

A. about one-third of the time
B. mainly at night
C. more than 80% of the time
D. practically all the time on weekends

50. After taking two alcoholic drinks, it is best NOT to drive until after you have 50.____

A. had a cup of black coffee B. waited three hours
C. eaten a full meal D. taken a half-hour nap

KEY (CORRECT ANSWERS)

1. D	11. B	21. D	31. C	41. D
2. A	12. C	22. A	32. C	42. B
3. C	13. A	23. B	33. A	43. C
4. D	14. A	24. B	34. C	44. C
5. B	15. A	25. B	35. B	45. D
6. B	16. C	26. A	36. D	46. D
7. C	17. A	27. D	37. B	47. B
8. C	18. D	28. D	38. C	48. C
9. D	19. B	29. B	39. D	49. A
10. D	20. C	30. C	40. A	50. B

TEST 3

DIRECTIONS: Each question or incomplete statement is followed by several suggested answers or completions. Select the one that BEST answers the question or completes the statement. *PRINT THE LETTER OF THE CORRECT ANSWER IN THE SPACE AT THE RIGHT.*

1. There has been talk of assigning police detectives to operate taxicabs. The PRINCIPAL reason for making such assignments would be to 1.____

   A. protect cab patrons against robbery
   B. give detectives a chance to learn their way about the city
   C. apprehend and arrest those who are robbing cabdrivers
   D. give the police department an idea of the type of people who use cabs

2. An employee of the Transit Authority must notify the office whenever he moves and changes his address. 2.____
   The logical reason for this requirement is to

   A. enable the Authority to furnish correct information to creditors
   B. enable the Authority to contact the employee in time of need
   C. prevent the holding of two jobs
   D. help the post office, if necessary

Questions 3-14.

DIRECTIONS: Questions 3 through 14 are to be answered on the basis of the following description of an automobile accident. Read the description carefully before answering these questions.

DESCRIPTION OF AUTOMOBILE ACCIDENT

Ten persons were injured, two critically, when a driverless automobile - its accelerator jammed - ran wild through the busy intersection at 8th Ave. and 42nd Street at 11:30 A.M. yesterday. The car struck a truck, overturned it, and mounted the sidewalk. Several persons were bowled over before the car was finally stopped by collision with a second truck. Police Officer Fred Black, Badge No. 82143, said that the freak accident occurred after the car's driver, Mrs. Mary Jones, 39, of Queens, got out of the car with her daughter, Gloria, aged 3, while the engine was still running. Mr. Herbert Field, 64, of the Bronx, a passenger in the car, accidently stepped on the accelerator when he tried to get out. This caused the car to shoot forward, because the shift was in *drive,* and 5 pedestrians were thrown to the ground.

3. This accident occurred 3.____

   A. late in the morning
   B. early in the morning
   C. early in the afternoon
   D. late in the evening

4. The number of persons who were injured, but not critically, is 4.____

   A. 2
   B. 5
   C. 8
   D. 10

5. This accident occurred a block away from 5.____

A. Grand Central Terminal
B. Times Square
C. Union Square
D. Pennsylvania Station

6. The runaway car was finally stopped just AFTER it 6.____

A. mounted the sidewalk
B. collided with a second truck
C. crossed the intersection
D. bowled over several persons

7. It can be inferred from the description that the driverless auto had 7.____

A. power brakes
B. power steering
C. a turn indicator
D. an automatic shift

8. The number on the police officer's badge is 8.____

A. 82314
B. 82413
C. 82143
D. 82341

9. The first name of the driver of the car is 9.____

A. Mary
B. Fred
C. Gloria
D. Herbert

10. According to the accident description, the adult passenger lives in 10.____

A. the Bronx, and so does the driver
B. Queens, and so does the driver
C. the Bronx, and the driver in Queens
D. Queens, and the driver in the Bronx

11. The number of pedestrians who were thrown to the ground is 11.____

A. 2
B. 5
C. 7
D. 10

12. The person who made a statement about the runaway car was 12.____

A. Herbert Field
B. Mary Jones
C. Gloria Jones
D. Fred Black

13. Herbert Field is older than Mary Jones by about ______ years. 13.____

A. 25
B. 35
C. 51
D. 61

14. The car shot forward immediately after 14.____

A. Mrs. Jones placed the shift in *drive*
B. Mr. Field stepped on the accelerator
C. Mrs. Jones stepped out of the car
D. Mr. Field got out of the car

15. Sudden stopping of a bus is to be avoided MAINLY because 15.____

A. some injury to passengers may result
B. some damage to the bus may result
C. this might tie up traffic
D. this might cause a skid

16. To make a smooth normal stop from a speed of 30 M.P.H. on a dry roadway, the operator of a bus should apply the brakes 16.____

A. using a pumping action, with heavy pressure on each application
B. and maintain steady brake pressure until the bus stops
C. and gradually increase the brake pressure as the bus comes to a stop
D. and then partially release them as the bus comes to a stop

17. A bus operator, making his last run for the day, notices that the reading of the engine oil pressure gauge has dropped to zero when he is about 20 blocks from the end of the run. He would do BEST to 17.____

A. complete the run and let the next operator report it
B. stop and make the necessary repairs
C. complete the run and report the condition on arrival
D. stop the bus and telephone headquarters

18. A man can drive safely only if he has good driver training, is alert, and is 18.____

A. less than 60 years old B. over 25 years old
C. familiar with the road he is on D. familiar with traffic laws

19. A particular bus seats 34 passengers and stands half that number. The TOTAL passenger capacity of the bus is 19.____

A. 41 B. 51 C. 61 D. 68

20. The fare register box on a bus shows the total number of cents collected. At the beginning of a run, the register reading of a certain box was 15750; and at the end of the run, the reading was 29750. The TOTAL number of $2 fares collected during the run was 20.____

A. 83 B. 85 C. 70 D. 95

Questions 21-29.

DIRECTIONS: Questions 21 through 29 are to be answered on the basis of the sketch shown on the following page showing the routes of the East Ave. (solid line) and the 8th St. (dotted line) buses. Refer to this sketch when answering these questions.

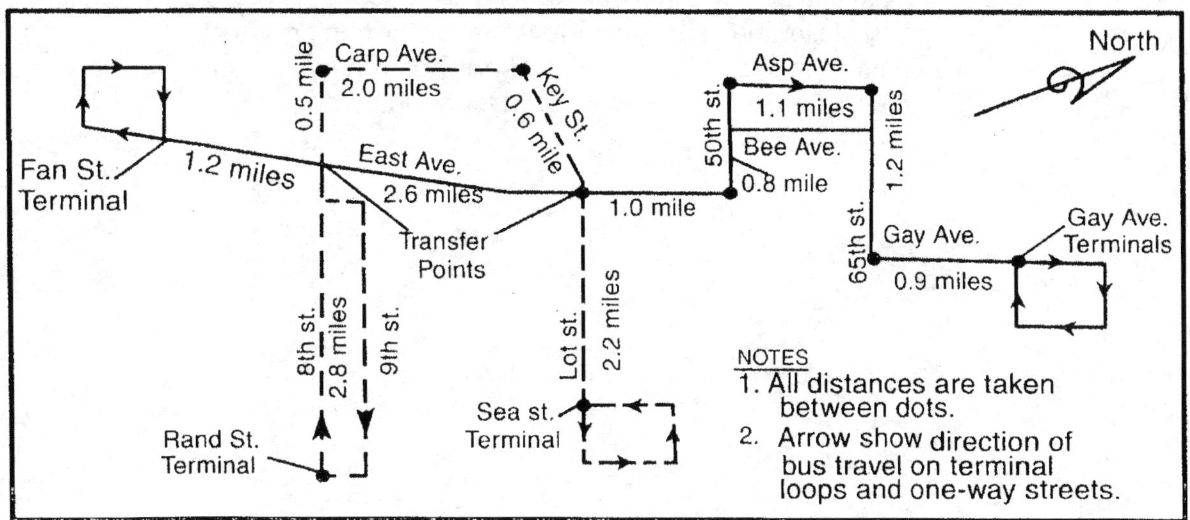

21. The bus route distance between the Fan St. and Gay Ave. terminals is ______ miles. 21.____

A. 6.8 B. 7.6 C. 8.0 D. 8.8

22. A passenger MUST transfer if he is going from Gay Ave. Terminal to ______ St. 22.____

A. Sea B. Fan C. 8th D. 50th

23. A bus on Key St. going toward Carp Ave. is moving 23.____

A. north B. east C. west D. south

24. Buses are NOT required to make even one left turn at the terminal at 24.____

A. Gay Ave. B. Fan St. C. Rand St. D. Sea St.

25. After discharging all passengers at the Sea St. Terminal before going around the loop, the number of right turns a bus must make to reach 8th St. is 25.____

A. 1 B. 2 C. 5 D. 6

26. From Rand St. Terminal to Carp Ave. via 8th St., a bus travels a TOTAL distance of ______ mile(s). 26.____

A. 0.3 B. 2.3 C. 2.8 D. 3.3

27. The street having the SHORTEST bus mileage is 27.____

A. 50th St. B. Gay Ave. C. Key St. D. 8th St.

28. One street used by buses operating in both directions is 28.____

A. 8th St. B. 9th St. C. Eagle St. D. Bee Ave.

29. The bus route distance between the Rand St. and Sea St. Terminals is ______ miles. 29.____

A. 7.6 B. 8.1 C. 8.6 D. 9.1

Questions 30-43.

DIRECTIONS: Questions 30 through 43 are to be answered on the basis of the sketch shown on the following page. Refer to this sketch when answering these questions. The sketch shows the situation shortly after the traffic lights have changed to green for east-west traffic and red for north-south traffic.

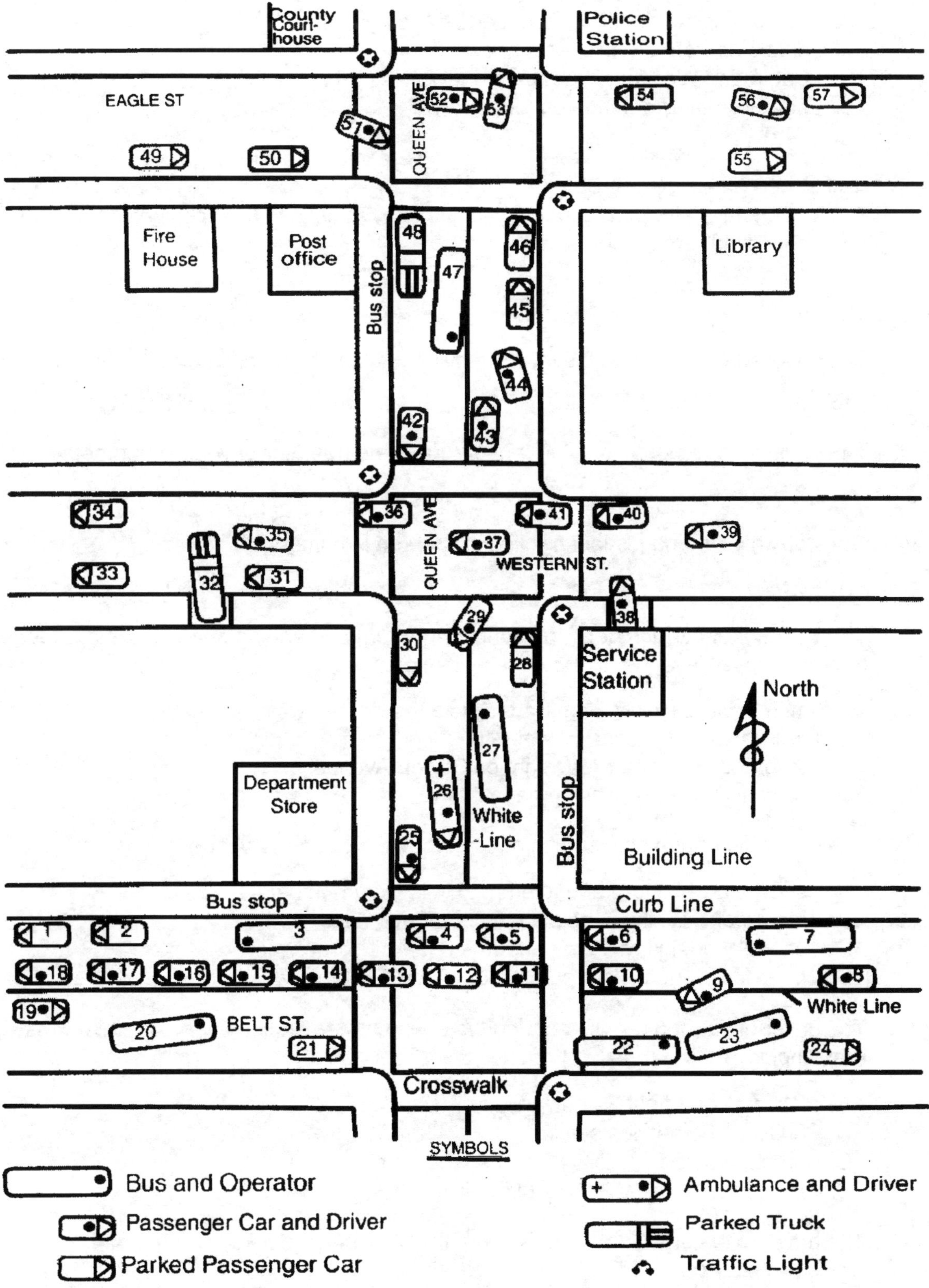
County Court-house
Police Station
EAGLE ST
QUEEN AVE
Fire House
Post office
Library
Bus stop
WESTERN ST.
Service Station
North
Department Store
White Line
Bus stop
Building Line
Curb Line
BELT ST.
White Line
Crosswalk
SYMBOLS
Bus and Operator
Passenger Car and Driver
Parked Passenger Car
Ambulance and Driver
Parked Truck
Traffic Light

30. After inspecting the sketch, one can see that 30.____

A. no commercial traffic is permitted on Western St.
B. buses operate on all streets shown
C. Eagle and Western Streets are one-way streets
D. no trucks are permitted on Queen Ave.

31. Car Nos. 15, 16, 17, and 18 and Bus No. 3 were in the positions shown before the traffic light turned green for Belt Street. 31.____
Cars which have all violated traffic regulations by moving to the positions shown, even on a green light, are numbers

A. 12, 13, 14, and 4
B. 11, 12, 13, 4, and 5
C. 4, 10, 11, and 12
D. 4, 5, 6, 10, 11, and 12

32. The driver who is violating the law by leaving his lane is the driver of car number 32.____

A. 9 B. 38 C. 44 D. 51

33. The driver who is clearly making a poor turn is the operator of vehicle number 33.____

A. 23 B. 29 C. 38 D. 51

34. One car which is unquestionably illegally parked is number 34.____

A. 33 B. 34 C. 49 D. 50

35. The operator of car number 41 making a right turn and seeing an eastbound pedestrian crossing Queen Avenue at about the white line should 35.____

A. inch forward slowly, prepared to yield the right-of-way
B. turn rapidly alongside number 43
C. stop and wait for a green light on Queen Avenue
D. blow his horn to hurry the pedestrian

36. The driver of car number 38 wishing to go north on Queen Avenue 36.____

A. show blow his horn and attempt to follow car number 41
B. must wait until the light is green for Queen Ave.
C. should work his way over after the other cars have moved
D. must first bring his car parallel to the curb of Western Street

37. The driver of car number 39, hearing the siren of a fire engine overtaking him from the rear, should 37.____

A. follow car number 29 down Queen Avenue
B. pull into the service station
C. proceed quickly across Queen Avenue
D. pull to the curb behind car number 40

38. The driver of the ambulance (vehicle number 26), seeing the congestion at Belt Street, would probably do BEST to 38.____

A. turn around and find another route
B. stop and wait until traffic opens up

C. sound his siren and make his way through the space that opens up
D. stop and telephone for public assistance

39. The operator of bus number 47, having found the bus stop occupied by vehicle number 48 (a U.S. Mail truck) should 39.____

A. make the stop where he is, to take on and discharge passengers
B. try to get the entire bus in to the curb
C. skip the stop
D. stop where he is but keep the doors closed until the mail truck leaves

40. Car numbers 52 and 53 have stopped in the positions shown. It is LEAST likely that car number 40.____

A. 52 *jumped the gun*
B. 53 passed a red signal
C. 52 was going to continue along Eagle St.
D. 53 was going to turn into Eagle St.

41. If car number 52 had struck car number 53 and injured an occupant, the drivers could obtain the necessary forms on which to report the accident at the 41.____

A. post office
B. library
C. police station
D. county court house

42. One car which is unquestionably illegally parked at a public building is car number 42.____

A. 48
B. 50
C. 54
D. 55

43. Three vehicles which are clearly in violation of the regulation against parking within 15 feet of a crosswalk are numbers 43.____

A. 6, 10, and 25
B. 28, 30, and 46
C. 30, 31, and 48
D. 22, 46, and 54

44. A driver should NOT permit his engine to run for long in an enclosed area MAINLY because gasoline engine exhaust is 44.____

A. irritating
B. explosive
C. corrosive
D. poisonous

45. Although lateness of any transit employee is undesirable, it is plain that a bus operator must make special effort to report for work on time MAINLY because 45.____

A. he might be delayed by traffic
B. his bus must be warmed up before leaving the garage
C. lateness is always an indication of operator carelessness
D. bus schedules cannot be maintained otherwise

46. Subway maps do NOT give information about the 46.____

A. waiting time between trains
B. location of transfer points
C. terminals of the various lines
D. relative positions of express stations

47. A bus requires 40 minutes to go from one terminal to another, and stops for 10 minutes at each terminal. 47.___
The MAXIMUM number of one-way trips that the bus can complete in 6 hours is

A. 6 B. 7 C. 8 D. 9

48. The officially CORRECT hand signal for a left turn is to extend the hand and arm 48.___

A. downward at about 45°
B. vertically downward
C. vertically upward
D. horizontally

49. The device which permits the two rear wheels of a car to turn at different speeds is the 49.___

A. differential
B. universal joint
C. torque converter
D. overdrive

50. A bus operator reports that, while proceeding north on a certain street, the middle of the left side of his bus was hit by a truck which was making a right turn from an eastbound street. 50.___
It follows that the bus was struck by the ______ corner of the truck.

A. front left
B. front right
C. rear left
D. rear right

KEY (CORRECT ANSWERS)

1. C	11. B	21. D	31. B	41. C
2. B	12. D	22. A	32. A	42. C
3. A	13. A	23. C	33. B	43. B
4. C	14. B	24. C	34. C	44. D
5. B	15. A	25. A	35. A	45. D
6. B	16. D	26. D	36. C	46. A
7. D	17. D	27. C	37. D	47. B
8. C	18. D	28. A	38. C	48. D
9. A	19. B	29. B	39. A	49. A
10. C	20. C	30. C	40. D	50. A

EXAMINATION SECTION
TEST 1

DIRECTIONS: Each question or incomplete statement is followed by several suggested answers or completions. Select the one that BEST answers the question or completes the statement. *PRINT THE LETTER OF THE CORRECT ANSWER IN THE SPACE AT THE RIGHT.*

1. The problem with driving the car in neutral is that 1.____

   A. you lose needed motor control
   B. the car will not go fast enough
   C. the car would not ride as smooth
   D. you would not be able to go up a hill

2. At 40 MPH, you should allow ______ car lengths between your car and the one ahead. 2.____

   A. four B. eight C. twelve D. sixteen

3. Your taillight must be visible at night for ______ feet. 3.____

   A. 200 B. 350 C. 500 D. 400

4. The driver's left hand and arm are extended upward. This hand signal means that the driver plans to 4.____

   A. turn left B. turn right
   C. come to a stop D. go straight ahead

5. Which of the following are used on some highways to direct drivers into the proper lanes for turns? 5.____

   A. Flashing red lights
   B. White lines on the side of the road
   C. White arrows in the middle of the lanes
   D. Flashing yellow lights

6. When you want to overtake and pass another vehicle, you should 6.____

   A. change lanes quickly so the other driver will see you
   B. signal and pass when safe to do so
   C. wait for a signal from the other driver
   D. stay close behind so you need less time to pass

7. If you drive past your exit on an expressway, you should 7.____

   A. drive to the next exit and leave the expressway
   B. make a U-turn at the nearest emergency turn area
   C. make a U-turn at the next service area
   D. pull onto the shoulder, then back up to the exit

8. A flashing yellow light means 8.____

   A. come to a full stop B. proceed with caution
   C. merging traffic D. pedestrian crossing

9. You are waiting in the intersection to complete a left turn. You should 9.____

A. drive around the rear of a car if it blocks you
B. signal and keep your wheels straight
C. flash your headlights so the driver will let you get through
D. signal and keep your wheels turned to the left

10. Alcohol affects 10.____

A. recovery from headlight glare
B. judgment of distances
C. reaction time
D. all of the above

11. A red and white triangular sign at an intersection means 11.____

A. always come to a full stop at the intersection
B. look both ways as you cross the intersection
C. slow down and be prepared to stop if necessary
D. slow down if an emergency vehicle is approaching

12. When driving at 60 MPH, a driver will be able to stop his car in ______ feet. 12.____

A. 67 B. 120 C. 190 D. 400

13. After you have passed a car, you should return to the right lane when you 13.____

A. see the front bumper of the other car in your mirror
B. see the other car's headlights come on
C. have put your turn signal on
D. have turned your headlights on

14. You may pass another vehicle on the right if it is waiting to 14.____

A. park at the curb
B. turn into a driveway on the right
C. turn right
D. turn left

15. Expressways have *expressway entrance lanes* (acceleration lanes) so that drivers can 15.____

A. reach the proper speed before blending with traffic
B. test their brakes before driving at expressway speeds
C. test the pickup of their cars
D. stop at the end to wait for a traffic opening

16. Night driving is dangerous because 16.____

A. some traffic signs are less visible at night
B. more vehicles are on the road at night
C. street lights tend to blur our vision
D. the distance we can see ahead is reduced

17. Assuming that the street is level, after you have finished parallel parking in a space between two other cars, you should 17.____

A. leave your front wheels turned toward the curb
B. straighten your front wheels and leave room between cars
C. move as far forward in the space as possible
D. make sure your car almost touches the car behind you

18. You drive along a street and hear a siren. You cannot immediately see the emergency vehicle. 18.____
You should

A. pull to the curb until you are sure it is not on your street
B. speed up and turn at the next intersection
C. keep driving until you see the vehicle
D. slow down but don't stop until you see it

19. If you leave ignition keys in an unattended vehicle, 19.____

A. you must leave the meter running
B. you commit a traffic infraction
C. it is alright as long as you have your parking brake set
D. you should leave them in the event the car has to be moved

20. The ones who *always* have the right of way are 20.____

A. motorists
B. pedestrians
C. cyclists
D. animals

21. On a road where there are no sidewalks, a pedestrian should walk 21.____

A. on the shoulder of the road, facing traffic
B. on the shoulder of the road, going with the traffic
C. in the gutter alongside of the road
D. in the nearest clear space next to the road

22. To signal for help on the New York State Thruway, 22.____

A. flash your headlights on and off
B. flash your brake lights on and off
C. tie a white cloth to the left hand door handle of the car
D. stand on the road and flag down the first oncoming car

23. The MAIN use to which a driver's horn should be put is 23.____

A. to let the other driver know the light is green
B. in passing other cars or as a warning
C. if the driver is in a hurry
D. so that pedestrians will give you the right of way

24. If a car is traveling at 40 MPH, it needs ______ feet to stop. 24.____

A. 30
B. 67
C. 120
D. 190

25. When a tire blows out, 25.____

A. take your foot from the gas and hold the steering wheel as steadily as possible
B. brake firmly until you bring the car to a stop
C. disengage your clutch and use your brakes to reduce speed
D. give more gas and hold the steering wheel as steadily as possible

---

KEY (CORRECT ANSWERS)

1. A
2. A
3. C
4. B
5. C

6. B
7. A
8. B
9. B
10. D

11. C
12. D
13. A
14. D
15. A

16. D
17. B
18. A
19. B
20. B

21. A
22. C
23. B
24. C
25. A

TEST 2

DIRECTIONS: Each question or incomplete statement is followed by several suggested answers or completions. Select the one that BEST answers the question or completes the statement. *PRINT THE LETTER OF THE CORRECT ANSWER IN THE SPACE AT THE RIGHT.*

1. When a driver sees or hears a vehicle with a flashing red light on, siren blowing, or bell ringing, he should 1.____

   A. give it the right of way
   B. speed up and drive on
   C. stop in his lane
   D. stop and direct traffic, if there is no police officer

2. When approaching a stopped school bus with red lights flashing, a driver should 2.____

   A. pass the bus with due caution
   B. pass the bus only on the left
   C. stop at least 8 feet behind and wait until the bus proceeds
   D. stop and then go if all is clear

3. Before making a turn, a driver should signal for ______ ft. 3.____

   A. 50 B. 100 C. 150 D. 75

4. The general rule with regard to right of way at intersections is that the car ______ has the right of way. 4.____

   A. going straight ahead B. on the main road
   C. on the right D. making a turn

5. You should be ______ ft. from a vehicle you are overtaking before switching your headlights to low beam. 5.____

   A. 100 B. 200 C. 250 D. 350

6. Unless a sign indicates otherwise, a driver must park ______ ft. from a fire hydrant. 6.____

   A. 5 B. 10 C. 15 D. 9

7. When parking parallel to the curb, the wheels must be no more than ______ inches away from the curb. 7.____

   A. 6 B. 12 C. 18 D. 24

8. If a police officer at an intersection gives a signal for you to proceed although the traffic signal is against you, the driver should obey 8.____

   A. the traffic signal
   B. whichever he wants
   C. the police officer
   D. the pedestrian who may be crossing

9. An octagonal (8-sided) sign means to 9.____

A. reduce speed
B. proceed with caution
C. yield the right of way
D. stop and proceed with caution

10. When approaching a flashing red traffic signal, a driver should 10.____

A. proceed with caution
B. stop and then proceed with caution
C. pull over to the side of the road
D. reduce speed

11. When nearing an intersection marked with a *Yield Right of Way* sign, the driver must 11.____

A. yield the right of way to pedestrians
B. yield the right of way to all commercial traffic
C. yield the right of way to all horse-drawn vehicles
D. slow down and allow all cross traffic to proceed before him

12. If a signal light changes from green to yellow as a driver nears an intersection, he should 12.____

A. try to get through the intersection before the red light comes on
B. prepare to stop
C. keep his speed the same
D. speed up and rush through the intersection

13. A flashing yellow or amber light differs in meaning from a flashing red light in that yellow means ______ while red means ______. 13.____

A. proceed with caution; stop and then proceed
B. try to stop; stop and then proceed
C. proceed with caution; stop
D. stop; proceed at will

14. Diamond-shaped signs indicate 14.____

A. cattle crossing ahead
B. stop and then proceed with caution
C. reduce speed for curves, hills or narrow bridges
D. railroad crossing ahead

15. The rectangular (square) signs mean 15.____

A. proceed with caution
B. railroad crossing ahead
C. yield right of way
D. danger, slow down

16. A broken line painted on the highway means that a driver 16.____

A. must not cross it at any time
B. may cross it to pass provided traffic permits
C. may cross it to pass, even on hills
D. must not cross it on weekends

17. A double solid line on the highway means that a driver 17.____

    A. may cross it any time
    B. may cross it only if he is on the main road
    C. must never cross it
    D. must never cross it unless traffic permits

18. The highway sign shaped like an inverted pyramid means 18.____

    A. stop
    B. slow down, and proceed with caution
    C. danger
    D. yield right of way

19. The shape of the highway sign which means that a driver is approaching a railroad crossing is 19.____

    A. square B. round
    C. diamond D. rectangular

20. A driver may follow a fire engine on its way to a fire ______ ft. in a city, ______ ft. in a rural area. 20.____

    A. 200; 500 B. 100; 500 C. 20; 400 D. 100; 50

21. Parking lights should be used when a driver 21.____

    A. is driving in well-lighted areas
    B. leaves the car parked in a driveway
    C. parks the car on a road facing traffic
    D. parks the car on a road going with the traffic

22. When passing a playground, park or other area where children are playing or walking, 22.____

    A. stop and then proceed with caution
    B. slow down and proceed with caution
    C. blow horn and make sure they see you
    D. blow horn, stop, and then proceed with caution

23. If a driver is parked parallel to the curb on a busy street, he may open the doors on the traffic side 23.____

    A. when the traffic light turns red
    B. between the hours of sunrise and sunset
    C. if he looks very carefully
    D. when no traffic is approaching

24. When following another car on a superhighway, 24.____

    A. do not tailgate
    B. try to follow at the same speed
    C. watch out for littering
    D. make sure you do not lose sight of it

25. When driving in heavy fog at night, a driver should use his 25.____

A. upper headlight beams
B. lower headlight beams
C. uppers, in addition to fog lights
D. lowers, in addition to fog lights

26. A driver may drive at the MAXIMUM speed limit whenever 26.____

A. his car is in good condition
B. there is an emergency
C. he is on a New York State road unless otherwise marked
D. he is escorted by a state policeman

27. At night when you meet an oncoming vehicle with blinding, bright lights, the SAFEST action to take is to 27.____

A. turn your head away so that you don't have to look at the lights
B. cast your gaze at the right side of the road, stay near it and slow down
C. put on your brightest lights so as to counteract his
D. put on your dark glasses

28. To get a car out of a skid, 28.____

A. press the gas gently as you turn the wheels in the direction of the skid
B. press the brakes and try to stop the vehicle
C. press the gas hard so as to pull out of the skid
D. turn the wheels as fast as you can in the direction you want

29. A driver should stay at least ______ car length(s) behind the car ahead of him for every ______ MPH. 29.____

A. 2; 20 B. 2; 10 C. 1; 20 D. 1; 10

30. A driver can avoid being poisoned by the monoxide gas from his exhaust by 30.____

A. always making sure he keeps the car windows closed
B. keeping a window of the car open to allow fresh air in
C. making sure he always uses the best grade gasoline
D. boring an extra hole in the exhaust pipe

KEY (CORRECT ANSWERS)

1.	A	16.	B
2.	C	17.	C
3.	B	18.	D
4.	C	19.	B
5.	B	20.	A
6.	C	21.	C
7.	B	22.	B
8.	C	23.	D
9.	D	24.	A
10.	B	25.	B
11.	D	26.	C
12.	B	27.	B
13.	A	28.	A
14.	C	29.	D
15.	A	30.	B

EMERGENCY DRIVING TECHNIQUES

TABLE OF CONTENTS

OBJECTIVES

1. Skid
2. Tire blowout
3. Brake loss
4. Obstruction in path of bus
5. Sudden loss of visibility

OVERVIEW

INSTRUCTOR GUIDELINES	CONTENT
	Expert drivers don't depend on their skill to get them out of tight spots. They depend on their judgment to avoid tight spots. IT'S A LOT EASIER TO STAY OUT OF TIGHT SPOTS THAN TO GET OUT OF THEM.* However, you may find yourself confronted with one of these five emergency conditions: 1. Skid 2. Tire blowout 3. Brake loss 4. Obstruction in the path of the bus 5. Sudden loss of visibility
Tell trainees that they'll be asked to "rehearse" the techniques in written form so they won't have to think about what they should do in an actual emergency.	Under these conditions, you must know what emergency driving techniques to use. Your responses must become automatic because you will not have much time to think about what you should do. The procedures in this unit are "last ditch" measures to avoid an accident if at all possible. Since it is impossible to completely eliminate human error in the performance of routine driving tasks, <u>your ability</u> to take appropriate and immediate action under emergency conditions becomes <u>critical</u>.

SKID CONTROL

INSTRUCTOR GUIDELINES	CONTENT
Explain that skids on snow-covered/icy downgrades may be prevented by shifting into lowest gear and accelerating slightly while going down the hill. This forces the wheels to keep turning and gives better traction than you'd get by braking or not accelerating in a higher gear. Also, drivers should downshift before they reach spots where skids are likely. Drivers should "try out" the road to test for skid conditions. They should test how their buses handle, since buses differ in their handling when they start to skid.	Any number of factors can cause a school bus to go into a skid. During a skid, the tires lose proper traction with the road surface. The normal means of controlling the bus are affected--steering, braking, decelerating, and accelerating. You must be able to detect a loss of traction in time to maintain or regain control of the bus. Loss of traction may include: • Skids caused by tire failure resulting from under inflation or sudden deflation from a blowout. • Front wheel skids resulting from faulty brakes. • Rear wheel skids resulting from faulty brakes, excessive acceleration or speed on curves, rough or slippery surfaces. • Four wheel locked brake skid resulting from inappropriate application of brake pressure. • Hydroplaning resulting from traveling too fast on a water covered roadway with lack of attention given to tires, tread, and pressure. • Skids caused by oil on the road after the first few minutes of rain. NOTES:

INSTRUCTOR GUIDELINES	CONTENT
	Once you lose traction and the bus goes into a skid, you must be able to regain directional control:
Emphasize that the phrase "steer in the direction of the skid" means you actually turn your wheels in the direction you want the bus to go.	1. STEERING--Immediately apply controlled steering (turn into the skid--usually this means steer the wheels in the direction you want to go). Follow by controlled counter-steering to dampen fish-tailing until steering control is re-established.
Explain when modified braking may be appropriate.	2. BRAKING--Apply <u>no</u> brake pressure or only <u>modified</u> braking, as appropriate, until steering control is re-established.
	3. DECELERATION--Remove pressure from the accelerator smoothly (not suddenly) and do not accelerate again until steering control is re-established.
Describe a local incident (if any) in which a bus driver experienced a skid. Put diagram on chalkboard. Ask members of the class what they would have done. Describe what action the bus driver took. Discuss results.	4. ACCELERATION--Once steering control is re-established, shift to a lower gear and accelerate gradually to maintain traction.
	NOTES:
Refer to Figure 1 and explain procedure for steering to get out of a skid. Explain how they would countersteer to prevent or control fish-tailing.	

(Read illustration from bottom to top)

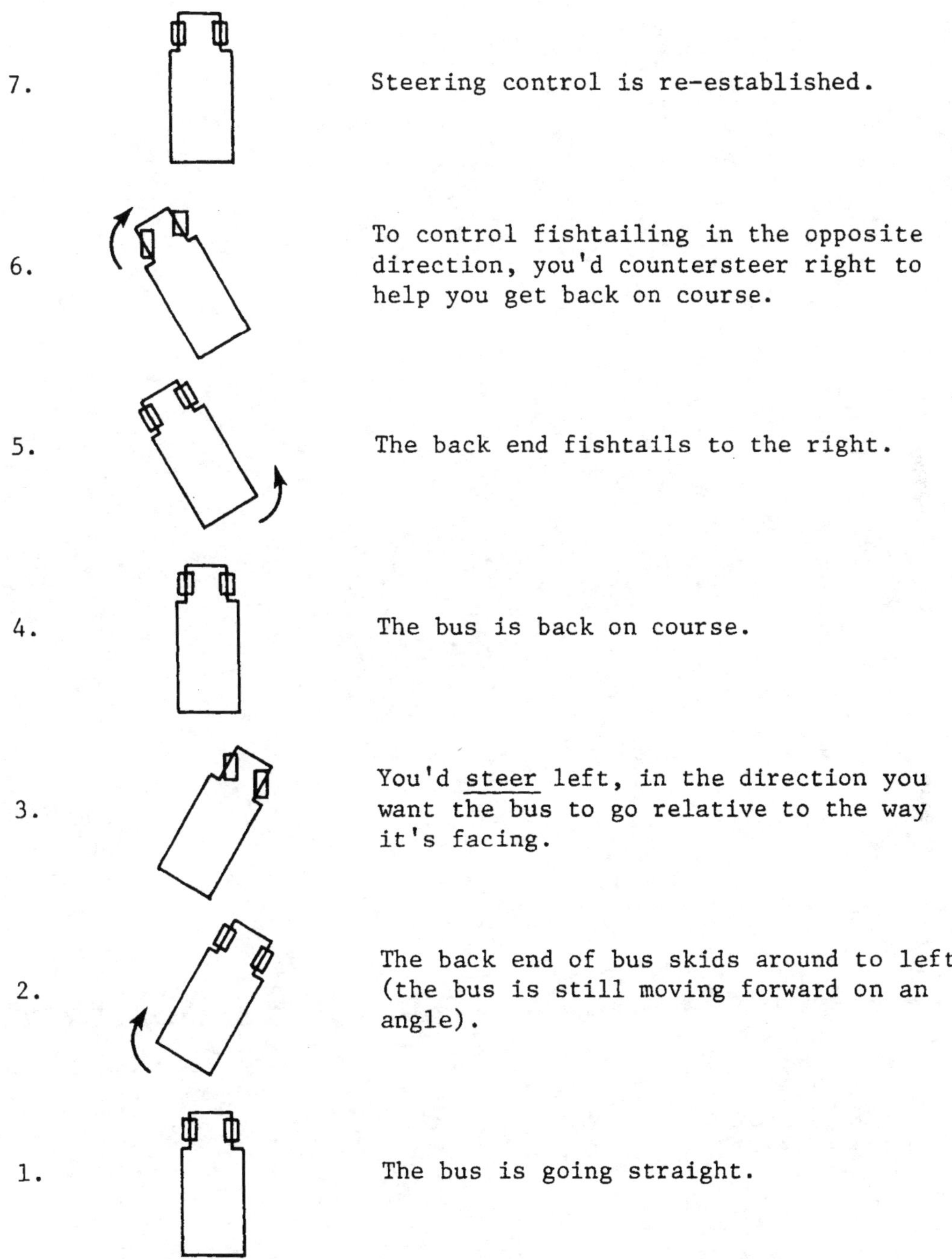

Figure 1. Steering to Get Out of a Skid

A-9

PRACTICE

INSTRUCTOR GUIDELINES	CONTENT
	To control a skid you must remember what to do about steering, braking, deceleration, and acceleration. Describe the procedure in your own words. STEERING: BRAKING: DECELERATION: ACCELERATION: Discuss your answers with the class.

WHAT WOULD YOU DO?

INSTRUCTOR GUIDELINES	CONTENT
	Suppose you're driving your bus on a road that's mostly dry with some wet spots. As you start up a hill, you hit a wet and oily spot. Your rear wheels spin and the rear of your bus slides toward the right side of the road. What would you do?
Ask one or two trainees what they wrote. Have class discuss. Answer should include major points of the emergency technique.	Discuss your answer with the class.

PROBABILITY OF SKIDDING

INSTRUCTOR GUIDELINES	CONTENT
Emphasize that preventing a skid is better than having to get out of a skid. Discuss the answers they check:	Check which condition in each set is more likely to get you into a skid:
	ENVIRONMENTAL CONDITIONS
A. wet road	A. ____ wet road or ____ dry road.
B. icy road	B. ____ wet road or ____ icy road.
C. snow-covered road. But, note, when snow melts, sand and cinders act like ball bearings on the pavement, so skid would be likely.	C. ____ cindered/sanded road or ____ snow-covered road.
D. loose gravel	D. ____ loose gravel or ____ smooth road surface.
E. curved road	E. ____ curved road or ____ straight road.
F. hilly road	F. ____ level road or ____ hilly road.
G. bridge	G. ____ bridge or ____ solid ground.
	BUS CONDITION
H. bald tires	H. ____ bald tires or ____ tires with good tread.
I. tire blowout	I. ____ tire with slow leak or ____ tire blowout.
J. low pressure	J. ____ tire with low pressure or ____ tire with chains.
	YOUR ACTIONS
K. locking brakes	K. ____ locking the brakes or ____ modulated braking.
L. sudden acceleration	L. ____ smooth acceleration or ____ sudden acceleration.
M. sudden deceleration	M. ____ smooth deceleration or ____ sudden deceleration.
N. driving fast	N. ____ driving fast or ____ driving slow.

INSTRUCTOR GUIDELINES	CONTENT
The behavior for all probable skid conditions is to slow down and increase caution in executing all maneuvers.	WHAT IS THE MAIN THING YOU SHOULD DO WHEN YOU THINK A SKID IS PROBABLE? NOTES:

TIRE BLOWOUT*

INSTRUCTOR GUIDELINES	CONTENT
Describe what it's like to have a tire blowout--the loud sound, the feel of the bus, the possibility of skidding. Emphasize that maintaining control is main goal. The blown tire acts like a brake only on one side, so the bus is likely to pull very hard to that side. Refer to Figure 2. Explain that a front tire blowout is worse than one in the rear because of the dual wheels on each side in the back.	1. Grip the steering wheel firmly and steer your vehicle straight down the center of your lane. 2. Do not apply your brakes. 3. Take your foot off accelerator. If bus starts to skid, follow skid procedure. 4. Activate right turn signal, move right slowly, out of the lane of traffic and stop. Watch out for soft shoulders which could make the control of the bus even more difficult. 5. Activate 4-way hazard lamps, not red flashing warning lights. 6. Decide whether to evacuate your children while the repair is being made.
You may want to review Procedures for Mechanical Breakdown from Core Unit C.	7. Follow procedures for Mechanical Breakdown. NOTES:
Describe a local incident (if any) in which a bus driver experienced a tire blowout. Put diagram on chalkboard, if you want. Ask members of class what they would have done. Describe what action the driver took. Discuss results.	

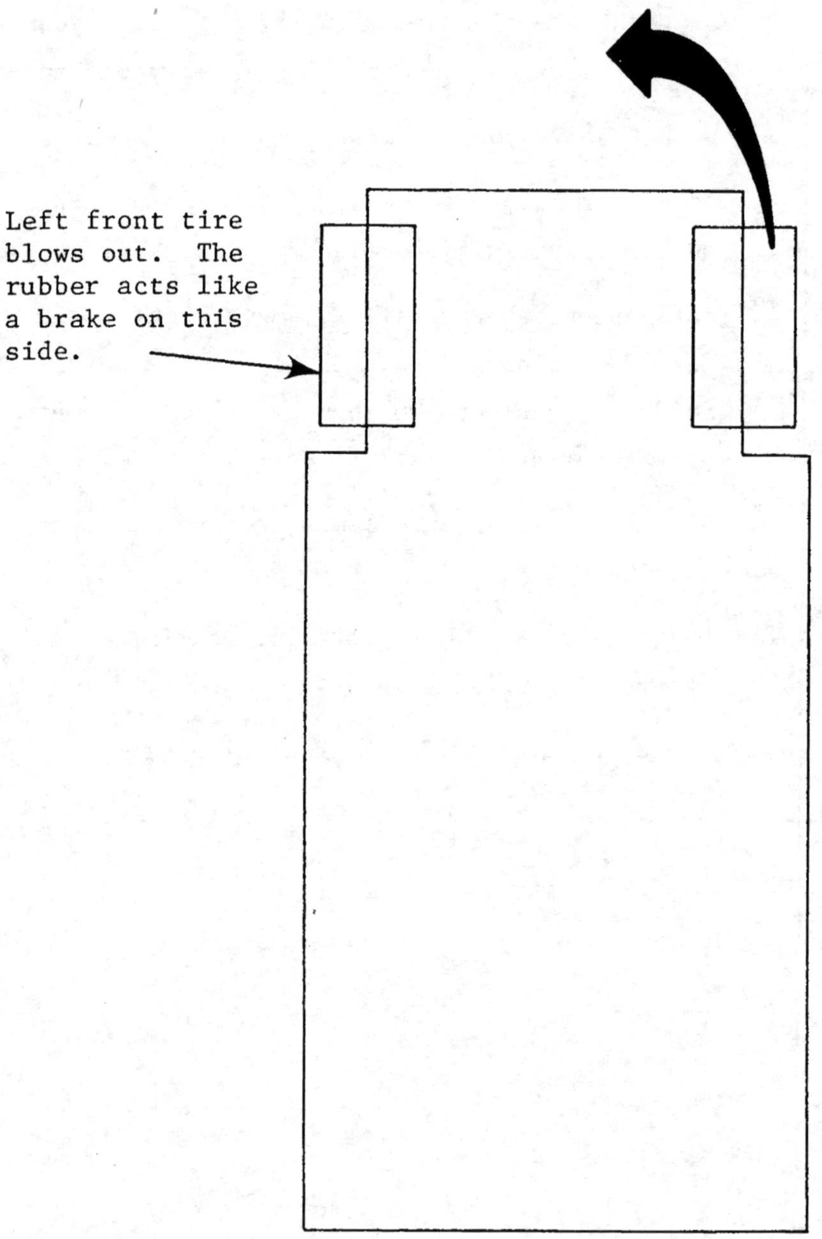

Figure 2. Left-front Tire Blowout

INSTRUCTOR GUIDELINES	CONTENT
	You're driving along an expressway at 50 mph when suddenly your right front tire blows out. HOW WILL YOU KNOW IT? WHAT WOULD YOU DO? <u>Steering</u>: <u>Braking</u>: <u>Stopping</u>:
Ask one or two trainees what they wrote. Have class discuss. Answer should include major points of the emergency techniques.	Discuss your answers with the class.

LOSS OF BRAKES

INSTRUCTOR GUIDELINES	CONTENT
NOTE: This does not apply to air brakes, which should lock <u>on</u>, when there is a brake failure. Discuss what to do if air brakes fail. Drivers may have to control a skid in such a case.	If you're ever confronted with a partial or total loss of brakes: 1. Pump the brake pedal and sound horn, flash headlights, etc.
There are practical limitations in how far a driver should try to downshift. The conditions dictate. Usually, 3rd gear is as far as you should try to downshift because, at fairly great speeds, e.g., over 30 mph, it's hard to get into 2nd gear. And it would be worse to get stuck in neutral and have no gear to hold the bus back. But if the driver is very experienced and the speed of the bus has not built up too much, he/she could attempt to downshift to second gear. Suggest they practice this.	2. Downshift to lowest gear possible. 3. If there is an upgrade within the assured clear distance ahead, stay on the road and allow the upgrade to slow the bus. Then select a path for leaving the roadway. 4. If no upgrade is within the assured clear distance ahead, select a path for leaving roadway that will minimize injuries and property damage. If you must go into a bank, turn into it at an angle. Otherwise, bus may flip over.
Explain that for partial brake loss or brake loss while going under 8 mph, the driver could choose to try the hand brake to help slow the bus. But, it's awkward to reach and has no great holding power. So, if the bus has built up speed, don't try the hand brake; reaching for it gives the driver less steering control and it would burn out within a minute or so anyway.	NOTES:
Describe a local incident (if any) in which a driver lost the brakes. Draw a diagram on the chalkboard. Ask class members what they would do. Describe what the driver did. Discuss results. Discuss alternatives for minimizing injuries and property damage.	

PRACTICE

INSTRUCTOR GUIDELINES	CONTENT
	You should remember four things if you lose your brakes. Describe them in your own words. BRAKE PEDAL, HORN, AND LIGHTS: SHIFTING: IF CLEAR UPGRADE: IF NO CLEAR UPGRADE:
Ask one or two trainees what they wrote. Have class discuss. Answer should include major points of the emergency technique.	Discuss your answers with the class.

INSTRUCTOR GUIDELINES	CONTENT
Refer to Figure 3.	You are following 100 feet behind another school bus, going 25 mph, down a steep grade. At the bottom of the hill is a stop sign. The road comes to a T-intersection with a highway which has a medium amount of traffic going in both directions. Across the highway is a wooden-fenced field. On your right is a concrete retainer wall. There are houses on the left side of the road. There are no vehicles in the oncoming lane. You apply your brakes and nothing happens.
Ask one or two trainees what they wrote. Have class discuss. Answer should include major points of the emergency technique. This situation was taken from an actual incident. The driver chose not to hit the bus in front but steer around and cross highway, through fence into field. Two of the cars on the highway were sideswiped, and the bus came to a stop beside the tree. No one was injured.	WHAT WOULD YOU DO?
	Discuss your answers with the class.

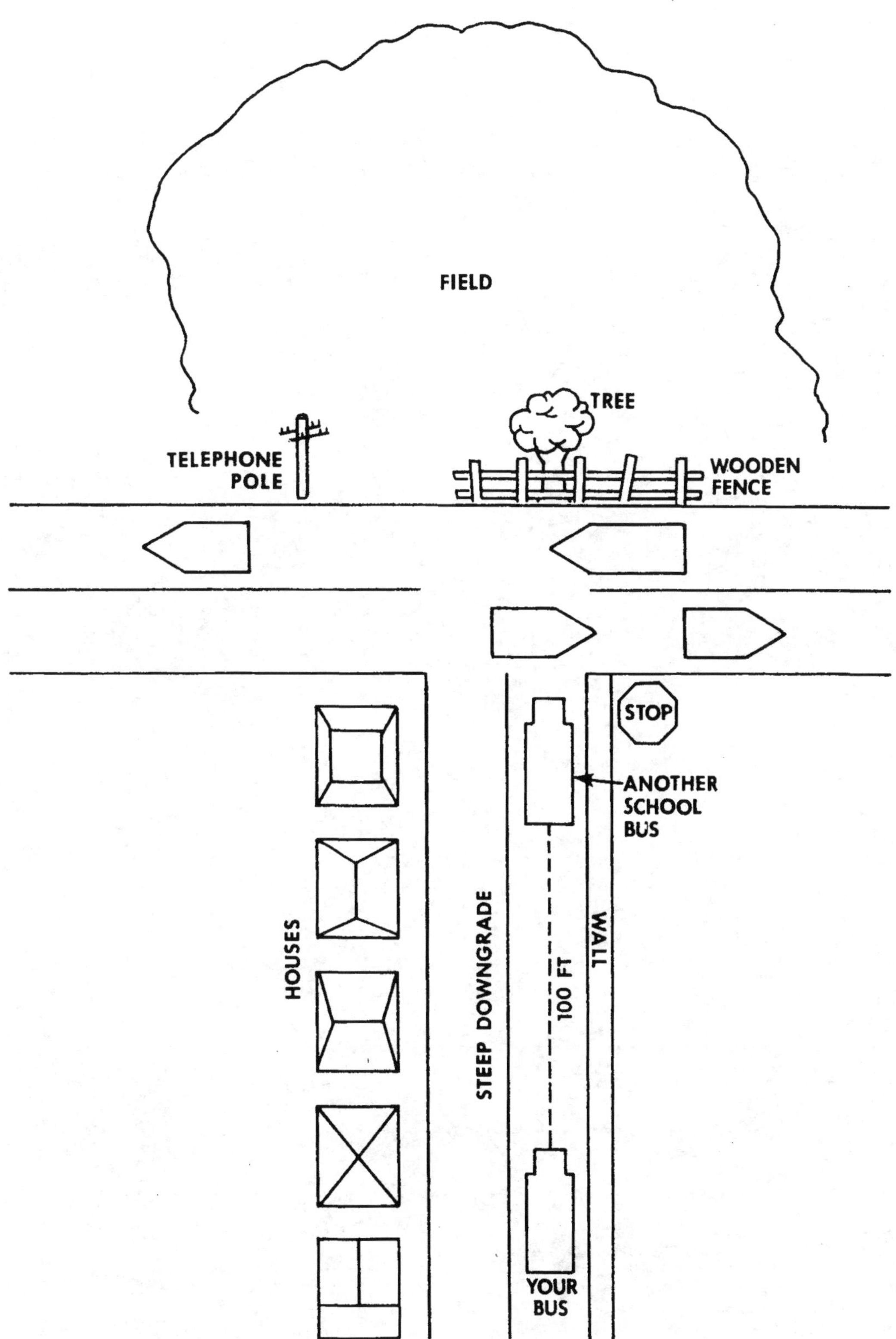

Figure 3. Brake Loss

OBSTRUCTION IN PATH OF BUS

INSTRUCTOR GUIDELINES	CONTENT
NOTE: Road conditions can increase the stress.	When you suddenly see an obstruction--a pedestrian, ball, another vehicle, construction barrier, etc.,--in the direct path of the bus, you must take evasive action to avoid hitting it. Evasive action is simply the exercise of your fundamental driving maneuvers under conditions of stress--limited time, space, and distance. You must decide which of these evasive actions you should perform to avoid hitting the obstruction. 1. Modulated braking. 2. Quick steering to the right, with or without braking. 3. Leaving the paved portion of roadway, with or without roadside hazards present. For effective evasive action, you must be able to inhibit the tendency to slam on the brakes. Generally, drivers tend to apply the brakes at the first sign of trouble. While effective in many instances, braking can lock the wheels and cause loss of steering control, making it impossible to steer away from a collision. You may decide that braking to a stop is the best evasive action you can take to avoid the obstruction. This will depend on how fast you're going, how far away the object is, how good your tires are, and whether the road is wet or dry.

INSTRUCTOR GUIDELINES	CONTENT
Ask members of the class, especially new drivers, how many "car lengths" are represented by the Total Stopping Distances in the chart. Ask them how a car performs under similar conditions. The rule of thumb is "buses take longer."	Recall the stopping distances for a bus under ideal conditions:

Maximum Safe Stopping Distances for
TRUCKS and BUSES
In Accordance with ICC Regulations

Speed Miles Per Hour	Feet Per Second	Vehicle Travels (One Second) Reaction Time	Braking Distance	Total Stopping Distance
20	29	29	30	59
30	44	44	67	111
40	59	59	120	179
50	73	73	188	261
60	88	88	270	358
Speed of vehicle.	No. of feet covered per second by vehicle.	Distance traveled in one second before brake can be applied after seeing danger (in feet).	Distance required to stop after brake is applied with good pavement and fair brakes (in feet).	Total feet covered after seeing danger (in feet). Reaction time plus stopping distance.

INSTRUCTOR GUIDELINES	CONTENT
Discuss local incidents of obstructions in the path of the bus. Include "near misses" where evasive action was effective. Include any accidents which may have been prevented by evasive action. Ask class members what they would do in situation. Describe what driver did. Discuss results, using diagrams on chalkboard. Cover each point.	Because the obstruction is an emergency, you won't have time to do lengthy calculations. If it's not instantly obvious that you can stop in time, you must choose to steer the bus in an alternate path. You must be able to recognize quickly the best "escape route." At a glance, decide: • Whether a possible escape path is free of hazardous obstacles.

INSTRUCTOR GUIDELINES	CONTENT
	• Whether clearances are sufficient to allow the bus to pass through them.
	• Whether an off-roadway surface will permit steering control.
	• Whether the obstruction is likely to move into your escape path.
Generally, a driver should not steer left to avoid hitting an object, since this would put him in further danger of collision with oncoming traffic or rear approaching traffic in left lane. Clearly, there are exceptions. E. G., one would steer left if there was a wall on the right but no oncoming cars visible in the assured clear distance ahead.	• Whether one escape route is safer than another. The size and weight of the bus limits its ability to swerve sharply to avoid an object or to leave the pavement with any great degree of control. Overturning is a danger. STEER FIRMLY AND AS GRADUALLY AS POSSIBLE TO STILL CLEAR THE OBSTRUCTION. USE ONLY MODULATED BRAKING. It can't be stressed enough that your decision will probably have to be a split-second one. Rehearse these points so that you can decide what evasive action is best.
Another way to estimate this distance is by 7 bus lengths or by 2 telephone poles. (There are 100 feet between each pole.)	• If you're traveling as fast as 40 mph, the obstruction has to be <u>at least</u> 200 feet away for you to stop safely. That's 2/3 of a football field! Any closer, and you'd better steer around it, or off the road.
	• Behind every rolling ball, there's likely to be a running child. Just because the ball clears your path in time doesn't mean you're out of danger.
	• If you're in a tight spot, hitting the obstacle might be the safest thing to do. For example, with heavy oncoming traffic,

INSTRUCTOR GUIDELINES	CONTENT
	heavy pedestrian traffic on sidewalk to your right, suppose a construction warning sign is the unexpected obstacle less than 10 feet away in your lane. You're going 25 mph. You can't stop in time, and steering left or right would create a worse collision. You may assess the relative dangers and decide it's better to demolish the sign. IN ANY CASE WHERE COLLISION IS ABSOLUTELY UNAVOIDABLE, TRY TO: • Avoid a head-on collision; collision at an angle reduces force of impact. • Avoid hitting human beings, especially young children. If you have a choice, it's better to hit inanimate objects than people or animals. Remember: You're more likely to avoid hitting any obstruction in the path of the bus if you always anticipate the unusual and practice effective evasive action so it becomes as automatic as possible. NOTES:

PRACTICE

INSTRUCTOR GUIDELINES	CONTENT
	What three basic forms of evasive action can you take to avoid hitting an obstruction in the path of the bus?
1. brake to stop 2. steer around 3. leave roadway	1. 2. 3.
Ask different class members what they wrote. Discuss with class. Make sure all points on pages 25-28 are covered.	What things influence your decision?
	Discuss your answers with the class.

WHAT WOULD YOU DO?

INSTRUCTOR GUIDELINES	CONTENT
Refer to Figure 4. Reproduce diagram on chalkboard or magnetic board. Ask two trainees (who have come up with different solutions) to come up and demonstrate their answer. Discuss with class. The best thing for this bus driver to do is to steer left. Within one second the bus will be halfway to the disabled vehicle, while the vehicle going 60 mph will have reached it, giving the bus driver room to pull back onto the freeway and avoïd hitting the disabled vehicle and pedestrian. Even if this weren't accomplished with perfect timing, it would be better to sideswipe the other vehicle or even push him into the left lane than to hit the obstruction--including the unprotected person--head on. Ask them if they would do anything different if the disabled vehicle were closer to the bus. E.g., what if it was 25 feet ahead? 35 feet? 40 feet? They can use the technique of multiplying 1.5 times mph to see how far the bus will travel in one second.	DISCUSSION QUESTION Suppose you were approaching a freeway exit as shown in Figure 4. The ramp goes down under the freeway. The guard rail to your right protects a steep drop off. You are traveling 30 mph and have entered the deceleration lane. In the lane to your left a car is passing you at 60 mph. Suddenly you spot a disabled vehicle 60 feet ahead on the exit ramp. A person beside it is changing a tire. (It would require 67 feet for you to stop.) What evasive action would you take? Why? a. Indicate evasive action on Figure 4. b. Explain why here:

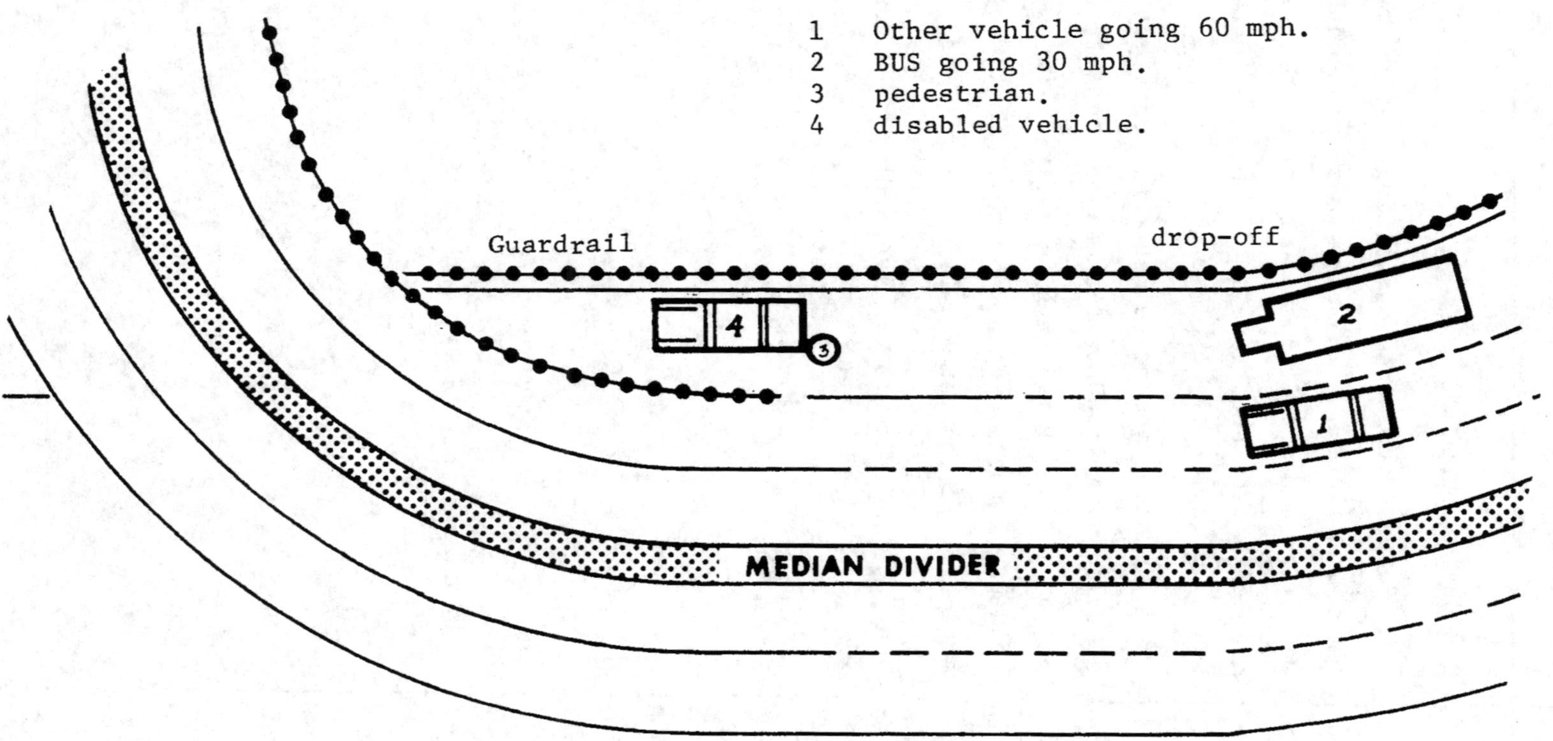

Figure 4. Obstruction in Path of the Bus

SUDDEN LOSS OF VISIBILITY

INSTRUCTOR GUIDELINES	CONTENT
Loss of visibility due to fog, etc., is covered in Advanced Unit G.	Several things can cause sudden loss of visibility--water splashed onto windshield, headlight failure, hood flies up, etc. You must know how to control the vehicle until you can regain normal visibility. You'll have to use clues other than the usual visual clues.
	IF THE HOOD FLIES UP:
Describe local incidents (if any) in which driver experienced sudden loss of visibility. Ask class members what they would do. Describe what actions the driver took. Discuss results.	1. Lower your head and try to look through the gap at the hinge. 2. Look out the left and right windows to help keep your sense of direction. 3. Apply brakes moderately. 4. Activate your right turn signal. 5. Steer out of the traffic lane and stop. 6. Activate four-way hazard lights (not red flashing warning lights).
	NOTES:
	IF THE HEADLIGHTS FAIL: 1. Immediately hit dimmer switch. 2. Activate right turn signal, four-way hazards. 3. Use available environmental light to keep sight of road.

INSTRUCTOR GUIDELINES	CONTENT
	4. Brake slowly and steer out of traffic lane and stop. NOTES:
Drivers should be able to activate all switches "blindfolded" so they can keep their eyes on the road.	IF WATER/SLUSH IS SPLASHED ON WINDSHIELD: 1. Apply brakes cautiously, look out side windows to keep sight of road. 2. Turn on wipers. NOTES:
	IF WINDSHIELD WIPERS FAIL DURING RAIN/SLEET/SNOW: 1. Look out side windows to keep sight of road. 2. Apply brakes cautiously. 3. Activate right turn signal. 4. Pull over as far to the right as possible, or off road, and stop. NOTES:

PRACTICE

INSTRUCTOR GUIDELINES	CONTENT
Look at road, street lights, etc., through side windows, or through gap in hood hinge.	If you suddenly lose your normal visibility through the windshield, what clues help you maintain directional control?
Carefully, modified.	How should you brake?
When visibility is not immediately restored.	When is it necessary to pull off the road?
Ask one or two trainees what they wrote. Have class discuss. Answers should include major points of the emergency technique.	Discuss your answers with the class.

FIRST AID

TABLE OF CONTENTS

OBJECTIVES

1. Set priorities for treating severe injuries.

2. Recognize and treat symptoms of severe bleeding, stoppage of breath, and shock.

OVERVIEW

INSTRUCTOR GUIDELINES	CONTENT
Present local situation in which a student requires first aid on the bus. The driver recognizes symptoms and administers proper treatment. The situation should be severe enough that the child's life is saved.	BUS DRIVER SAVES A LIFE
	YOUR RESPONSIBILITY TO RENDER FIRST AID* The first objective of first aid is to save life. You must know how to apply the principles of first aid. First aid is the immediate and temporary care given to the victim of an accident or sudden illness until the services of a physician can be obtained. A victim will respond much more readily to treatment if he recognizes that a competent person is administering that treatment. Practicing the procedures in this unit will increase your competence in rendering first aid. Common sense and a few simple rules are the keys to effective first aid. It is as important to know what not to do, as to know what to do. In case of an emergency, making mistakes could be disastrous to the injured person. You are more likely to act promptly and correctly if you learn only a few simple principles but learn them well. Emphasis is placed on problems you may confront on the road. The procedures in this unit include: 1. Evaluation of injury and setting of priorities for treatment.

INSTRUCTOR GUIDELINES	CONTENT
	2. Evaluation and treatment of bleeding. 3. Maintenance of airway and respiration. 4. Evaluation and control of shock. Other first aid topics that are important but not urgent in the saving of life will be discussed only briefly to provide you with a general knowledge of first aid. Little attention has been given the contents of the first aid kit and its use, because the most important equipment you have is your knowledge of first aid, not the number and types of splints, bandages, and ointments in the first aid kit. Where references are made to bandages or other equipment, use the cleanest materials available but <u>do not delay</u> first aid if clean bandages are not available. However, the first aid kit should contain a supply of 4" x 4" pads and similar clean bandages for covering wounds and stopping bleeding.

FIRST AID KIT

INSTRUCTOR GUIDELINES	CONTENT
Give local details on these three topics. Have trainees take notes.	CONTENTS
	LOCATION
	WHERE TO GET NEW SUPPLIES

SETTING OF PRIORITIES FOR TREATMENT

INSTRUCTOR GUIDELINES	CONTENT
	You must make three evaluations in establishing priorities for treatment: condition of scene, types of injuries, and need for immediate treatment. EVALUATION OF THE SCENE Several types of situations require high priority action. For example, if fire is present, the most urgent action is to remove everyone from its danger. Don't give any first aid treatment until everyone is safe. If someone has been electrocuted, the most urgent action for a first aider is to remove him from the electrical source while simultaneously protecting himself and others from also being electrocuted. Use a completely dry stick to lift off an offending wire. Do not touch the injured until he is removed from contact with the electrical source. If a person has drowned or is in the presence of a dangerous gas, such as chlorine or ammonia, do not attempt to rescue him unless you are sure that you can do so without becoming a victim yourself. Often, a few seconds delay will give you enough time to find an alternate, safer way to rescue the person. EVALUATION OF INJURIES At least three types of injuries require prompt attention: 1. *Severe bleeding.* If a person is bleeding profusely, he may be dead in less than two minutes.

INSTRUCTOR GUIDELINES	CONTENT
	2. *Blocked airway or stoppage of breath.* Most people can be saved if they start breathing on their own or artificially within two minutes. If breathing has been stopped for five minutes, there is only a 25 percent chance of saving the victim. It is, therefore, important to note the time at which breathing stopped. 3. *Shock.* In shock the vital body functions are depressed. Death may result if not treated promptly, even though the injury which caused the shock is not severe enough to cause death. PRIORITY FOR TREATMENT A school bus accident may involve injury to a number of people. If several people are injured and the scene permits you to begin treatment promptly, treat severe bleeding first, then move quickly to those who have stopped breathing and still have a chance for survival. Then, move to less urgent injuries. Whenever possible, treat a person where he is found. Before you move any sick or injured person, bleeding should be stopped, breathing should be established, and shock should be treated. If there is great urgency to move an injured person, drag him on the long axis of his body pulling him by his hands (stretched back behind his head), or by the shoulders. If possible, place beneath him a coat or a blanket on which he can ride or be pulled.

INSTRUCTOR GUIDELINES	CONTENT
	There is always the possibility that you may be injured in the accident also. You should, therefore, be able to direct students in first aid practices in the event you are injured. Decide which of your regular passengers might be most capable of assisting you during an emergency.
Add any comments you feel are important before they actually get to the first aid procedures.	NOTES:

EVALUATION AND TREATMENT OF BLEEDING

INSTRUCTOR GUIDELINES	CONTENT
	Use the following procedures in the evaluation and treatment of bleeding. EVALUATION OF BLEEDING When treating a bleeding injury, determine the type of bleeding and the amount of blood lost. You must be able to recognize three types of external bleeding: 1. *Capillary oozing*. Injuries to capillaries or small veins is indicated by a steady ooze of dark-colored blood. 2. *Venous bleeding*. Bleeding from a vein is indicated by a flow of dark-colored blood at a steady rate. 3. *Arterial bleeding*. Bleeding from an artery is indicated by bright red blood, flowing swiftly in spurts or jets. This may sometimes be mixed with venous bleeding, in which case the blood will be slightly darker in color. When evaluating the severity of bleeding, remember: • Blood dripping slowly from the wound is generally not serious and can be controlled. • Blood flowing in a small, steady stream or in small spurts may be serious and can be controlled. • Blood flowing in a heavy stream or in large spurts indicates a serious condition, and a

INSTRUCTOR GUIDELINES	CONTENT
	first aider must attempt to bring it under control immediately. Bleeding needs immediate attention. Even the loss of small amounts of blood will produce weakness and can cause shock. The loss of as much as a pint of blood by a child, or a quart of blood by an adult, may have disastrous results. CONTROL OF BLEEDING *Direct pressure*. The main step in controlling bleeding is for the first aider to exert direct pressure over the wound area. This is done by placing the cleanest material available (preferably a pad of sterile gauze) against the bleeding point and applying firm pressure with the hand until a bandage can be applied. To bring bleeding under control, follow these steps:
Refer to Figure 1. ↓	1. Apply dressing or pad directly over wound. 2. Apply direct, even pressure, using bare hand if necessary when bleeding is serious and when dressing is not immediately available. 3. Leave dressing in place. 4. Continue pressure by applying bandage. 5. Secure bandage in place, checking to be sure bandage is not too tight and thus cutting off circulation. 6. Elevate limb above heart level except when there is a possible broken bone.

To stop bleeding, apply a dressing pad or a bare hand directly over the wound and apply pressure.

Continue the pressure until the bleeding has stopped or slowed to the point that you will be able to apply a bandage. Do not hurry to remove the pressure.

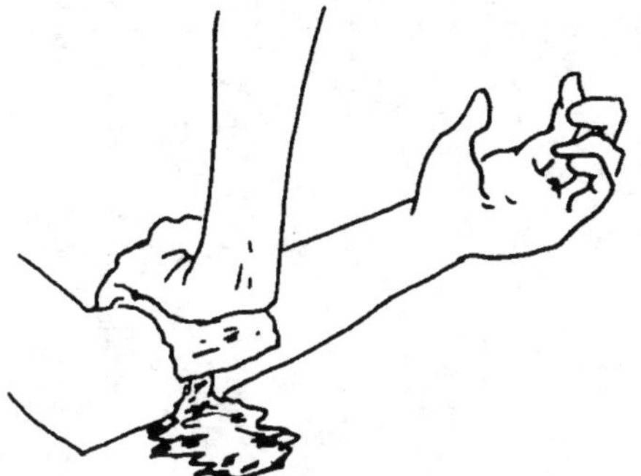

Then apply a bandage over the dressing to continue the pressure and thus control the bleeding. Check the bandage after the knot is tied to be sure it is not too tight and is not cutting off the circulation.

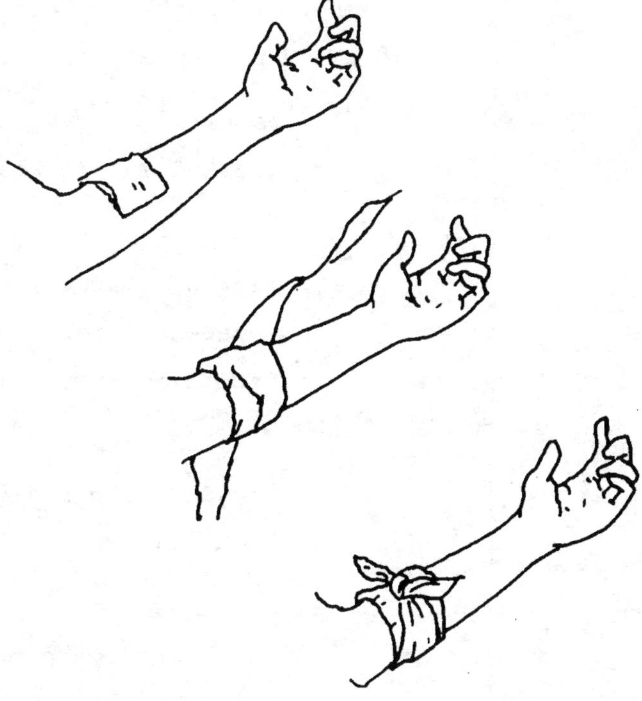

Figure 1. Using Direct Pressure to Control Bleeding*

INSTRUCTOR GUIDELINES	CONTENT
	7. Treat for shock. 8. If blood soaks through dressing, do not remove but apply more dressings
Answer any questions trainees may ask.	NOTES:
	Pressure points. If direct pressure does not control bleeding, pressure on an artery (pressure point) close to the wound is necessary.
Refer to Figure 2.	The point selected must be between the heart and the injury. To control bleeding in this manner, find one of these pressure points: 1. *Temporal artery*. The temporal artery is located in the hollow just in front of the ear. 2. *Facial artery*. The facial artery is located in the small crevice about one inch from the angle of the jaw. 3. *Carotid artery*. The carotid artery is located deep and back on each side of the Adam's apple. 4. *Subclavian artery*. The subclavian artery is located deep and down in the hollow near the collarbone. 5. *Brachial artery*. The brachial artery is located on the inner side of the upper arm about three inches below the armpit.

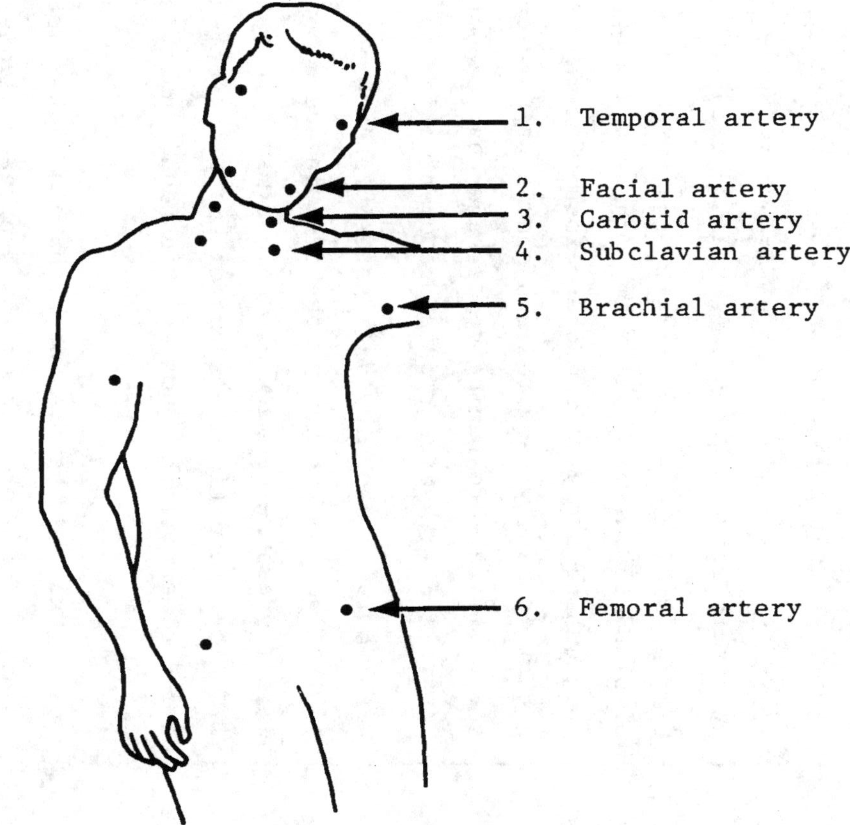

Figure 2. Pressure Points for Applying Arterial Pressure

INSTRUCTOR GUIDELINES	CONTENT
	6. *Femoral artery*. The femoral artery is located midway in the groin, between the crotch and the hip.
Emphasize. ⇨	*Tourniquet warning*. A tourniquet applied to control bleeding is mentioned here principally to discourage its use. It is dangerous to apply, dangerous to leave on, and dangerous to remove. It will cause tissue injury and stoppage of the entire supply of blood to the part below it. This causes gangrene and, subsequently, could cause loss of limb. A tourniquet is rarely required and should be used only for severe, life-threatening hemorrhage that cannot be controlled with direct pressure or arterial pressure.
	Applying the bandage. After bleeding has been controlled, do not remove the dressing used to apply direct pressure, even though blood may have saturated it. Apply additional layers of cloth to form a good-sized covering; then bandage the wound snugly and firmly.
	A bandage that is too tight can cause further injury. Therefore, check the bandage periodically. Look for swelling around the wound. If it seems that the bandage is interfering with the circulation of the blood, loosen it.
	Treating for shock. Anyone who has lost much blood will need treatment for shock. Even if the symptoms of shock are not evident, the patient should be kept warm and quiet.
	NOTES:

PRACTICE IN CONTROLLING BLEEDING

INSTRUCTOR GUIDELINES	CONTENT
	Your instructor will first demonstrate the control of bleeding using direct pressure. Watch how he does it.
	Now observe the location of the six pressure points and how to apply arterial pressure.
Ask for a volunteer from the class to act as the injured person. Demonstrate the direct pressure method and arterial pressure method of controlling bleeding.	Now you practice each method on another class member.
Explain how to apply and tie bandage.	Suppose you notice a student with severe arterial bleeding at the wrist. Demonstrate what you would do to control bleeding.
Break class into pairs. Have each pair take turns practicing each method. Assist where necessary. Have them tell you when they feel competent to be checked. Check each method and provide feedback.	NOTES:

MAINTENANCE OF AIRWAY AND RESPIRATION*

INSTRUCTOR GUIDELINES	CONTENT
	Breathing may stop for three reasons: 1. The mouth or windpipe is blocked (by the tongue, blood, or mucus). 2. The brain centers that control breathing have stopped (drowning, electrocution, head injury, or poisoning). 3. There is a sucking sound of the chest that prevents the lungs from expanding (obvious by looking at the chest). With the first two, the person may be blue in color and respiration may appear to have stopped, or he may be choking. ARTIFICIAL RESPIRATION Most persons can live about six minutes after breathing stops. Therefore, artificial respiration must begin as soon as possible after natural breathing has been interrupted, or when natural breathing is so irregular or so shallow as to be ineffective. Artificial respiration is a method of getting air into and out of a person's lungs until he can breathe for himself. *Mouth-to-mouth method*. One of the simplest and most effective ways to give artificial respiration is by the mouth-to-mouth (or mouth-to-nose) method. This method is effective for both children and adults and can be used even when there are injuries to the chest and arms. Follow these steps: 1. Place the person who has stopped breathing on his back.

INSTRUCTOR GUIDELINES	CONTENT
	2. Open his mouth and clear out foreign matter (food, dirt, and so forth) with the fingers. If the person has false teeth, remove them. 3. Tilt his head back so that his chin points upward and tilt his lower jaw beneath and behind so that it juts out. This moves the base of the tongue away from the back of the throat so it does not block the air passage to the lungs. Unless this air passage is open, no amount of effort will get air in. 4. Blow air into a person's lungs through either his mouth or nose. Open your mouth wide and place it tightly over the person's mouth. Pinch his nostrils shut. Or close the victim's mouth and place your mouth over his nose. With an infant or small child, place your mouth over both his nose and mouth making an airproof seal. Air can be blown into a person's mouth even through clenched teeth. 5. Blow into the mouth or nose, continuing to hold the unconscious person's lower jaw so that it juts out to keep the air passage open. 6. Remove your mouth from the patient's mouth. Turn your head to the side and listen for the return outflow of air coming from the patient's lungs. If you hear it, you will know that an exchange of air has occurred.

INSTRUCTOR GUIDELINES	CONTENT
	7. Continue breathing for the patient. Blow vigorously into his mouth or nose about 12 times each minute. Remove your mouth after each breath and listen for the exchange of air. In the case of an infant or child, blow less vigorously, using shallower breaths about 20 times a minute.
Refer to Figure 3.	8. If there is not an exchange of air, turn the person on his side and strike him several times between the shoulder blades, using considerable force. This will help dislodge any obstruction in the air passages. Check the position of the head and jaw. Finally, make sure there is no foreign matter in his mouth.
	Normal breathing may begin again after 15 minutes of artificial respiration. But if it does not, continue the procedure until medical aid arrives. Alternate with other persons, if possible, to maintain maximum efficiency. Cases of electric shock and drug or carbon monoxide poisoning may require artificial respiration for longer periods.
	The first sign of restored breathing may be a sigh or a gasp. Breathing may be irregular at first, therefore, artificial respiration should be continued until regular breathing resumes.
	When normal breathing resumes, the person usually recovers rapidly. However, be prepared in case he stops breathing again.
	NOTES:

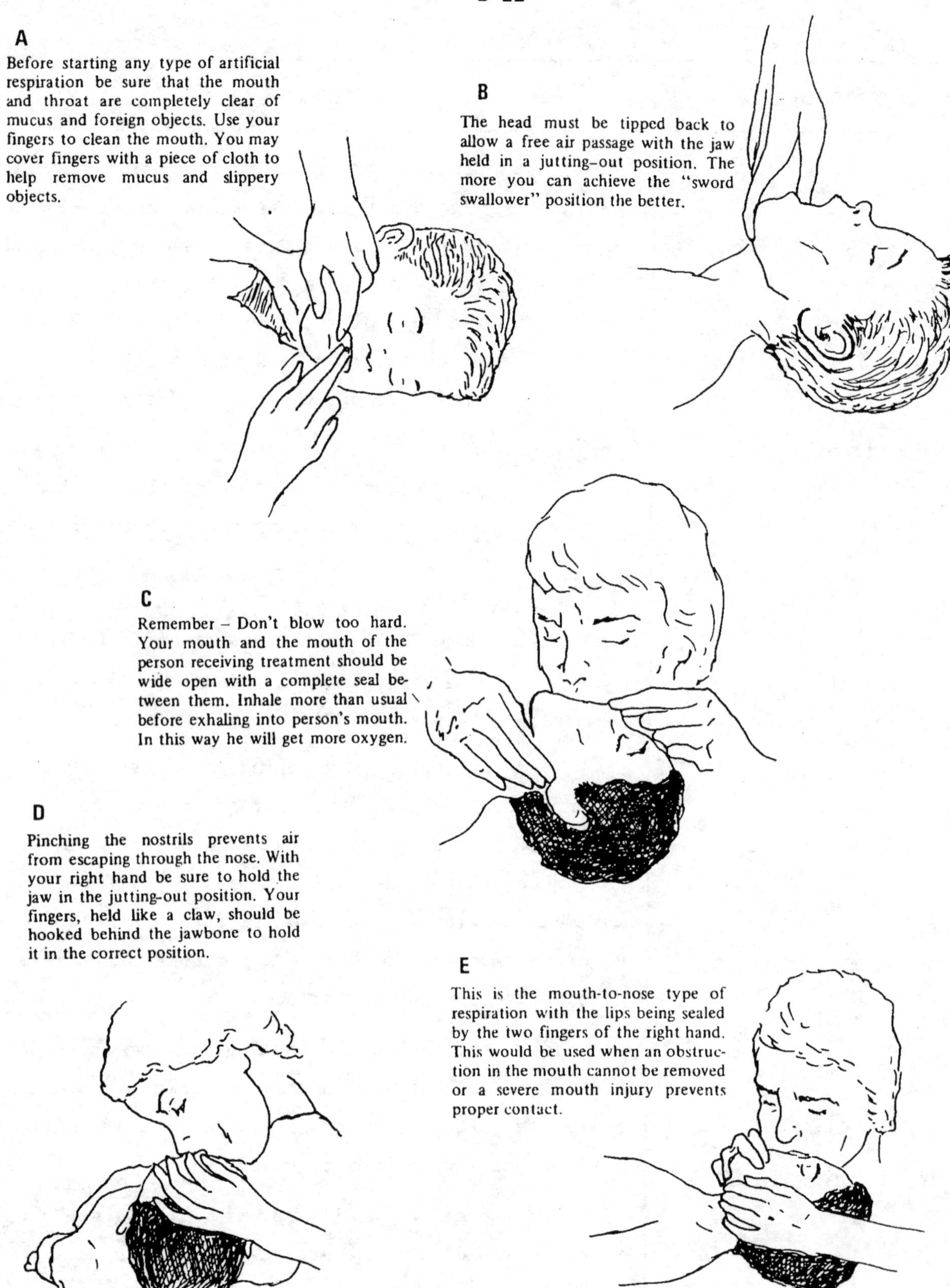

Figure 3. Mouth-to-Mouth and Mouth-to-Nose Method*

INSTRUCTOR GUIDELINES	CONTENT
Refer to Figure 4. Emphasize that this method is not as effective as mouth-to-mouth. Back-pressure method should only be used when mouth injuries, etc., prevent use of mouth-to-mouth method.	*Back-pressure, arm-lift method.* This is the second most desirable method of artificial respiration. It should be used only when injuries to the head or face prevent the use of mouth-to-mouth or mouth-to-nose method. If a person has injuries both to the face and chest so you cannot use either method, one should not hesitate to open the victim's mouth and keep the windpipe clear of blood, mucus, broken teeth, or obstructing tongue. It is better to move a broken jaw, broken nose, or broken teeth and keep the person alive by letting him breathe than to keep the broken bones from moving and have the person die.
Add any comments about artificial respiration you feel are necessary. Answer any questions trainees may ask.	NOTES:

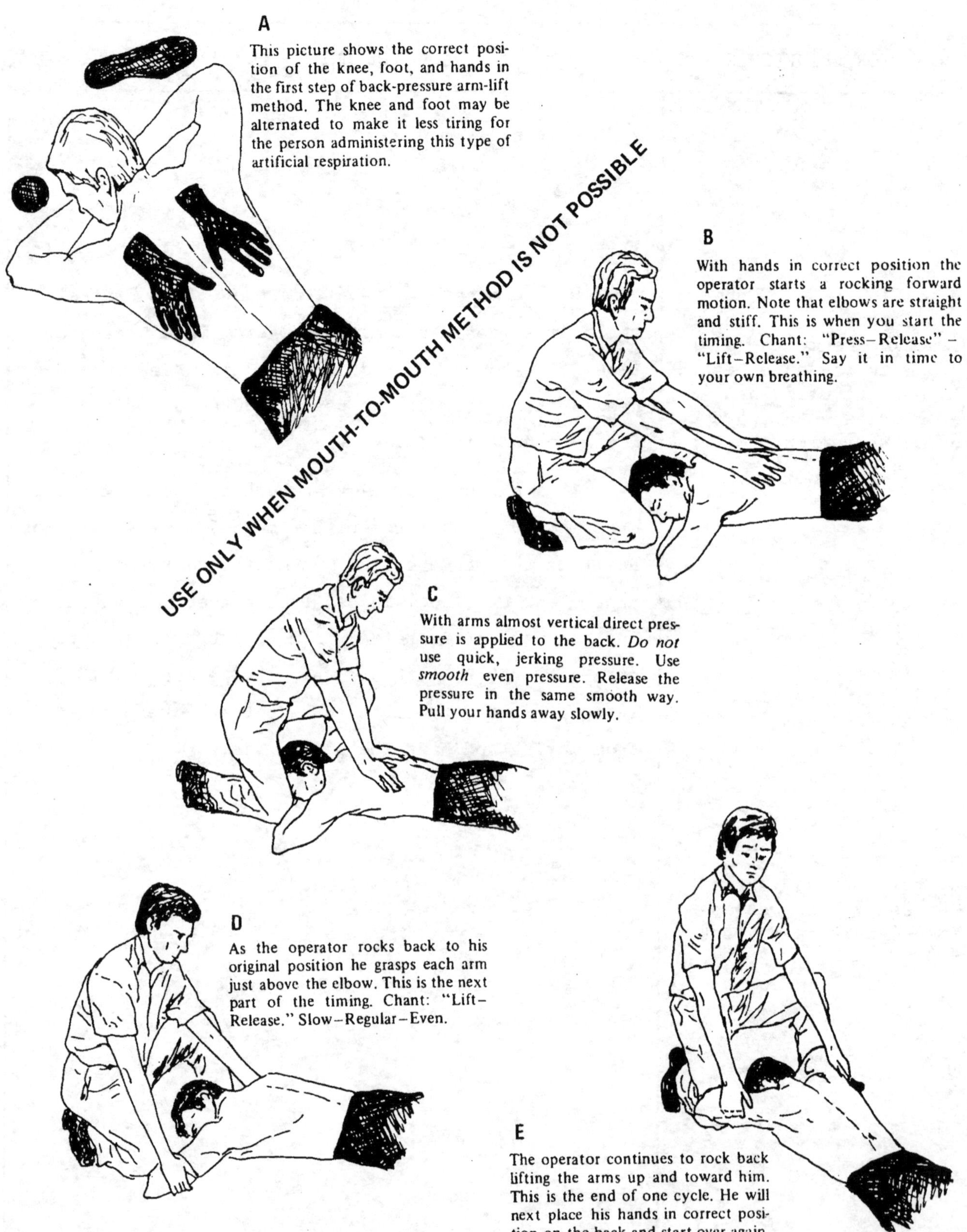

Figure 4. Back-Pressure Arm-Lift Method

PRACTICE IN ARTIFICIAL RESPIRATION

INSTRUCTOR GUIDELINES	CONTENT
If you did not show the film, "First Aid on the Spot," use a volunteer from the class to demonstrate the mouth-to-mouth method of artificial respiration. Also demonstrate the back-pressure arm-lift method. Comment as you go.	Your instructor will now show you the two methods of artificial respiration. When would you use the back-pressure arm-lift method? How does the mouth-to-mouth method differ when the injured person is a small child?
Break class into pairs. Have each pair take turns practicing each method. Assist where necessary. Have them tell you when they feel competent to be checked. Check each method and provide feedback.	Now you take turns practicing each method with another member of the class. Your instructor will be around to observe. NOTES:

EVALUATION AND CONTROL OF SHOCK

INSTRUCTOR GUIDELINES	CONTENT
It is not recommended that bus drivers attempt to splint a fractured bone. Keeping the person immobile, comfortable, and treating him for shock are usually the best actions until medical help arrives.	Shock may cause death if not treated promptly, even though the injury which caused it may not itself be enough to cause death. The three most common causes of severe shock are inadequate breathing, excessive bleeding, and unsplinted fractures. Correction of these will do much to correct the shock. RECOGNIZING SHOCK Shock is easily recognized: The skin is pale and clammy with small drops of sweat particularly around the lips and forehead; the person may complain of nausea and dizziness; the pulse may be fast and weak and the breathing shallow and irregular; the eyes may be dull with enlarged pupils. A person may be unconscious or unaware of the seriousness of the injury, and then suddenly collapse.

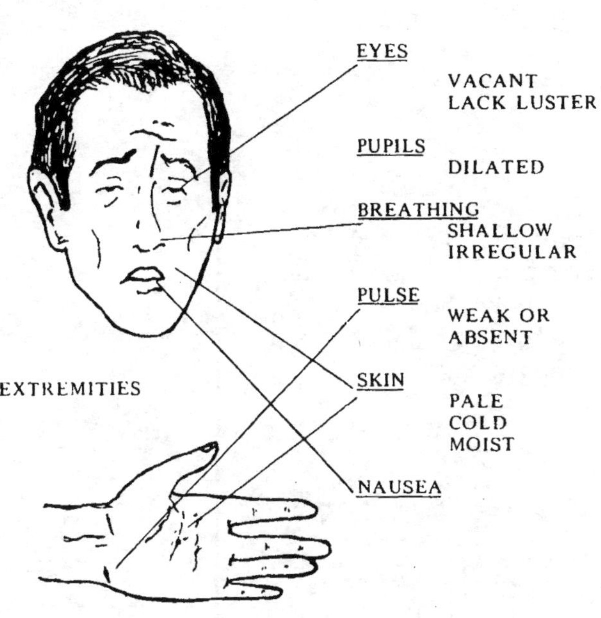

INSTRUCTOR GUIDELINES	CONTENT
	You should treat all seriously injured persons for shock, even though all of these symptoms have not appeared and the person seems normal and alert.
	CONTROL OF SHOCK
	When treating for shock, follow these steps:
	1. Have the injured person lie down.
	2. Elevate his feet and legs 12 inches or more. This helps the flow of blood to his heart and head. If the person has received a head or chest injury, or if he has difficulty breathing, elevate his head and chest rather than his feet.
Usually a first aider would use a blanket, but drivers must use what is available on the bus.	3. Keep the person warm, but not hot. Place a coat, jacket, newspapers, or any available covering under him. Depending on the weather, also cover him. Avoid getting him so hot that he perspires, because this draws blood to the skin and away from the interior of his body where it is needed. On warm days or in a hot room, no covering is necessary.
Feet may be elevated by placing the child on the floor of the bus with his feet raised up to rest on a bus seat.	

INSTRUCTOR GUIDELINES	CONTENT
Generally, water won't be available on the bus. De-emphasize this point. In any case, don't send other students to search for water. It's better to keep them on the bus and do without the water until help arrives.	4. If water is available, give him some every 15 minutes in small amounts if his condition permits. If he is unconscious, do not attempt to give anything to drink. If he vomits or is nauseated, postpone giving liquid until the nausea disappears. 5. Keep the person quiet. See that bleeding is controlled and injured parts are kept still. Assure him that he will get the best care you can give. Reassurance is a potent medicine.
 Add any comments you may have on the treatment of shock. Answer any questions trainees may ask.	NOTES:

PRACTICE IN TREATING SHOCK

INSTRUCTOR GUIDELINES	CONTENT
Demonstrate how to check for symptoms of shock, using a volunteer from the class. Demonstrate how to treat shock. Comment and question trainees on when you should elevate the feet and when you you should elevate the head and shoulders. Break class into pairs and have each member "treat" the other for shock. Observe each pair, and provide feed-back.	Your instructor will now show you how to treat an injured person who has gone into shock (or who is in danger of going into shock). Now, you practice the treatment on another class member. NOTES:

GUIDELINES ON OTHER INJURIES AND CONDITIONS

INSTRUCTOR GUIDELINES	CONTENT
Federal Standards recommend that school bus drivers take a Standard American Red Cross First Aid course. Therefore, procedures for other injuries and conditions are not included here. However, you may want to include procedures for certain injuries that are more likely in your area (for example, snake bites and scorpion bites). Or, your local policy may advise that drivers who have not yet taken Red Cross courses must know how to treat eye injuries, burns, etc., before they transport children. Expand this section to fit your own needs. Insert extra pages if necessary.	Can you think of any injuries or conditions that have not been covered?
Administer Unit Review Questions. Provide feedback. Provide remedial review and practice for anyone who does not meet criterion.	

FIELD TRIPS

TABLE OF CONTENTS

OBJECTIVES

1. Learning an unfamiliar route.
2. Working with chaperones.
3. Students unfamiliar with bus rules of conduct.
4. Excesses in behavior due to nature of the trip.
5. Extra and oversize equipment.

OVERVIEW

INSTRUCTOR GUIDELINES	CONTENT
	You may be called on to make special trips with various groups. Several things about driving on a field trip are different from the things you do on your regular route. Consider two examples of these special trips.
	FIELD TRIP OVERNIGHT
Provide a brief description (purpose, destination, etc.) of each example from your locale. Include differences pertaining to route, students, chaperones, student conduct, and equipment.	ACTIVITY TRIP TO FOOTBALL GAME
Ask trainees to "spot differences." Lead discussion and ask trainees for other examples of field trips and special activity trips. Have them describe differences between these trips and their normal run.	How many differences can you spot?

INSTRUCTOR GUIDELINES	CONTENT
	Consider at least these five differences. You may have to know what to do about: 1. An unfamiliar route. 2. Chaperones and their responsibilities. 3. Students who aren't familiar with bus riding rules. 4. Excesses in behavior due to the nature of the trip. 5. Extra and oversize equipment.
Ask trainees to write in their best guesses (or list a real experience) for each of the five items. Then lead discussion, having them volunteer, and compare their answers.	What do these five differences imply for you as the bus driver? 1. 2. 3. 4. 5.

SPECIAL FIELD TRIP PROCEDURES

INSTRUCTOR GUIDELINES	CONTENT
"Dry runs" are the best method. Usually, it's the Transportation Supervisor's job to give route directions to bus drivers.	1. Review route of trip, mentally, by use of a map, or by driving a private vehicle to the destination prior to the trip.
Refer to Figure 1. Substitute your own form, if any.	2. Prepare special trip AUTHORIZATION REPORT including on it: a. Destination and date. b. Nature and purpose of trip. c. Departure and expected return times. d. Number of pupils to be transported. e. Rest stops and overnight arrangements, if any. f. Signature of appropriate supervisory person for authorization.
Lead brief discussion of each of these items.	3. When loading for special trips, check to see that only students and authorized adults get on the bus.
Rosters may be attached to trip report, or back of report could be used for listing students assigned to bus. An additional vehicle, e.g., a van, could be used for extra equipment.	4. If band instruments or other large items must be transported, store them in the proper space under the bus; if there is no storage area, check that all items are kept on the bus away from the front, behind the stanchion bars, and not blocking the emergency door(s).
	5. Request chaperones to be responsible for maintaining order on the bus.
	6. When destination has been reached, make sure that all students know which bus they are to board and at what time.

SPECIAL TRIP AUTHORIZATION REPORT

School District: ______________________ Bus Number: ____________

Destination: ______________________ Bus Driver: ____________

____

____

Date of Trip: ______________

Nature and Purpose of Trip: ______________________

____

____

Departure Time: ____________ Expected Time of Arrival: ____________

Expected Return Departure Time: ________ Expected Time of Return: ________

Number of Pupils to be Transported: ______________________

Rest stops, if any: ______________________

Overnight Arrangements, if any: ______________________

____

Chaperones, if any: ______________________

____

____

Supervisory Person Authorizing Trip: ______________________
(Signature)

Problems Encountered:

(use back of sheet, if necessary)

Total Mileage: ________ I hereby verify that trip was completed as authorized.

Return Time: ________

____
(Bus Driver's Signature)

Figure 1. Sample Special Trip Authorization Report Form

INSTRUCTOR GUIDELINES	CONTENT
	7. Check that no student(s) board the bus at any time unless authorized by you or by a chaperone. 8. When the trip has been completed, enter the following information on the special trip AUTHORIZATION REPORT: a. Mileage. b. Time returned. c. Problems encountered, if any. d. Signature beneath statement that the trip was completed as authorized.
Provide filled-in examples of your local special trip AUTHORIZATION REPORT forms, if any.	NOTES:

GUIDELINES AND LOCAL POLICY

INSTRUCTOR GUIDELINES	CONTENT
Most school districts have their own guidelines and policies on field trips. Use these topics to structure how your district handles each area. Be specific and list concrete things the driver should do. For example, "Pass out list of special instructions to all passengers. Explain each instruction and answer any questions students may have."	HOW TO ADAPT TO AN UNFAMILIAR ROUTE Reported Hazards, Conditions Use of Maps Dry Runs
The question is sometimes asked as to who is the "boss" on the bus; the chaperone or the bus driver? It would seem reasonable that the chaperone, who is expected to be a competent adult, should have general charge of the group in all matters except where there is some conflict or interference with the bus driver's job of driving the bus in the safe manner expected of him: If students do not remain in their seats, if the noise level is such as to interfere with his effective driving, if the language overheard is improper. In other words, if the chaperone is ineffective and not doing his job, the driver certainly must have final authority.	HOW TO WORK WITH CHAPERONES Their Responsibility-- Your Responsibility--

INSTRUCTOR GUIDELINES	CONTENT
	HOW TO MANAGE STUDENTS WHO ARE UNFAMILIAR WITH RULES FOR SCHOOL BUS CONDUCT Special Instructions-- HOW TO MANAGE EXCESSES IN BEHAVIOR DUE TO NATURE OF TRIP Cheering-- Singing-- Rocking the Bus-- Leaning Out Windows-- Other--

INSTRUCTOR GUIDELINES	CONTENT
	HOW TO HANDLE EXTRA OR OVERSIZE EQUIPMENT Loading-- Securing for Transport (aisles and exits clear)--
Add here any special topics not covered that you usually emphasize in preparing school bus drivers to complete a field trip safely. Other topics you may want to include: 1. Seniority policy, if applicable. 2. Bus preparation. 3. Overnight trips. 4. Parking after the bus arrives at its destination. 5. Policy on size of loads that can be taken. 6. Student supervision ratio (how many children per adult, if applicable). 7. Any other item that will fit this subject.	OTHER POLICIES IN EFFECT IN YOUR DISTRICT

LOCAL RECORDS

INSTRUCTOR GUIDELINES	CONTENT
Distribute all record forms used in your district (or by your company). Have sample forms filled out.	INSTRUCTIONS ON RIDERS, DESTINATION, SCHEDULE, FOOD/ REST STOPS, BUSES IN CONVOY, ETC.
Prepare a handout description of a field trip that a "bus driver" has completed. Have trainees fill in trip report and/or other necessary records, using the information on the handout they receive.	
Distribute model forms for comparison.	
Clarify any items about forms they receive and forms they are to turn in.	NUMBER OF HOURS AND MILES DRIVEN
	TRIP REPORTS

PLANNING FOR FIELD TRIPS

INSTRUCTOR GUIDELINES	CONTENT
Give each trainee a special field trip "assignment." Provide details and clues that give him a basis for making plans on how to handle the trip. NOTE: Make sure each trainee writes a plan and has a turn to present it to the class. Ask them to jot down what problems they might have, plans for necessary activities, forms needed to work with, etc. Then have each trainee read his assignment to the class and tell them his "plan." You and the other trainees can question him, e.g., "what would you do about ________________," etc., if he hasn't considered all appropriate items. Each plan should conform to local policy on any of the five topics covered (unfamiliar route, chaperones, etc.) plus any topic(s) you added. His presentation must meet your approval (as well as the majority of the class) as to whether his plan is appropriate to the trip assignment. Administer Unit Review Questions. Provide feedback.	Your instructor will give you a field trip "assignment." YOUR PLAN:

TRANSPORTING EXCEPTIONAL STUDENTS

TABLE OF CONTENTS

OBJECTIVES

1. Identify the physical characteristics and behavioral tendencies of different types of exceptional students.

2. Describe special loading/unloading procedures.

3. Describe special methods of controlling exceptional children.

4. State ways of communicating with parents of exceptional children.

OVERVIEW

INSTRUCTOR GUIDELINES	CONTENT
Stress that the bus driver's attitude is of utmost importance in dealing with exceptional students. Many problems can arise if the driver does not act as if he has a favorable attitude toward each child. For example, if a driver would scold or ridicule a child who has an "accident" on the bus, the problem will be worse. The child feels guilty and embarrassed enough without further aggravation by the driver. Or, consider the negative effect on a handicapped child if he hears two adults arguing about who is going to lift him out of the bus. Any remarks about how heavy he is or how hard it is on the driver's back, etc. are examples of negative attitude "in action."* It is important that bus drivers have a positive influence on the exceptional children they transport. Any child who feels his abilities are inadequate (and many exceptional children do have this feeling) need to have their self-worth developed. How is a child's self-esteem built up? Words, gestures, and facial expressions tell anyone if he is accepted or not. Criticism, blame, and ridicule also serve as indications of others' feelings toward him. To a child who doubts his self-worth these negative responses can be very damaging.	Attitude. The success of programs for exceptional children depends upon the people who have daily contact with the children. Such people should possess characteristics which are different in kind and degree from the average. They should have extra patience, mental alertness, flexibility, resourcefulness, enthusiasm, emotional stability, personal warmth, friendliness, understanding, and sympathy. As a bus driver, you should be able to develop and maintain rapport with children, and be able to exercise mature judgment in relation to both the care of exceptional children and the responsibilities of driving. You should be aware of, and be willing to conform to, the objectives of the child's therapeutic needs. You should be able to accept the exceptional child and his problems as you would accept any child. You should treat exceptional children as you would want your own children to be treated. The daily bus ride to school can be an important part of a child's progress toward independence. The child will learn how to leave his home to meet the bus, how to cross a street, and how to behave on the bus. You will explain the bus rules to him and the child will learn to obey them. You play an important role in determining behavior patterns of children. In fact, you can start the child's day off right or wrong. The bus ride to and from school can be a pleasant experience which a child anticipates eagerly or it can become a dreaded experience. You should be thoughtful and careful about such routine matters as assigning a seat or seatmate, the presentation and purpose of a seatbelt, and about using discipline.

INSTRUCTOR GUIDELINES	CONTENT
Praise, encouragement, and smiles are the best ways to support a child's self-worth. Bus drivers should see themselves as a part of a co-operative team who can help the students tremendously. For many exceptional children, the bus ride is the "highlight" of the day and a sincere, warm, bus driver can add much to their day.*	Remember, however, that your primary purpose is to take children to and from school safely and dependably. Therefore, while you make allowances for specific problems of exceptional children, a child's social adjustment will be of less importance than getting to school on time and the safety of the other children, the driver, and the bus.

YOUR RESPONSIBILITY

INSTRUCTOR GUIDELINES	CONTENT
	Qualifications. Besides driver qualifications regarding age, health, past experience, knowledge of vehicles and maintenance, safe driving practices, etc., you should be able to operate specially equipped or adapted vehicles. You should have a knowledge of first aid and be familiar with the use of wheelchairs, braces, crutches, etc. Information. You should be aware of the problems of each of the children who ride your bus; you should be familiar with the medical and physical aspects of disabilities of each child. You should, through communication with school personnel and parents, know when a child is on medication and what the effects of the medication will be. You should be able to determine when a child is behaving abnormally for his condition. You have the responsibility of reporting to the school authorities or to parents specific incidents, attitudes, etc., which may be significant in the treatment of the child. You should know what special steps to take in case of a traffic accident or breakdown because the comfort and emotional well-being of these children are your responsibility while they are in your charge. You may spend much time learning how to care for each child under the many circumstances that might occur while the children are on your bus.

COMMONLY USED SPECIAL EDUCATION TERMS

INSTRUCTOR GUIDELINES	CONTENT
Go over the definitions of these terms briefly. Trainees are not expected to learn all definitions. They are provided for their orientation and may become a useful reference in communicating with special education teachers and parents. 	Acting out - overt expression of strong feelings, nature of which is not always understood by the child. Aggression - a forceful action, usually directed toward another, often unprovoked, and out of proportion to the situation. Antisocial - behavior which is hostile to the well-being of society. Anxiety - feeling of apprehension, the source of which is frequently unrecognized. Aphasia - defect or loss of the power of expression by speech, writing, or signs, or of comprehending spoken or written language, due to injury or disease of the brain centers. Birth injuries - injuries occurring in the organism at birth. The central nervous system is more commonly affected, but bones, joints, and muscles may be involved. Brain-injured child (Strauss Syndrome) - a child who before, during, or after birth has received injury to or suffered infection of the brain. As a result of such organic impairment there may or may not be defects of the neuro-motor system but this child may show disturbance in perception, thinking, and emotional behavior. These disturbances may occur alone or in combination. C.N.S. - central nervous system. Cerebral palsy - a condition resulting from neurological damage occurring before, at, or shortly after birth, which interferes with normal control of the motor system.

INSTRUCTOR GUIDELINES	CONTENT
	<u>Convulsion</u> - violent involuntary contraction of muscles. <u>Distractibility</u> - an abnormal variation of attention. Inability to fix attention on any one subject for an appropriate amount of time, due to C.N.S. impairment which prohibits necessary monitoring of stimuli. <u>Dull-normal child</u> - an individual at the lower end of the average range of intelligence. Can function as majority of children except in academic subjects. Usually 1-2 years retarded according to age grade level. <u>Educable mentally retarded</u> - mentally retarded children whose retardation ranges from mild to moderate. Usually have I.Q. scores between 50-75. Most of these children can be taught useful reading and number skills and some academic content. Usually will not achieve beyond 4th or 5th grade academically. Capable of integration in society and becoming at least partially self-sustaining. <u>Encephalitis</u> - inflammation of the brain. There are many types, most of which are due to virus infections and which can damage one or many parts of the brain. It is a frequent cause of learning and behavior disorders because of the resultant brain dysfunctioning. <u>Epilepsy</u> - a chronic functional nervous disorder, characterized by attacks of unconsciousness or convulsions or both. <u>Exceptional child</u> - term refers to a child who is different from the average child. A child showing abnormality either physical or mental could be considered in this category. Sometimes the term "exceptional" is used to designate a child of more

INSTRUCTOR GUIDELINES	CONTENT
	than usual ability. May include the handicapped and gifted who deviate from the average to such an extent that they require specialized treatment. Hearing impairment - a sensory neuro loss resulting in slight to profound hearing loss and learning difficulties. The hearing loss is often associated with language retardation and speech difficulties. Hydrocephalus - (a clinical type) an enlarged cranium is a clinical sign of this condition which involves an accumulation of cerebro-spinal fluid, within the ventricles of the brain. Degree of mental defect depends upon degree of cortical destruction, not size of skull. Hyperactive (hyperkinesis) - a characteristic of brain-injured children. Abnormally increased motor activity. Hypoactivity - abnormally diminished motor activity or function. Intelligence quotient (IQ) - expressed mental development in relation to chronological age; obtained by dividing mental age by the chronological age and multiplying by 100. The chronological age is often fixed at a certain maximum, most commonly 16 years, when growth of intelligence due to maturation has been assured to cease; this may vary in different tests, however, from 14 to 18 years. Kinesthetic - pertaining to the sense by which muscular motion, weight, position, space orientation, etc., are perceived. Laterality - the tendency, in voluntary motor acts, to use preferentially the organs (hands, feet, ears, eyes) of the same side.

INSTRUCTOR GUIDELINES	CONTENT
	Mental age (MA) - the level of a person's mental ability expressed in terms of norms based on the median mental age of a group of persons having the same chronological age; thus, if a child's mental ability is equal to that of the average nine-year-old, he has a mental age of nine years, regardless of his actual chronological age. In class, the teacher should teach on basis of MA, not IQ. Mentally retarded - usually considered a general term meaning all degrees of mental retardation from profound mental deficiency to borderline mental defect or to upper limits of dull normalcy. Frequently considered a synonym for mentally handicapped. Minimal brain dysfunction - this diagnostic category refers to children of average or above general intelligence with learning and/or behavior difficulties ranging from mild to severe, which are due to subtle deviations arising from genetic variations, perinatal brain insults, metabolic imbalances, biochemical irregularities, and/or illnesses and injuries sustained during the years critical for the development and maturation of those parts of the central nervous system having to do with perception, language, inhibition of impulses and motor control. Mongoloid child (Mongolis, a clinical type of feebleminded person or child with Downs Syndrome) - physically and mentally defective at birth. Characterized by eyes obliquely placed; fold of skin at inner edge of eye; flat, round face; round cheeks and large flat lips; large long tongue usually protruding from mouth; small nose. Multiple-handicapped - a child who has two or more disabilities.

INSTRUCTOR GUIDELINES	CONTENT
	Nystagmus - an involuntary rapid movement of the eyeball, which may be horizontal, vertical, rotary, or mixed, i.e., of two varieties. Orthopedics - branch of medicine dealing with deformities and diseases of the bones and joints. Perception - the receiving, integration, and interpretation of impressions and sensations through the senses. Perceptual disturbances - a characteristic of brain-injured children who are attracted to the details of an object rather than the whole object. May occur in visual-perceptual field, tactual field, and auditory field. Requires special educational procedures. Perseveration - a perceptual disturbance occurring in brain-injured children may be present when child continually repeats what he has done, like repeating the same word, letter, action, or number over and over again. Requires specific educational procedures to aid child. Sense training - games, exercises, and materials to develop those senses relating to sight, hearing, muscular coordination, taste, touch, and smell. Special classes (homogeneous) - a segregated class in a regular grade school organized according to a small range of C. A. and mental age abilities. Strabismus - deviation of the eye which the individual cannot overcome. The visual axes assumes a position relative to each other different from that required by the physiological conditions. Squint or crossed eyes. Visually defective - one whose sight is imperfect.

INSTRUCTOR GUIDELINES	CONTENT
Include here any terms the trainees may encounter in your district's special education programs.	OTHER TERMS USED IN YOUR DISTRICT

GUIDELINES FOR HANDLING BEHAVIOR PATTERNS*

INSTRUCTOR GUIDELINES	CONTENT
Be accepting and tolerant of individual problems which may be unpleasant, such as drooling, wet or soiled clothing.	Behavior patterns of each child with these conditions are individual problems and should be understood. Each driver must treat each child separately. For example, don't give a general direction to the entire busload of children. You can't assume everyone would understand this direction. Behavior patterns of these children for any given day or hour of the day can be caused or changed by the actions of many people: · You, the school bus driver · Parents or members of the family · Teacher or aide · Other bus passengers These people affect <u>any</u> child but they can compound the trouble that a special child may already have. The person handling the youngster can understand what may have caused the problem and be able to correct it in the right manner. Additional problems could be created if the situations were handled badly. When you correct a child, take into consideration, regardless of the age and size of the youngster, his or her attention span. With some children, this can be rather short. Be consistent when you correct a child. A student may behave differently from day to day because of medication which he may be taking. Many students are extremely hyperactive and use their excess energy to get attention from you or from someone else.

INSTRUCTOR GUIDELINES	CONTENT
	It is difficult to give guidelines for handling all situations. However, these are some courses of action that should prove helpful: 1. Work with the child's parents by talking over any problems. 2. Work with the teacher. 3. Work with your supervisor. 4. Work with the child. It can also be of help to move the child to another seat away from a student who may be causing problems.
Stress that discretion is important when discussing a child's problems with parents.	NOTES:

BEHAVIOR PATTERNS*

INSTRUCTOR GUIDELINES	CONTENT
OPTION: Arrange for teacher(s) of special education classes to conduct this section. The teacher can lead the discussion questions.	Usually, your exceptional students will fall into one of three categories: · Physically handicapped · Mentally retarded · Educationally handicapped The children with these different types of handicaps may act quite differently. So, you should learn to recognize these differences and learn how to handle them. The following descriptions of behavior patterns are average and, of course, there will be many variations and degrees which are not covered here.

PHYSICALLY HANDICAPPED STUDENTS

INSTRUCTOR GUIDELINES	CONTENT
Describe situations in which trainees decide what they would do. For example, how would they communicate the bus rules of conduct to a deaf child? What if the child can't read? Discuss with class and provide feedback.	The Physically Handicapped Child--Deaf and Hard-of Hearing. Hard-of-hearing children are those with slight or moderate hearing loss; the sense of hearing is still functional, with or without a hearing aid. Deaf children must be taught through their other senses. A hearing handicapped child's educational progress depends upon his intelligence, the degree of his hearing loss, and the age at which his hearing became impaired. The greatest handicap created by loss of hearing is the difficulty of learning speech and language. Because of this handicap, deaf children may be from two to five years retarded in educational subjects. A deaf child learns to respond to lip movement, facial expression and head movement, as well as to gestures, signs, and finger spelling.
How would trainees explain a new seating arrangement on the bus to a blind child? What would they do if a blind child trips and becomes disoriented trying to find his seat? Discuss with class and provide feedback.	The Physically Handicapped Child--Blind and Partially Blind. The educational development of partially blind children probably does not deviate from that of seeing children; however, a severe deficit in any sensory area does create adjustment patterns which are different from those of non-handicapped children. Personality and social maladjustment can be caused by pain and discomfort, the likelihood of undue parental concern, negative attitudes of other children, teachers, or parents. Totally blind children are usually not deficient in language usage. They are taught to read braille, but in other school subjects such as arithmetic and spelling, they are educationally retarded. The blind child's knowledge is gained primarily through hearing and touch. The ease with which the blind child can move about, find objects and places, and orient himself to new situations is crucial; controlling himself

INSTRUCTOR GUIDELINES	CONTENT
	and his environment are essential to the development of poise and independence.
How would trainees react to a child who, in trying to tell the driver something, cannot make himself understood? What would they do if other bus passengers laughed or mimicked the child? Discuss with class and provide feedback.	<u>The Physically Handicapped Child--Speech Handicapped</u>. Defective speech may be defined as any speech which differs from the average so far as to draw unfavorable attention to the speaker. Speech defects are classified into: 1. Articulatory disorders, or those involving tongue, teeth, lips, palates, or jaws. 2. Vocal disorders, or those of pitch, vocal intensity, vocal quality. 3. Delayed speech, as when a child does not learn to speak at the normal age. This includes aphasia, in which the child cannot understand language or its symbols due to cerebral disorder, and dysphasia, which is a disturbance of language. 4. Speech disorders associated with hearing impairment, cleft palate, or cerebral palsy.
What would trainees do if a child's crutches caught on seat and child fell in aisle? How should driver decide whether to assist a crippled child onto the bus or whether to let him struggle through the process himself? What is the advantage of letting the child do it himself? Disadvantages? Discuss with class and provide feedback.	<u>The Physically Handicapped Child--Orthopedic and Other Health Problems</u>. The crippled child is one who has an orthopedic impairment interfering with the functions of the bones, joints, or muscles. The child may have been born with the condition, or it may have been caused by an accident or by an infection such as polio or tuberculosis of the bones, or by muscular dystrophy, etc. The provisions which must be made for these children are for physical and medical reasons rather than for educational accomplishment; they have physical and emotional problems to conquer but their learning process is the same as that of

INSTRUCTOR GUIDELINES	CONTENT
	non-crippled children. The crippled child's restricted activity and the resulting frustration make it necessary for him to find other ways of attaining satisfaction within his abilities. He needs help in attaining a healthy concept of himself in spite of his disability. He may try to prolong his dependency upon other people in order to feel secure; he should be taught to become as independent as his condition permits.
	CEREBRAL PALSY
	Cerebral palsy is defined as any abnormal alteration of movement caused by defect, injury, or disease of the brain. Cerebral palsy may also include learning difficulties, psychological problems, sensory defects, convulsive and behavioral disorders.
How would trainees decide which of these types of cerebral palsied children they should assist:	It takes different forms such as:
In routine movements?	1. Spastic paralysis, in which muscles remain in a state of tension. The muscles can be moved voluntarily but the movement is slow, explosive, and poorly formed. Different groups of muscles can be affected by this paralysis.
Activities requiring special effort?	
Discuss with class and provide feedback.	2. Ataxia, in which the child is unsteady in his movements and falls easily. Sometimes his eyes are uncoordinated and move in a jerky manner.
What special problems does the child with multiple handicaps have?	3. Athetosis, in which the child walks in a lurching, writhing manner. Posture is uncontrolled. Athetotic movements such as facial grimaces and uncontrolled movements intensify as the child's conscious effort increases.

INSTRUCTOR GUIDELINES	CONTENT
	4. Tremor and rigidity, in which the body shows involuntary vibrating movements. This child is more predictable and consistent. Cerebral palsied children may or may not be mentally retarded, or they may have visual or hearing defects. All these children need to feel accepted and secure; they should be encouraged to be as self-sufficient and independent as their conditions allow.

MENTALLY RETARDED STUDENTS

INSTRUCTOR GUIDELINES	CONTENT
Suppose John were an educable mentally retarded child, 12 years old, with a mental age of 6. One particular day after school he's crying, hostile to any attempts to touch him, and shows signs of becoming aggressive to his seatmate. Some of your other passengers explain that some "regular" students his own age had grabbed his books at the bus stop and made fun of him for reading "baby books." What would you do? Discuss with class and provide feedback.	The Educable Mentally Retarded Child. These children are considered minimally educable in academic subjects in school, in social adjustment in the community, and in the occupational field at an unskilled or semi-skilled level. Their height, weight, and motor coordination are close to average but their development in mental, social, and academic areas are one-half to three-fourths that of average children. Such children, at age 12, will have a mental age between 6 and 9 years. An educable mentally retarded child is usually not recognized as such until he enters school and begins to fail at learning required subjects. He is slower to learn and remains longer at each stage. Behavior problems develop and are usually the result of the discrepancy between the child's capacity to perform and the requirements of his environment. He is easily frustrated because he repeatedly fails to perform according to his chronological age. If materials and methods are geared to his ability to succeed, he becomes frustrated less easily. It is important for such a child to experience success and to know he has succeeded.
What would trainees do if a child soiled himself on the bus? What if other passengers complain, cry, and become upset by the incident? Discuss with class and provide feedback.	The Trainable Mentally Retarded Child. These children have been defined as those who, because of subnormal intelligence, cannot learn in classes with the educable mentally retarded but who have the potential to learn self-care, adjustment to home and neighborhood, and economic usefulness at home or in an institution. These children develop at the rate of one-third to one-half that of normal children. NOTES:

EDUCATIONALLY HANDICAPPED STUDENTS

INSTRUCTOR GUIDELINES	CONTENT
What would trainees do if some seemingly innocent remark of theirs touched off a fight between two children? What would they do if an emotionally disturbed child hit them? Discuss with class and provide feedback.	<u>The Educationally Handicapped Child</u>. These children are defined as neurologically and/or emotionally handicapped. They often have behavior problems based on inner tensions which create anxiety, frustrations, fears, and impulsive behavior; social maladjustment, including incorrigibility, truancy, predelinquency, and delinquency. Normal mental health depends to a large degree on developing feelings of security, adequacy, and the ability to meet frustrations calmly.
	NOTES:
Socially/emotionally maladjusted students who are also mentally retarded have a dual handicap; retardation is the primary deficit.	

LOADING AND UNLOADING*

INSTRUCTOR GUIDELINES	CONTENT
Specify whether your district has a different policy. Use of bus attendants, if you have them, will be covered later.	Most transportation systems load and unload special education youngsters in front of each child's home due to the fact that the child cannot be left unattended. These children sometimes need a driver's assistance to board the bus and must be held during this process. Eye-to-eye contact with some children is a must. Most buses used for this purpose are equipped with seat belts which should be used if possible. Care is needed at all times to keep these children on the bus when other children are being loaded or unloaded. The child that must have special equipment such as a wheelchair, braces, crutches, etc., has problems during the loading and unloading process and it is your responsibility to learn these problems and know how to handle them. Remember, care and protection are two things which the parents and children expect from you.
Review loading and unloading procedures if necessary. (See Core Unit B.)	Usually, you will follow the same routine loading and unloading procedures for controlling the bus as you would when transporting regular passengers.
Fill in number of feet, as specified by state or local regulations.	· Activate amber flashing lamps (if any) ______ feet from student's home. · Approach the stop slowly, and stop the bus. · Activate the red flashing warning lamps.

INSTRUCTOR GUIDELINES	CONTENT
NOTE: There may be reasons for not following the same loading and unloading procedures that are used for regular passengers. The bus may load in a driveway or other off-street area where traffic control is not necessary. Also, with long stops at each residence, traffic often won't wait for flashing red lights to go off before they pass the bus. Federal Standards are flexible on this and do not require the use of the red flashing warning lights at every stop, if special loading conditions make it more practical not to use them. Add, delete, or change any steps which differ in your local procedures. OPTION: Demonstrate how to get a child in a wheelchair onto the bus. Show use of ramp, if available, and how to carry student and secure him in seat belt. Show how to collapse wheelchair and store it safely during the ride. Have trainees practice, with a "live" child, if possible.	Then, follow these steps : 1. If an attendant is assigned to the bus: a. Be sure each person knows his role; in the case of misunderstanding, don't argue. Carry on any discussion out of the students' presence. b. Direct him (her) to carry or guide the student onto the bus. c. When the use of seat belts is required or available, check to see that they are securely fastened before putting the bus into motion again. d. When specially equipped buses are used to accommodate wheelchairs, etc., with the use of a ramp, supervise the attendant in guiding the chair onto the bus and securing it in place inside the bus. 2. If an attendant is not used: a. Put the bus in "park" neutral; turn off the motor and take the keys out of the ignition. b. Leave the bus and carry or guide the handicapped student onto the bus. (The student should be brought to the bus by a parent or other responsible person from the house.) c. After securing the seat belt for the student, start the bus again,

INSTRUCTOR GUIDELINES	CONTENT
	following the proper procedures for entering the flow of traffic. 3. Check that the ramp and side door have been securely fastened into a locked position after the student has entered the bus. 4. Unloading on the school grounds: a. Carry or guide each student off the bus into the charge of a teacher or other school attendant. b. Check that all belongings of each student are taken off the bus. 5. Unloading at home of the passenger: a. Carry or guide each student off the bus into the charge of a parent or other responsible person. b. Check that all belongings of each student are taken off the bus. c. Report to the parent any observations which may be appropriate, whether medical or behavioral observations. d. If an authorized person is not at home to receive the student, keep him or her on the bus; after the run is completed, make arrangements with the school or transportation officials to care for the student until the parent (or other responsible person) has been contacted.

ON THE ROAD

INSTRUCTOR GUIDELINES	CONTENT
	1. Assign the bus attendant (if any) to watch that all passengers remain safely seated (if no bus attendant, make periodic checks yourself). Occasionally a particular student's needs require more than you can provide as one who must be responsible for the safety of all passengers. DO NOT allow students to continually demand your attention when you are driving.
	2. If any student shows symptoms of illness that requires immediate attention, pull bus as far to the right of the road as possible and stop; activate four-way hazard lamps.
Suppose you had no bus accident. What behavior or occurrences would make it necessary for you to pull over and stop the bus? Discuss with class and provide feedback.	3. If a radio is available, notify the proper authorities; otherwise assign the attendant or passing motorist to call them from a phone booth or nearby private home.
	4. Watch for unusual behavior that should be expected to occur, i.e., petit mal epilepsy attacks, erratic behavior of emotionally disturbed or mentally retarded students, etc.
	NOTES:

GET THE FACTS

INSTRUCTOR GUIDELINES	CONTENT
	You must have pertinent information about each of your passengers and be a special observer of behavior on your vehicle. You are often the source of information which is vitally important to your supervisor, the student's teacher, and parents. All your passengers should have medical identification bracelets specifying special care or medication limitations. Secure pertinent information about and identification picture of each student you transport. Make a confidential card file form to be kept on your bus and in your supervisor's office. A 3" x 5" card is suggested.
Provide filled-in samples of local forms used, if any. Discuss how, where, and when to get this information and where to keep it.	Name Last First Telephone # (home) Primary disability Secondary Disability Directions to driver (controlling or directing the child) EMERGENCY HEALTH CARE INFORMATION What medication is the student Under? Student's Doctor Doctor's telephone # Special information when time delays occur:

EMERGENCIES

INSTRUCTOR GUIDELINES	CONTENT
OPTION: You may want to refer trainees back to Core Unit C (Accidents and Emergencies) to review procedures, depending on how much time has elapsed since they were trained in accident and emergency procedures. OPTION: Discuss advantages and practical difficulties of holding evacuation drill for exceptional students. How would you plan it, explain it, execute it?	Due to the emotional reaction of your riders during time delays and emergency situations, expect passenger disruption. You should prepare a "line of action" in handling the particular student's needs and controlling the rest of your passengers when the following conditions occur: · Broken bones - keep broken bone and joints above and below break from moving. Get medical assistance. · Fainting - keep the person lying down until recovery. Loosen tight clothing. Secure medical assistance if condition persists. · Seizure** 1. Steer bus to side of roadway and stop vehicle. 2. Know and follow directions on child's 3" x 5" card. 3. Remain calm. Students will assume the same emotional reaction that you display. The seizure is painless to the child. Do not try to restrain the child. There is nothing you can do to stop a seizure once it has begun. It must run its course. Clear the area around him so that he does not injure himself on hard or sharp objects. Try not to interfere with his movements in any way. Special care should be taken to protect the head.

INSTRUCTOR GUIDELINES	CONTENT
Emphasize 4. Formerly, most people thought you should put something between the teeth. The new advice is not to; more damage can be caused by pencils, tongue depressors, etc., than is usually caused by tongue biting.	4. Don't force anything between his teeth. If his mouth is already open, you might place a soft object like a handkerchief between his side teeth in the back of the mouth.
	5. It isn't generally necessary to call a doctor unless the attack is followed almost immediately by another major seizure, or if the seizure lasts more than about ten minutes.
	6. When the seizure is over, let the child rest if he wants to.
	7. The child's parents and physician should be informed of the seizure.
The recognition and treatment of shock is covered in more detail in Advanced Unit B (First Aid).	· Shock - depression of body function. 1. Loosen tight clothing. 2. Keep the person lying down. 3. Guard against body heat loss. 4. Secure medical assistance.
Provide here any emergency treatment required in special cases in your district.	· Other

INSTRUCTOR GUIDELINES	CONTENT
	Report circumstances of illness or injury to your supervisor as quickly as possible. Planning for emergencies should include: 1. An "in-bus" list of telephone numbers for assistance in case of fire, respiratory or heart failure, and mechanical breakdown. 2. First aid equipment including a blanket. 3. Information on each child with parent's and physician's telephone numbers.
Discuss each question as it is usually handled in your district.	A plan should be worked out between the parents and the school or driver to deal with emergencies that may arise. For example: 1. What is to be done if the parents are not at home to receive the child at the end of the day? 2. What is to be done if the bus, for some reason, cannot reach the home? One such reason could be due to weather conditions. 3. Have a back up plan. Example: A second home, such as a friend or relative, where the child can be taken in such emergencies. 4. What is to be done if the child needs medical attention while being transported?

PARENT RESPONSIBILITY

INSTRUCTOR GUIDELINES	CONTENT
Discuss how parents are informed of their responsibility in your district. 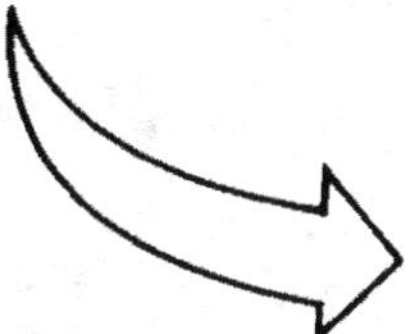	Parents play a tremendous role in the preparation of their child for his busy day. Hopefully, everything goes well during this preparation so that you can receive the child happy and ready to go on time. The parents have the responsibility to: 1. Feed. 2. Properly clothe. 3. See that any special equipment such as wheelchair, etc. is ready and in good working order. 4. Make certain that all bodily needs are performed. 5. Have the child at the designated place on time so that you can assist the child in boarding the bus.
What would trainees do if child insists that he can now walk by himself when the instructions on his card say, "assistance in walking at all times." How would you find out if the change is authorized? How would they remind parents to tell them of authorized changes in routine? Discuss with class and provide feedback.	6. Give you any instructions or information that is necessary if there is to be any change of plans from normal routine. 7. Wave the bus on if the child is not attending school that day. 8. Notify, in advance, the transportation department or school if there are to be any changes. Parents must know the following if they are to cooperate with you. 1. The time you will pick up their child.

INSTRUCTOR GUIDELINES	CONTENT
Discuss how drivers should communicate these things to parents.	2. The time they can expect their child to return home so that someone will be there. 3. The exact location where he will be picked up and returned. 4. If arrangements must be made in the event of bad weather. 5. Where to call if they have problems and need additional information.

STATE AND LOCAL POLICIES

INSTRUCTOR GUIDELINES	CONTENT
Provide the details of your state and local regulations or policies on both 1. and 2. Have trainees take notes. Ask whether they have any questions. If so, review answers.	As a partner in the transportation system, you must take an active role in encouraging a system which is designed to aid you in meeting your students' needs by: 1. Asking for clarification of parent and driver responsibilities with respect to loading and unloading procedures. NOTES: 2. Seeking information as to what part you are to take in communicating needs to parents, teachers, supervisor, and students. NOTES:

DETECTING HAZARDS

TABLE OF CONTENTS

OBJECTIVES

1. Use clues to detect potential hazards.

2. Determine degree of actual hazards.

3. Select what action they should take to avoid hazards.

OVERVIEW*

INSTRUCTOR GUIDELINES	CONTENT
	You've heard it said that every time you get into the bus, you take your life in your hands. Yours and every one of your passengers. With the recent emphasis on defensive driving, more and more drivers are becoming aware that just about every driving situation has potential hazards. It's not enough just to know what you're doing. You have to know what everyone else is doing, too. If you've been driving a school bus for any length of time, you are aware of some of the hazards involved in your daily run. Some hazards are obvious; some aren't. Some are always there, like the sharp curve. And, some appear out of nowhere, depending on the changing traffic situation. Do you consciously search for hazards as you drive?
Have trainees read text. Emphasize main points. Lead class discussion. Give overview of types of hazards they'll be learning to detect: 1. roadway hazards 2. off road hazards 3. single vehicle hazards 4. multiple vehicle hazards 5. other road users hazards 6. combination vehicle/ roadway hazards	In this unit, you'll practice a systematic technique for detecting hazards. You'll use most of your senses to pick up clues that indicate potential and actual dangers. And, you'll make decisions about how you should adjust your driving to minimize or avoid hazards. You should get into the habit of being an "automatic hazard detector." Expert school bus drivers drive well because they find the hazards before the hazards find them. You should develop a "mental image" of the clues associated with each hazard. The habit of detecting clues must be strong enough that you can: 1. Distinguish clues within a complex, changing traffic situation.

INSTRUCTOR GUIDELINES	CONTENT
	2. Identify them within the short period of time your eyes are focused upon the situation in normal scanning. 3. Detect them even when you are not consciously looking for them. Failure to recognize hazards in time is a major cause of accidents.
Reminder: Drivers should memorize their route beforehand. Dry runs are advisable so they can make note of chronic hazards.	• Passenger distraction, inattention, and misinterpretation of traffic sounds have caused drivers to react late to auditory clues of an impending crash. • Safe drivers tend to assure themselves of information 8 to 12 seconds ahead. The smallest lead time experienced drivers tend to allow is 1-3/4 seconds. • Even after several months, new drivers tend to spend more time monitoring only the road straight ahead than experienced drivers. Accident fatalities and rear-end collisions can be expected to be high in urban areas as a result of the increase of pedestrian and motor vehicle traffic. Approximately 12-15 percent of all urban school bus accidents are rear-end collisions.

SEARCHING FOR CLUES

INSTRUCTOR GUIDELINES	CONTENT
Explain "scanning," e.g., rapid surveillance of areas all around the bus, mostly with eye movement, using mirrors, not necessarily moving the head around. Much of the scanning can be done with peripheral vision, i.e., that which can be seen to the sides, outside the direct path of vision. To indicate how to judge how far a half-mile is, give some guidelines such as the distance of 25 telephone poles (100 feet between each pole) or the time it takes to reach a spot a half mile away would be about 1 minute at 30 mph. This distance would be decreased, of course, in areas where there are many curves or hills. Emphasize that in looking far down the road they will also make a <u>conscious effort</u> to observe everything between where they are and where they are looking.	Scan the environment for clues of potential hazards: 1. Continuously scan surroundings on and off the roadway, shifting your gaze frequently. Look well ahead in the lane to focus distance relative to the bus' speed and the roadway location. Specifically: a. Focus at farther distances as your speed increases. b. View the road ahead one full block in a city. c. Focus at farther distances down the road in rural areas than you would in urban areas. 2. <u>Avoid fixing your eyes on the road surface</u> immediately forward of the bus hood. 3. <u>An unobstructed view is important</u>. a. In a moderate number of accidents, collisions occurred at intersections where vision was reportedly obstructed or limited by buildings, vegetation, or parked cars. b. Roadside features that obscure your vision at intersections should be treated as if they were traffic lights and signs requiring you to stop. By stopping, you have an opportunity to study the traffic situation more carefully before proceeding rather than haphazardly continuing. 4. <u>Observe other drivers</u>. a. Accidents relating to overtaking vehicles have been caused frequently by the driver's

INSTRUCTOR GUIDELINES	CONTENT
	failure to note the actions of vehicles ahead. For example, a moderate number of accidents are caused by a driver's failure to note traffic stopped ahead for a left turn.
	b. Another cited cause is failure to check traffic in the adjacent lane prior to entering it to pass and/or to avoid impact with a stopped vehicle.
	5. You must know how to gather critical clues.
	a. The driver who keeps abreast of the driving situation by continuous surveillance of traffic, traffic controls, and the surrounding environment will be more likely to recognize hazards while there is time to avoid them.
Explain how central vision differs from peripheral (indirect) vision. A quick method of checking what can be seen via peripheral vision is to hold up the index finger of each hand at eye level with arms extended out to the sides of the body. Slowly bring the fingers forward and note at what point they can be seen while looking straight ahead.	b. You receive the vast majority of the clues you use through your eyes. The more intently you fix your central vision on a particular object, the less aware you will be of clues from your larger field of indirect vision.
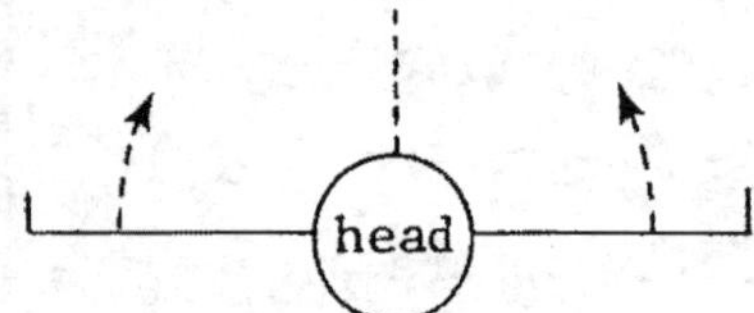 	6. <u>You must know the demands imposed on you when driving in urban or congested areas</u>.
	a. Visual demands on the driver appear to be about three times as much at 20 miles per hour in the city as at higher speeds on a modern divided highway. The mere presence of pedestrians and children increases your surveillance requirements.
	b. The greater need for surveillance in the city is partially due to the greater

INSTRUCTOR GUIDELINES	CONTENT
	concentration of other vehicles. Traffic controls and pedestrian traffic also contribute to making city driving a difficult task.
	7. <u>You must know the primary sources of potential trouble, and their clues, to be prepared for sudden actions by others.</u>
Emphasize sudden actions of others.	a. Driving alongside parked vehicles is potentially hazardous because your view is limited and hazards can appear when there is little time or space for evasive action.
	b. Three key sources of hazards are: • The spaces between parked vehicles through which pedestrians and animals may dart into the street. • The parked vehicle that may suddenly move into the bus' path. • Occupants of parked vehicles who may open the vehicle doors to get out without first checking the traffic situation. Positioning the bus at least four feet out from the parked vehicle will place it beyond the arc of a door being opened. • People stepping out from between parked vehicles.

INSTRUCTOR GUIDELINES	CONTENT
	8. Usually, there are clues from parked vehicles of impending entry into a driving lane. Among the clues you will find useful are: a. Exhaust fumes. These indicate the engine is running. b. Back-up lights. For these lights to be activated, the ignition must be on and the gearshift lever in reverse. The appearance of back-up lights is often followed by a shift to a forward gear. c. Brake lights. Most drivers depress the brake pedal, thus activating the brake lights, just prior to shifting to a forward gear. d. Front wheels. The direction toward which the front wheels are pointed may indicate whether the vehicle is ready to leave the space or still maneuvering into a good position for leaving. e. Steering wheel. The steering wheel of vehicles parked to the right of the bus can be seen from some distance. If a steering wheel is not visible, it may mean the driver is behind the wheel. A separation of at least a car width from a vehicle that is being parallel parked is recommended to accommodate the wide leftward swing of the vehicle's front end as it backs to the right. 9. You should know that you have an active, not passive, role when being passed. Continuously assess the chances for the other driver to

INSTRUCTOR GUIDELINES	CONTENT
	safely complete the pass within the distance available. Make adjustments in the bus' speed and position to accommodate the passing vehicle. You can flick your high beams at night to signal other drivers that it's safe to pass. 10. <u>Develop the surveillance habit of scanning 360° around the bus.</u> 360°

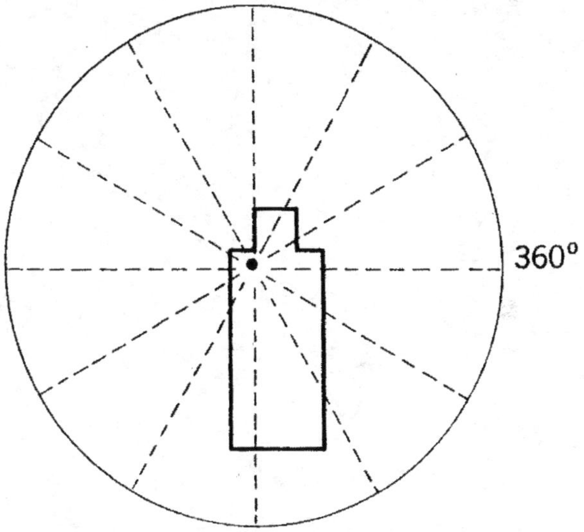

DETECTING ROADWAY HAZARDS CLUES

INSTRUCTOR GUIDELINES	CONTENT
Review the six sources of hazards before they read the text: Roadway hazards Off road hazards Single vehicle hazards Multiple vehicle hazards Other road users hazards Combination vehicle/ roadway hazards Add or highlight specific clues in each hazard. One method is to ask trainees what other clues they should look for. Emphasize that some clues will be heard, felt, and possibly smelled. After the trainees identify each clue, ask them for specific situations they've experienced where these clues have indicated a real hazard. Have them tell how bad the hazard is/was and what they did about it. Continue this method for each type of hazard.	ROADWAY HAZARDS 1. <u>Sight Distance Limitations</u> a. Curves (1) Watch the road ahead for indications of a curve. (2) When approaching a curve, estimate a safe speed (if not posted) from the degree of curvature and banking. b. Hills and Dips (1) Watch the road and roadside conditions (e.g., trees and poles) for signs of hills. (2) In approaching a downgrade, identify a grade which is steep enough to require downshifting. (3) Identify the presence of dips which may obscure another vehicle. 2. <u>Maneuvering Limitations</u>. Detect the following potential maneuvering limitations: a. Narrow or narrowing lanes. b. Roadway construction that is difficult to detect. c. When road surface ruts are present in gravel or dirt roads, you will: (1) Assess the road surface characteristics adjacent to the rut. (2) Assess the depth of the rut.

INSTRUCTOR GUIDELINES	CONTENT
	3. <u>Traction Limitations</u> a. Rough Surfaces (1) Detect surface irregularities on asphalt and concrete, such as potholes, cracked pavement, etc. (2) On a wooden surface, look for cracks, holes, and nails. (3) On a brick road, look for holes, bumps, cracks, loose bricks, and slippery spots. (4) "Washboard" conditions, e.g., continuous ruts. b. Slippery Surfaces. Anticipate potentially slippery surfaces: (1) Anticipate the smoothness of concrete or asphalt road surfaces at intersections. (2) Recognize areas of the roadway which are soaked with oil or grease. (3) Estimate depth and extent of deep water which partially or totally covers the roadway. (4) When driving on snow- or ice-covered roadways: (a) Judge the effect of traffic and temperature on road surface friction. (b) Observe closely the movement of vehicles approaching on side streets. (c) Note whether vehicle wheels are skidding.

INSTRUCTOR GUIDELINES	CONTENT
	(5) If ice is melting on the roadway: (a) Be alert for ice patches near shaded areas (e.g., underpasses and buildings). (b) Note spots where direct sunlight may have accelerated melting. (c) Look for additional ice patches ahead on the roadway. c. Loose Surfaces. Detect the signs of the following loose surfaces: (1) Gravel (2) Soft sand (3) Wet leaves 4. <u>Traffic Conflict Points</u> a. Recognize potentially hazardous roadway conditions when approaching and emerging from toll plazas: (1) Look for erratic driving from other drivers whose attention may be diverted while fumbling for money. (2) When emerging from the toll plaza, look for other drivers accelerating rapidly and cutting in to get ahead of the "pack." b. If driving on an entrance ramp, be alert for vehicles which are stopped or slowing down on the on-ramp. c. If driving on a long entrance ramp with an acceleration lane that continues on as an off-ramp or deceleration lane, be aware that

INSTRUCTOR GUIDELINES	CONTENT
	vehicles may leave the main roadway and cross over to merge onto the acceleration lane. Out-of-state drivers may be unfamiliar with exits and merge at the last minute. d. When approaching and entering an off-ramp: (1) Be alert for vehicles entering the deceleration lane, if that lane is also part of the acceleration lane for vehicles entering the roadway. (2) When nearing the end of the off-ramp, look for other vehicles which may be stopped or waiting in line at the end of the off-ramp. e. When approaching and passing interchanges on the freeway, note vehicles in the deceleration lane swinging back into the lane at the last minute. f. Look for lead vehicle deceleration at the following locations: (1) Uncontrolled intersection. (2) Entrances to highway (e.g., on-ramps), including short acceleration lanes and left-hand entrances. (3) Highway exits (e.g., off-ramps), including short deceleration lanes and left-hand exits. (4) Divergence points (forks in the road).

INSTRUCTOR GUIDELINES	CONTENT
Add here descriptions or pictures of local "roadway hazards" trainees might encounter. Have them pick out clues, judge how bad the hazard is and what they would do about it. Lead class discussion and provide feedback.	LOCAL ROADWAY HAZARDS:

DETECTING OFF ROAD HAZARD CLUES

INSTRUCTOR GUIDELINES	CONTENT
	OFF ROAD HAZARDS 1. <u>Sight Limitations</u> a. When driving on general highways, be alert for hidden traffic, pedestrians or animals obscured from view by nearby roadside structures, trees, or dense vegetation. b. When driving in urban areas: (1) Minimize distractions from the environment by seeking out traffic lights possibly "embedded" in lights from neon signs. (2) In commercial areas, be alert for vehicles emerging from driveways and alleys obscured by buildings, parked vehicles, or pedestrian traffic on the sidewalk. 2. <u>Maneuver Limitations</u>. When driving on roads with shoulders, periodically observe the conditions of the shoulders, including: a. Width b. Surface condition c. Alignment with pavement d. Presence of obstructions (e.g., signs, guardrails) e. Pitch of the roadbed 3. <u>Traffic Entry Points</u> a. Vehicle Entry Points (1) When approaching entrances to driveways, alleys, and parking lots, look ahead to determine their location.

INSTRUCTOR GUIDELINES	CONTENT
	(2) When driving in off-street areas, be alert for vehicles in or crossing the car's path. (3) Be alert for vehicles backing up to the exit or entering a parking space. b. Pedestrian Entry Point (1) When approaching a commercial bus stop: (a) Look for pedestrians crossing the street to board the bus or streetcar. (b) Check to see that pedestrians have reached safety before starting. (2) Near playgrounds, residential areas, schools: (a) Be alert for children playing or darting into the path of your bus from behind vehicles, structures, or vegetation. (b) Look for children sledding or otherwise playing in the snow or on the ice. (c) When driving in an off-street area, be alert for vehicle and pedestrian traffic that may be entering or crossing the traffic aisle from any direction.
Add here descriptions or pictures of local "off road hazards" trainees might encounter. Have them pick out clues, judge how bad the hazard is and what they would do about it. Lead class discussion and provide feedback.	LOCAL OFF ROAD HAZARDS:

DETECTING SINGLE VEHICLE HAZARD CLUES

INSTRUCTOR GUIDELINES	CONTENT
	SINGLE VEHICLE HAZARDS You should be able to recognize clues predictive of traffic hazards involving the motion of an individual vehicle. 1. General - In general, when surveying traffic, observe other drivers' driving behavior so that you can watch for clues to how they react: a. Note drivers who frequently change lanes as opposed to those who remain in the lane. b. Note drivers who operate their vehicles with frequent changes in speed as opposed to those who maintain a steady speed. c. Note those drivers who do not signal prior to a maneuver as opposed to those drivers who do signal consistently. d. Note those drivers who stop suddenly in non-emergency situations as opposed to those drivers who decelerate gradually to stop. e. Note out-of-state license plates; drivers may be unfamiliar with locations and road conditions. 2. Losing Control - Recognize clues indicating that another driver may lose proper control of vehicle: a. Surface conditions that might adversely influence oncoming

INSTRUCTOR GUIDELINES	CONTENT
	vehicle control (e.g., slippery surface, ruts, deep snow, etc.). b. Movements of the other vehicle including the following: (1) Turning too fast, e.g., if on-coming driver is turning too sharply after an off-road recovery. (2) Approaching from the side too fast to stop or turn. (3) Closing too fast from the rear. c. Movements of your bus, e.g., stopped too quickly to allow a following vehicle to stop. 3. <u>Lack of Communication by Other Drivers</u> - Look for clues or situations in which the driver of another vehicle may execute a maneuver without signalling. a. Whenever a turn may be made, e.g., an oncoming car may suddenly turn left particularly when: (1) The vehicle is slowing, or (2) The other driver is not attending to your oncoming bus. b. When a stopped vehicle gives an indication of imminent movement, e.g., parked car with driver in seat, exhaust, or turned wheels. c. When a driver may be giving a false indication, e.g., moving to the left

INSTRUCTOR GUIDELINES	CONTENT
	near an intersection when he intends to turn right. Any turn signal may be uncancelled from previous maneuver. 4. <u>Failure of the Other Driver to Observe</u> - When there are clues indicating that another driver may not have observed the bus and, therefore, may not be prepared to yield the right-of-way. These clues include the following: a. Driver not responding, e.g., approaching intersection from the side without slowing. b. Driver's vision obscured, e.g., posts, windows. c. Driver's view restricted, e.g., the vehicle is partially hidden by trees, detectable to you only by reflection or dust. d. Your bus may not readily be seen, e.g., when sun is in other driver's eyes, etc. 5. <u>Inadequate Adjustment by the Other Driver</u> - Look for indications that another driver is not adjusting properly to a situation. Impatience causes many improper actions. He or she may execute a maneuver that will cause hazard to you, including the following: a. Other driver isn't adjusting to an obstruction, such as a pothole or barrier.

INSTRUCTOR GUIDELINES	CONTENT
	b. Other driver isn't adjusting to a surface condition such as ice or snow. c. Other driver isn't adjusting to a pedestrian, e.g., turning a corner into a street blocked by pedestrians. d. Other driver isn't adjusting to another vehicle, e.g., passing vehicles forced to cut back abruptly. 6. Slow Moving or Stopping Vehicles - Watch for indications that another vehicle is slowing or may stop suddenly. a. Slow-moving vehicles: · Farm vehicles · Underpowered vehicles · Trucks on hills b. Frequently stopping vehicles: · Buses, including other school buses · Buses and trucks carrying inflammables at railroad crossings · Postal delivery vehicles c. Vehicles that are engaged in the following maneuvers: · Turning or exiting · Entering the roadway · Merging with other vehicles · Approaching controlled intersections or railroad crossings

INSTRUCTOR GUIDELINES	CONTENT
Add here descriptions or pictures of local "single vehicle hazards" trainees might encounter. Have them pick out clues, judge how bad the hazard is, and what they would do about it. Lead class discussion and provide feedback.	LOCAL SINGLE VEHICLE HAZARDS:

DETECTING MULTIPLE VEHICLE HAZARDS

INSTRUCTOR GUIDELINES	CONTENT
	MULTIPLE VEHICLE HAZARDS You should be able to recognize the clues in a traffic pattern that are predictive of a potential conflict. 1. Traffic Convergence. One or more vehicles converging on a traffic stream may force another vehicle into a conflict. a. May force another vehicle to change lanes, including entering from side of road, driveway, freeway ramps, etc. b. May cause other vehicles to stop suddenly. 2. Vehicle Obstructions. A vehicle slowing or stopping may cause another vehicle to drive around it, causing a conflict. a. Drivers tailgating, indicating a chance of a sudden pass. b. Slow-moving or stopped vehicles encourage other vehicles attempting to pass. c. A vehicle entering into the roadway, forcing other vehicles around it. 3. Limited Traffic Visibility. One vehicle may limit another's visibility, allowing the other driver to enter a potential conflict, e.g., an oncoming driver turns left.

INSTRUCTOR GUIDELINES	CONTENT
Add here descriptions or pictures of local "multiple vehicle hazards" trainees might encounter. Have them pick out clues, judge how bad the hazard is, and what they would do about it. Lead class discussion and provide feedback.	LOCAL MULTIPLE VEHICLE HAZARDS:

DETECTING OTHER ROAD USERS HAZARDS

INSTRUCTOR GUIDELINES	CONTENT
	OTHER ROAD USERS HAZARDS You should be able to recognize clues of potential conflict with other road users, including pedestrians, cyclists, and animals. Clues will include the following: 1. <u>Position of Road User Relative to Roadway</u> a. Pedestrians near roadway. b. Cyclist in roadway. 2. <u>Motion of Road User</u> a. Pedestrian running toward roadway. b. Children at play. c. Cyclist moving toward roadway. 3. <u>Road User's Ability to See</u> a. Road user's vision, e.g., pedestrian carrying packages, umbrella. b. Line of sight, e.g., driver alighting from a parked vehicle. 4. <u>Attentiveness of Road User</u> a. Activity, e.g., child chasing ball. b. Attention, e.g., pedestrian looking the other way, talking, etc. 5. <u>Lack of Control</u>, e.g., motorcyclist turning on a slippery surface, gravel, etc.
Add here descriptions or pictures of local "other road users hazards" trainees might encounter. Have them pick out clues, judge how bad the hazard is, and what they would do about it. Lead class discussion and provide feedback.	LOCAL OTHER ROAD USERS HAZARDS:

DETECTING COMBINATION VEHICLE/ROADWAY HAZARDS

INSTRUCTOR GUIDELINES	CONTENT
	COMBINATION VEHICLE/ROADWAY HAZARDS You should be able to identify potential hazards arising out of the interaction between vehicles and roadway. 1. Decision Point. Any point in the roadway at which drivers are confronted with decisions represents a potential point of conflict, e.g., a vehicle starting to exit from a freeway may suddenly return to the freeway; drivers unfamiliar with route signs may be in the wrong lane for their destination and change lanes suddenly as two major routes split. 2. Compression Point. Any point at which the roadway is compressed represents a potential source of conflicts, e.g., a vehicle approaching a point where 4 lanes become 2, may suddenly change lanes.
Add here descriptions or pictures of local "combination vehicle/roadway hazards" trainees might encounter. Have them pick out clues, judge how bad the hazard is and what they would do about it. Lead class discussion and provide feedback.	LOCAL COMBINATION VEHICLE/ROADWAY HAZARDS:

PRACTICE ON PAPER

INSTRUCTOR GUIDELINES	CONTENT
Supervise the worksheet activity and provide help if necessary. Trainees may look back through the unit for general descriptions of each hazard. You may run this activity as a group exercise. Lead class discussion after exercise is complete. Provide feedback.	Now you'll practice detecting hazards "on paper" before actually going out on the road for "real life" practice. Use the HAZARD DETECTION WORKSHEETS which follow. You'll find a numbered worksheet for each of the six types of hazards. Follow these steps: 1. Read the hazard situation in the left block. EXAMPLE: SINGLE VEHICLE HAZARD — Loss of Control — *There is a car ahead driven by an intoxicated person. The car is partially out of control.* 2. In the second block, read the usual and unusual clues that indicate the hazard. EXAMPLE: USUAL AND UNUSUAL CLUES — *The vehicle's left wheels keep going over the center line into oncoming lane. The car then crosses back to the right lane with a weaving motion. Car scrapes the right retaining wall and keeps going. Driver does not respond to bus' horn or the blinking of the bus headlights.* 3. Decide how bad the hazard is and write your judgment in the third block. EXAMPLE: HOW BAD IS IT? — *Seems really bad.* 4. Write in YOUR ACTION--what you'd do to avoid or minimize the danger of the hazard. EXAMPLE: YOUR ACTION — *Slow down and keep far behind him.*

INSTRUCTOR GUIDELINES	CONTENT
	The first few have been done for you as examples. Use these as a take off point for discussion before you fill in the rest of the worksheets. Discuss your completed worksheets with the entire class.

HAZARD DETECTION WORKSHEET #1

ROADWAY HAZARDS	USUAL AND UNUSUAL CLUES	HOW BAD IS IT?	YOUR ACTION
Sight Distance Limitations *You are coming up to a blind intersection.*	*There is no traffic light or stop sign. A building on the left corner is under construction, blocking your view of traffic coming from the left. Traffic is heavy in both directions.*	*Moderately bad, but not impossible to negotiate safely.*	*Stop at intersection. When there's a gap in traffic from left, edge forward until you can see around building. When gap in traffic from both sides, sound horn and proceed.*
Maneuvering Limitations *You are directed by a detour sign on to an unfamiliar road which has a hairpin curve.*	*You can see a road sign illustrating the direction and angle of curve and a caution sign.*	*Not too serious*	*Slow down to 5 mph and be sure to start the turn with enough room to clear it safely.*
Traction Limitations *You are crossing a bridge in snowy weather.*	*The car ahead of you is fishtailing slightly; the bridge surface looks glazed.*	*Could be very bad.*	*Ease off on accelerator and allow engine to slow bus; keep accelerating enough to keep the wheels turning.*
Traffic Conflict Point *You are approaching a traffic circle that is fed by 4 roads in each direction.*	*Cars are entering the circle from every road and there is a truck in the circle approaching from the left.*	*Potentially bad.*	*Wait for an acceptable gap in traffic from the left. Also, wait until vehicles coming from the left, and signalling to turn right into your road, have actually started to turn. Then proceed.*

HAZARD DETECTION WORKSHEET #2

OFF-ROAD HAZARDS	USUAL AND UNUSUAL CLUES	HOW BAD IS IT?	YOUR ACTION
Sight Limitations *You are approaching a hidden driveway 65 feet ahead on your right.*	*You are going 20 mph. You see a vehicle backing out onto the road; the car is half-hidden by hedges. You've noticed other driveways along this road. The car doesn't have his brake lights on.*	*Pretty bad, his view of the road is blocked, and he's still backing.*	*Sound horn. Take evasive action to avoid hitting the backing car: brake. You should stop within about 60 feet.*
Maneuvering Limitations *You must pull into the museum driveway.*	*The driveway is a narrow semi-circle There are 2 cars stopped in the driveway, blocking passage of a vehicle the size of your bus.*		
Traffic Entry Points *You are approaching a shopping center on your left.*	*There is no traffic light to control the flow of traffic in and out of the shopping center. Several cars are waiting to enter the road. The car nearest the road has his left turn signal on and the driver is looking to the left.*		

HAZARD DETECTION WORKSHEET #3

SINGLE VEHICLE HAZARD	USUAL AND UNUSUAL CLUES	HOW BAD IS IT?	YOUR ACTION
Loss of Control *There is a car ahead driven by an intoxicated person. The car is partially out of control.*	*The vehicle's left wheels keep going over the center line into oncoming lane. The car then crosses back to the right lane with a weaving motion. Car scrapes the right retaining wall and keeps going. Driver does not respond to bus' horn or the blinking of the bus headlights.*		
Lack of Communication *There is a motorcycle slowing down in front of you. The motorcyclist gives no hand signal.*	*You are approaching an intersection. The cyclist pulls left close to the center line and his brake lights come on.*		
Lack of Observation *A car that has passed you starts to cut back in front of you.*	*There is a car about one car length in front of you, going 40 mph. You are going 40 mph. The passing car is going 45 mph.*		

HAZARD DETECTION WORKSHEET # 3 (continued)

SINGLE VEHICLE HAZARD	USUAL AND UNUSUAL CLUES	HOW BAD IS IT?	YOUR ACTION
Inadequate Adjustment *The car behind you is closing.*	*You are going 30 mph. It looks like he is traveling much faster. You are on a two-lane road and a truck is in the oncoming lane.*		
Slow Moving or Stopped Vehicles *You are following a tractor.*	*The tractor looks like he is traveling 15 mph. He has his flashers on.*		

HAZARD DETECTION WORKSHEET #4

MULTIPLE VEHICLE HAZARDS	USUAL AND UNUSUAL CLUES	HOW BAD IS IT?	YOUR ACTION
Traffic Convergence *You are on an expressway approaching an entrance ramp.*	*You see a MERGE sign. Several cars are stopped on the entrance ramp looking for a gap in traffic. You are 100 feet from the entrance.*		
Vehicle Obstructions *A car that has overheated is stopped ahead in your lane on a 4-lane road.*	*Several cars ahead are stopped with left turn signals on, waiting to merge into the passing lane.*		
Visibility Limited by Traffic *An ambulance is approaching but you can't see it.*	*There is a truck behind you and a steady stream of oncoming traffic. You can hear the siren. Cars in the oncoming lane are pulling to the side of the road.*		

HAZARD DETECTION WORKSHEET #5

OTHER ROAD USERS HAZARDS	USUAL AND UNUSUAL CLUES	HOW BAD IS IT?	YOUR ACTION
Road User's Position *You are approaching a school zone and see a policeman in the middle of the road.*	*You have passed a flashing yellow sign saying 15 mph. The policeman directing traffic waves everyone to go straight. You have your turn signal on.*		
Road User's Motion *A woman on a bicycle is traveling with traffic in the same direction you are going.*	*You are closing on the bicycle which is to your right. She gives a left hand signal and starts to swerve left.*		
Road User's Ability to See *A child is waiting to cross the street.*	*The child turns his head right and left but the hood on his snowsuit partially blocks his view. He is not at a crosswalk. He steps off the curb.*		

HAZARD DETECTION WORKSHEET #5 (continued)

OTHER ROAD USERS HAZARDS	USUAL AND UNUSUAL CLUES	HOW BAD IS IT?	YOUR ACTION
Attentiveness of Road User *An elderly man is crossing the street.*	*You have the green light. He is crossing at an intersection against the DON'T WALK sign. You are going 15 mph. and are 40 feet from intersection.*		
Road User's Lack of Control *A car is pulling a boat and trying to pass you.*	*The boat begins to fishtail as the car picks up speed. The car's brake lights go on.*		

HAZARD DETECTION WORKSHEET #6

VEHICLE/ROADWAY HAZARDS	USUAL AND UNUSUAL CLUES	HOW BAD IS IT?	YOUR ACTION
Decision Points *You are coming to an unmarked fork in the road.*	*Your route takes off to the left road in the fork. You are following a car with an out of state license plate. His brake lights go on.*		
Compression Points *The road ahead goes from a 4-lane road into a 2-lane road.*	*You see a sign like this:* *You are in the right lane.*		

INSTRUCTOR GUIDELINES	CONTENT
Provide each trainee the opportunity for on-the-road practice in detecting and reacting to hazards. Plan a route where each of the six types of hazards are either known to exist or are likely to occur. Distribute a handout outlining the route. Have trainee drive and use surveillance habits to search for clues. Have them tell you the clues by using the "Commentary Driving Technique." Provide feedback on their performance, filling in any significant clues they miss. In heavy areas, not all clues can be verbalized, so have them comment on the most important ones--clues that will most likely have an impact on their driving decisions.	Now you're ready to detect hazards on the road. Your instructor will describe the route you will follow. Search for clues and announce them to your instructor as you go, using the following COMMENTARY DRIVING TECHNIQUE: 1. Talk out loud to yourself, identifying every usual and unusual clue that indicates a potential hazard. 2. Use the clues to decide how bad the hazard is. Decide whether it's really bad, moderately dangerous, o.k. to proceed, or whether there's not enough information to tell. 3. Say what you should do--proceed, slow down, go around, take an alternate path, or stop. 4. Act on your decision if instructor agrees. NOTE: Sometimes the hazard will appear so fast that Steps 1 through 3 will have to be done "in your head." So act, then talk over with your instructor the thought process you went through.

CONTROLLING THE POSITION OF THE BUS

TABLE OF CONTENTS

OBJECTIVES

1. Estimating required space for the bus.

2. Observing the position of other vehicles.

3. Making sure other drivers observe them.

4. Maintaining adequate separation between the bus and all other objects and pedestrians.

OVERVIEW

INSTRUCTOR GUIDELINES	CONTENT
Observing • Review traffic areas where vehicles and other road users are likely to enter the path of the bus. • Review hidden hazards. • Emphasize that early observation of other vehicles prevents probability of accidents. • Emphasize also: a. The need for active process of observation. b. The importance of frequent observation to accommodate rapidly changing patterns of traffic. c. The relation of speed to the need for observation.	Observing You must be prepared to observe and respond to other vehicles in the following situations: 1. When unusual noises occur. 2. Vehicles approaching from ahead. a. Approaching intersections and interchanges. b. Before attempting to pass. c. When overtaking cars ahead. d. Approaching parked cars. e. When entering traffic. 3. Vehicles following from behind. a. General. b. When changing lanes. c. When preparing to pass. d. When leaving traffic. e. When entering traffic. f. At intersections and interchanges. g. When slowing or stopping. 4. Cross traffic. 5. Other road users. NOTES:

INSTRUCTOR GUIDELINES	CONTENT
<u>Being Observed</u> Emphasize/discuss the following: . The importance of communicating significant intentions to other drivers. · Failure to signal properly causes many accidents.	<u>Being Observed</u> Make sure that you are observed by other drivers and road users through the following: 1. Use of brake lights when slowing or stopping. 2. Use of hand or turn signals when changing lanes. 3. Use of lights, horn, and appropriate acceleration when passing. NOTES:
<u>Separation</u> Emphasize/discuss the following: · The importance to accident prevention of maintaining a speed that does not interrupt traffic flow. · The importance to accident prevention of maintaining a longitudinal separation from cars ahead that will allow ample stopping distance, should the vehicle ahead stop abruptly. (Explain that "longitudinal" refers to areas ahead of and behind bus; "lateral" refers to areas at the sides of the bus.)	<u>Separation</u> You must maintain adequate separation--a safe margin of space between your bus and other vehicles, as follows: 1. Longitudinal separation a. Following distance b. Overtaking 2. Lateral separation a. Passing b. Being passed c. Approaching oncoming vehicles d. Approaching parked vehicles

INSTRUCTOR GUIDELINES	CONTENT
• The importance to accident prevention of maintaining a maximum lateral separation. • The reasons underlying laws relating to legal right of way. • The importance of allowing additional separation in the case of highly vulnerable road users (e.g., cyclists) or unpredictable road users (e.g., drunk or reckless drivers or speeders).	e. Approaching turning vehicles f. Approaching other road users NOTES:

SKILLS YOU WILL NEED

INSTRUCTOR GUIDELINES	CONTENT
Emphasize/discuss: • The appropriate point at which to keep the eyes focused in order to obtain the greatest amount of information and the greatest lead time. • The major sources of error in estimating the speed of other vehicles.	You must develop the following <u>perceptual skills</u>: 1. The ability to determine roadway limitations through peripheral vision, in order to be able to position the bus properly while attending to traffic. 2. The ability to maintain an appropriate separation from the car ahead when following. 3. The ability to judge closing rate with the cars approaching from ahead, behind, and the side. You must develop (or improve) your <u>manipulative skills</u> in controlling the longitudinal and lateral motion of the bus while attending to general traffic and roadway conditions. NOTES:

ESTIMATING REQUIRED SPACE

INSTRUCTOR GUIDELINES	CONTENT
To use time as a method of estimating space, (rather than feet or bus lengths), driver should note when a lead vehicle passes a reference point on the roadside (e.g., a telephone pole) and immediately begin counting seconds. Say 1001, 1002, etc., out loud. If the bus reaches the reference point at 1004, for instance, the following distance is 4 seconds.	1. You must be able to attain and maintain an appropriate, stable margin of space between the bus and any moving or stationary object. To do so, you will have to perceive changes in the separation distance or apparent object size, depending upon the distance involved, and adjust the bus speed and/or position.
Three seconds is the recommended minimum interval between a school bus and any lead vehicle. A four-second interval is even better; it provides a greater margin of safety.	2. Skill must be developed in using peripheral and central vision to accomplish the finer steering control required to keep the bus within its lane while maintaining a safe distance from parked vehicles, etc.
Refer to Figure 1. 	3. You must be able to judge the rate at which your bus is closing with the vehicle ahead in order to adjust your speed or initiate a pass at the proper time. a. The primary perceptual clue in the daytime is the change in apparent size of the lead vehicle.
Remind trainees that foreign or compact cars have taillights closer together than standard-size cars. So, they may <u>appear</u> farther away than they really are.	b. At night the primary clue is the distance between the taillights. c. Size or brightness of the taillights are <u>not</u> useful clues.
	4. You must be able to judge: a. If the closing rate and distance of following vehicles in other lanes and the traffic flow will give you a safe opportunity to change lanes. b. The speed and distance of leading vehicles. Speed changes must be estimated quickly if changing into the lane is to be done safely.

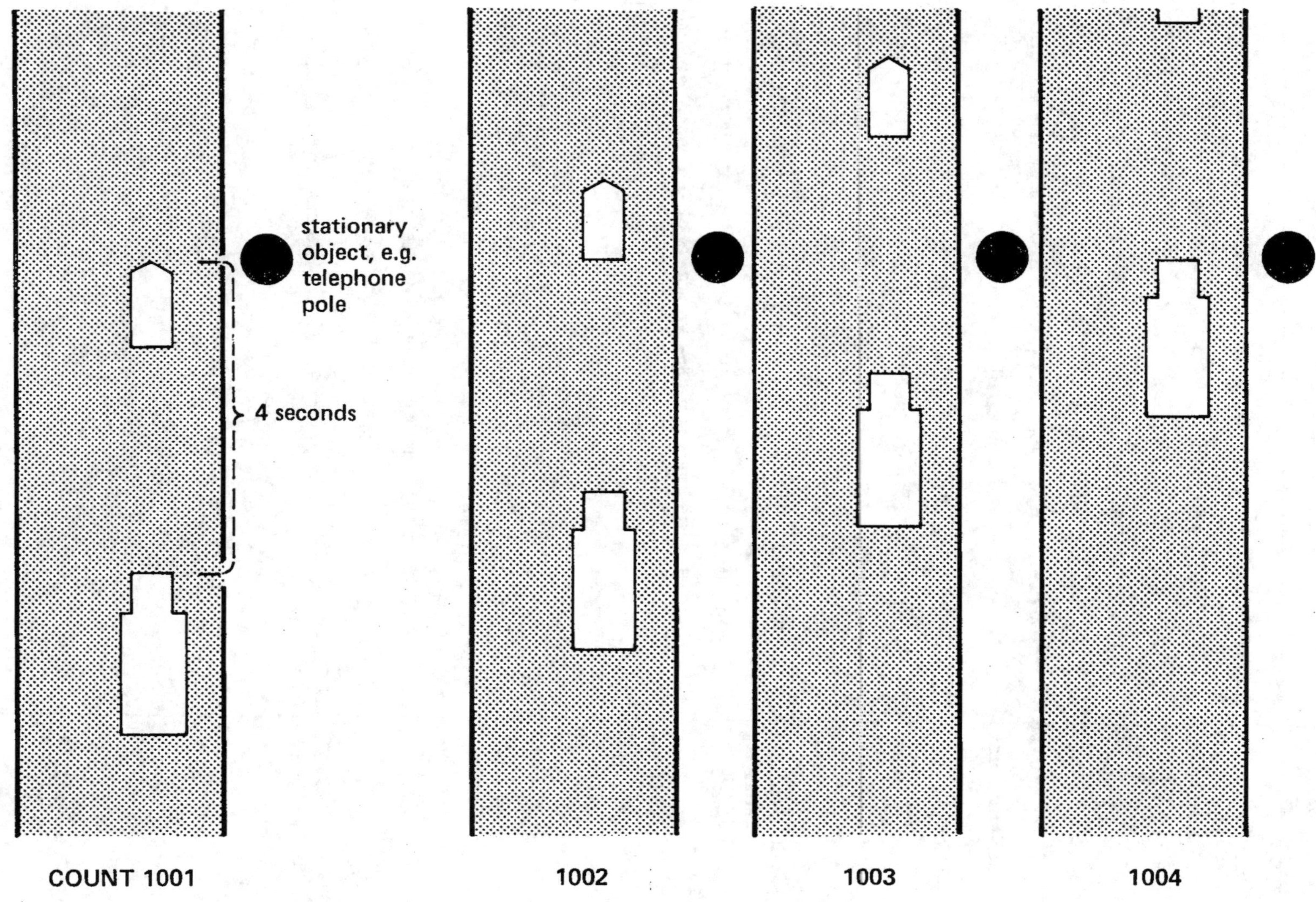

Figure 1. Four Second Timed Interval

INSTRUCTOR GUIDELINES	CONTENT
	c. Before changing lanes, you must be able to: (1) Keep traffic to your front, side, and rear under constant surveillance and simultaneously steer the bus within its lane. (2) Accomplish the change in a smooth continuous movement with very slight steering corrections and accelerator reversals. 5. You must: a. Develop the visual surveillance habit of scanning 360° around the bus. b. Develop coordination between control movements and eye movements. c. Be able to use peripheral vision for lateral control. d. Develop the ability to adjust your position to avoid hazards you detect. 6. You must know that appropriate and stable following distances maintain safe traffic flow, and certain conditions call for a greater than normal following distance. a. Following another vehicle requires a margin of space of sufficient size for you to adjust to unexpected moves by the vehicle ahead or to fluctuations in the traffic ahead without being forced into sudden swerves or stops. b. One rule that can be used to maintain safe following distances is to keep a distance between vehicles that is traveled in at least

INSTRUCTOR GUIDELINES	CONTENT
	three seconds. The three-second separation time interval can be estimated by using the procedure described in Figure 1, p. 10.
Illustrate bus lengths on chalkboard using a scale of 1 inch per 10 feet. Or use scaled toy vehicles on magnetic board.	c. A traditional rule of thumb has been one bus length for every 10 miles per hour of speed.
	d. Some circumstances call for greater following distance:
	(1) When increasing speed. As speed increases, so does the distance required to come to a stop. To allow for the greater stopping distance, a greater headway between the bus and vehicle ahead is needed.
	(2) When driving on wet or icy roads, which also increases the stopping distance.
	(3) When driving at night or during weather conditions that adversely affect your ability to see roadway and traffic conditions ahead. Vehicles may decelerate sharply during poor visibility. A greater following distance is required to allow a safety cushion for responding to sudden actions by the vehicle(s) ahead.
	(4) When fatigued. This causes a person to respond to situations more slowly than when he is fresh. The longer you take to react, the greater is the distance required to stop the car. To accommodate this poorer performance, allow a greater headway from the vehicle in front.

INSTRUCTOR GUIDELINES	CONTENT
	(5) When following emergency vehicles. Most states require a separation of at least 500 feet from emergency vehicles. (6) When following dual-wheeled vehicles, which may cause debris to be thrown from between the wheels. Also, the vehicle's larger size tends to block the view ahead if followed closely. (7) Following two-wheeled vehicles. Because of their lighter weight, two-wheeled vehicles can stop within a much shorter distance than the bus. Usually, they can also stop within a shorter distance than a car. e. Unstable spacing between vehicles adversely affects the flow of following traffic. 7. Drivers seem to underestimate distance in feet by 30 to 40 percent on the average, at highway speeds. In one study, drivers, on the average, were 20 percent off in attempting to maintain an 80-foot following distance at 45 miles per hour. Following too closely is a significant factor for accidents. For example: a. Driver failure to maintain an appropriate interval while following a lead vehicle in traffic was a significant factor in rear-end collisions in a moderately high percentage of accident reports reviewed. b. Maintaining "proper" following distance prior to changing lanes permits deceleration and reentry to the right lane if necessary. Independent studies of accidents and near

INSTRUCTOR GUIDELINES	CONTENT
	accidents among professional drivers attributed these situations largely to following too closely before changing lanes to pass. 8. The length of a sufficient gap in traffic will be defined differently by different drivers. Generally, a seven- to eight-second gap or lag in the flow of traffic is required before you enter an intersection. During peak traffic hours, this gap may be reduced by a second or two. 9. Drivers tend to underestimate gaps in traffic from the left and overestimate gaps in traffic from the right, owing to differences in angle of view. During peak hours, drivers in a hurry tend not to allow sufficient gaps in traffic from the right. NOTES:

STRUCTURES WITH RESTRICTED SPACE

INSTRUCTOR GUIDELINES	CONTENT
	When approaching a bridge, tunnel, or underpass, you should: 1. Decelerate for better control.
Trainees must know approximate weight of a loaded and an unloaded bus, how wide it is and how high it is.	2. Look for signs indicating load, width, and height limits; or estimate whether required clearance is available. BUS DIMENSIONS:
	3. Decide whether to proceed. 4. Yield to oncoming vehicles if structure is narrower than normal roadway.
For bridges, drivers should note whether other heavy vehicles are already on the bridge. The weight of that vehicle plus the weight of the bus may exceed the load capacity of the bridge. If so, wait until the other vehicle has crossed before going onto the bridge.	5. Avoid stopping in or on the structure except in response to traffic flow or an emergency. 6. Maintain appropriate speed, taking into account the surface grade, weather conditions and traffic. 7. Stay as far right as possible until you clear the structure.

OBSERVING PROCEDURES

INSTRUCTOR GUIDELINES	CONTENT
	OBSERVING
Ask trainees to give other examples of the following key words listed beside each procedure:	1. You must be able to respond to specific AUDITORY CLUES from the environment (which includes other traffic, pedestrians, and animals) in order to drive safely.
1. Auditory clues	a. Attempt to identify the sources of unusual sounds, including sounds of emergency vehicles, screeching tires, horns, and whistles.
	b. Look in the direction of the noise, using the mirrors to help locate the sound.
	c. Note whether the noise is continuous or intermittent, or whether its intensity is increasing or decreasing as an indication of whether the source of the sound is approaching or leaving, or completely irrelevant to the intended path of your bus.
	d. Open the window to improve the audibility of noise. In addition, to improve the detection of warning signals, minimize passenger noise level within the bus.
2. Vehicles ahead	2. Observe VEHICLES AHEAD in order to drive safely.
	a. When negotiating intersections:
	(1) Observe the oncoming traffic for an indication of a left turn.
	(2) If turning left, check to make sure that the oncoming traffic has not anticipated a green light.

INSTRUCTOR GUIDELINES	CONTENT
	b. Look ahead and note indications of vehicles leaving parking spaces by: (1) Observing the vehicle driver's hand signals or activated directional turn signals. (2) Noting the vehicle's lighted back-up lights or brake lights.
	c. Observe other traffic when negotiating a safe exit from parking spaces. (1) If parked at an angle and backing out, check the traffic behind and the vehicles to each side of the bus.
Remember: Backing is not recommended. If the bus must park so that backing out is necessary, it is recommended that an outside adult observer check that the way is clear. It is, however, much preferred that drivers park where they can pull straight ahead to leave parking space.	(2) If parked at an angle and exiting facing a traffic lane from a perpendicular space, check the traffic to both sides of the front of the bus. (3) If parallel parked and a parked vehicle is ahead, check for traffic before entering the roadway.
NOTE: These passing cautions were presented in Core Unit E (Driving Fundamentals). They are reviewed here for additional emphasis.	d. Observe the vehicle ahead and do not pass if the lead vehicle is: (1) Signalling or otherwise indicating a left turn. (2) Changing lanes preparatory to passing. (3) Weaving or wandering. In this case, sound the horn or flash the headlights to alert the driver of the lead vehicle. If the weaving does not cease, wait until you can pass with at least one-half lane separation.

INSTRUCTOR GUIDELINES	CONTENT
	(4) Decelerating suddenly. (5) Passing children, cyclists, or animals. (6) Being passed by another vehicle. In this case, wait until the lead vehicle has been passed, your view of the road ahead is clear, and an acceptable gap is present. e. Adjust your speed to changes in the speed of the lead vehicle. Note indications of reduced speed, such as: (1) Hand signals from the lead vehicle driver. (2) Activation of the lead vehicle's brake lights or directional turn signals. (3) Vehicles in front of the lead vehicle which are changing speed, causing the lead vehicle's velocity to change. f. Watch for slow-moving vehicles on a long or steep upgrade and downshift. Some states require vehicles going less than 40 mph to use their emergency flashers. g. Check the traffic to the front and rear when entering traffic. Specifically: (1) Yield to the rear-approaching traffic. (2) Look for a suitable gap in the traffic.

INSTRUCTOR GUIDELINES	CONTENT
	(3) Note the vehicle that you plan to enter behind and activate the turn signal as that vehicle passes.
3. Vehicles behind	3. <u>Observe VEHICLES BEHIND in order to drive safely</u>. a. In general, you should be able to react appropriately to <u>being followed</u>. Specifically: (1) Make smooth gradual stops and observe the roadway and traffic ahead to anticipate stop requirements. (2) Check the rearview mirror frequently to assess the traffic situation behind. Watch for tailgating vehicles and for the following vehicle's directional signals indicating an intent to pass. (3) Avoid looking at the mirrors if being followed closely at night by a vehicle with high beams on. b. Look for rear-approaching traffic in the new lane when <u>deciding to change lanes</u>. You should: (1) Look out the window to check your blind spot, moving your head enough to see around the blind spot. (2) On multi-lane roads, look for vehicles about to enter the new lane from the far adjacent lane. (3) Check all mirrors to observe vehicles passing in the new lane, following

INSTRUCTOR GUIDELINES	CONTENT
	vehicles closing fast from the rear in the new lane, and following vehicles about to enter the new lane. c. <u>When approaching an upgrade</u>, check the traffic for trucks or other heavy vehicles that may be "highballing," i.e., approaching a long or steep hill with excessive speed. d. When <u>negotiating a downgrade</u>, periodically observe the traffic behind for vehicles which may be accelerating excessively.
4. Cross traffic	4. <u>Observe CROSS TRAFFIC in order to drive safely</u>. a. Observe the traffic ahead and from the left and right when approaching and traversing intersections. Specifically: (1) Watch for vehicles which are close, and fast approaching the intersection, and decelerate or stop to permit those vehicles to clear the intersection. (2) Watch for vehicles approaching from the left and signalling a right turn, and decelerate and prepare to enter the intersection only after the vehicle has begun the turn. (3) If your vision is obscured (e.g., by buildings, trees, parked vehicles, etc.), stop at the intersection and edge forward slowly.

INSTRUCTOR GUIDELINES	CONTENT
	b. Observe other traffic when moving with traffic. Specifically: (1) Scan the traffic situation and the roadway contour well ahead, in addition to watching vehicles surrounding the bus. (2) Periodically observe vehicles in adjacent lane(s) in case that lane is needed for maneuvering or passing.
5. Pedestrians and animals	5. Observe PEDESTRIANS AND ANIMALS in order to drive safely. a. You should respond to pedestrians and animals appropriately. Specifically: (1) Watch for pedestrians or animals entering the roadway from the front of or between parked vehicles. (2) Watch for pedestrians near intersections, crosswalks, and school crossings. Decelerate and proceed cautiously if pedestrians are near the corner of an intersection. (3) When stopped at intersections and noting pedestrians waiting to cross with large or heavy objects, remain stopped to allow the pedestrians to proceed. b. Watch out for animals (domestic and wildlife) in the roadway. c. When in danger of striking a pedestrian or cyclist, check the traffic for space to take evasive action.

INSTRUCTOR GUIDELINES	CONTENT
	Add here any particular observation techniques you find useful. Include other things to observe that are pertinent in your area if they aren't covered in this section. NOTES:

MAKING SURE YOU ARE OBSERVED

INSTRUCTOR GUIDELINES	CONTENT
Emphasize/discuss that it is the responsibility of bus drivers to communicate their intentions (as well as their mere presence) to other drivers and pedestrians. If your district's buses have the eight light warning system, emphasize when to activate flashing amber warning lights in preparation for stopping to load/unload passengers. →	You must be able to utilize signaling devices and techniques to ensure that other drivers are aware of your intentions and to warn other drivers of potential hazards. 1. Signal appropriately to traffic behind you under the circumstances indicated: a. Signal your intention to decelerate or stop, by using brake lights-- (1) When determining the suitability of a parking space. (2) When preparing to park parallel or to exit from a parking space. (3) When parking at an angle. (4) In response to the actions of the vehicles ahead. b. Signal your intention to change lanes or direction, by using directional turn signals well in advance. 2. Signal your intention to pass: a. To the lead vehicle--by flicking your headlights at night, or by sounding the horn: (1) When the lead vehicle's vision to the rear is obscured by a trailer, open trunk lid, ice or snow on the rear window, or objects in the rear window. (2) When the lead vehicle is about to pull out and pass.

INSTRUCTOR GUIDELINES	CONTENT
	(3) When the lead vehicle moves laterally toward the car. (4) When the driver of the lead vehicle appears inattentive. b. To traffic following--by activating the left turn signal well in advance of initiating the passing procedure.
<u>Being Observed</u> Emphasize/discuss the following: 1. Laws regarding giving signals to other drivers. 2. The appropriate point at which to give signals in order to avoid confusion. 3. Motions of the car that are most likely to be misinterpreted by other drivers.	3. <u>Signal appropriately your intention to turn, using directional signals</u>: a. When leaving a parallel parking space to enter traffic. b. When leaving traffic. c. At intersections at the appropriate time. d. When approaching and entering an off-ramp without a deceleration lane. e. When leaving an off-street area facing traffic. f. When preparing to change lanes or direction.
	4. <u>As a warning to other drivers</u>: a. Tap the brake pedal lightly-- (1) To signal following traffic (and to reduce speed) if the lead vehicle changes speed. (2) To signal following traffic if an oncoming vehicle starts across the center line.

INSTRUCTOR GUIDELINES	CONTENT
	b. Flash headlight beams or sound the horn-- (1) To signal an oncoming vehicle that he has crossed the center line. (2) When the occupants of a parked car are about to exit on the roadway side. c. Sound the horn-- (1) When passing a stopped vehicle in the roadway. (2) When approaching the crest of a hill on a narrow road, in order to alert oncoming vehicles. 5. <u>Sound the horn</u>: a. To alert animals (domestic and wild-life) in the roadway of the car's approach. b. When in danger of striking a pedes-trian or cyclist.
Add here any other methods of communication accepted in your own district.	NOTES:

LONGITUDINAL SEPARATION PROCEDURES

INSTRUCTOR GUIDELINES	CONTENT
Emphasize that maintaining separation keeps a margin of space around the bus. This is sometimes referred to as a "space cushion" or an "extra margin of safety."	Maintain adequate LONGITUDINAL separation from other traffic. 1. In maintaining an appropriate following distance behind the lead vehicle: a. Allow enough distance for stopping the bus before the lead vehicle stops, if necessary. b. Decelerate early and gradually for required stop maneuvers to avoid jamming on the brakes. 2. Increase longitudinal separation: a. When following-- . Oversized vehicles that obscure your visibility. . Gasoline or inflammable/explosive carriers. . Vehicles that stop frequently--e.g., other school buses, delivery vans, mail carriers. . Two-wheeled vehicles--e.g., motorcycles and bicycles. . Vehicles carrying protruding loads. . Vehicles being driven erratically. . Emergency vehicles. b. On wet or icy roads. c. Under conditions of reduced visibility--fog, snow, smoke or haze. d. Under conditions of darkness.

INSTRUCTOR GUIDELINES	CONTENT
	e. Where traffic intersects, merges, or diverges. f. When the road ahead is not visible. 3. Accelerate to increase separation distance with the vehicle following, if the driver of the vehicle exhibits erratic behavior. 4. Decelerate and be prepared to stop in order to maintain appropriate longitudinal separation: a. When the lead vehicle reduces speed. b. When a vehicle is stopped on the roadway ahead. Stop well behind the overtaken vehicle so that you can pass the vehicle without having to back up. c. When approaching a parked vehicle with the hood up. d. When the driver(s) of the vehicle(s) behind, including one that may be tailgating, indicates he wishes to pass. e. When following slow-moving vehicles. Deceleration should be initiated in sufficient time-- • To avoid emergency stops ("panic stops") • To assure at least a three-second separation from the vehicle ahead. f. When following or approaching special vehicles, such as another school bus, trolley or transit bus, engaged in picking up and/or discharging passengers.

INSTRUCTOR GUIDELINES	CONTENT
	g. When an emergency vehicle, such as an ambulance, fire truck, or police vehicle is approaching from any direction.
	h. When flashing red lights or flashing yellow lights are noted on the vehicle ahead.
	i. When following a convoy, such as a funeral procession.
	j. When following a driver exhibiting erratic behavior.
	k. When approaching hidden driveways that are heavily used, e.g., plant exits.
	5. Be prepared to stop or to change lanes when the vehicle ahead is about to enter or exit a parking space.
	a. If you decide to stop, allow the driver of the other vehicle sufficient clearance to complete his maneuver without crowding.
Ask whether trainees have questions. If so, discuss with class.	b. If you decide to change lanes, allow a full car width between the bus and the vehicle that is parallel parking.

LATERAL SEPARATION PROCEDURES

INSTRUCTOR GUIDELINES	CONTENT
Emphasize that buses are wider than cars and thus take up more lateral space.	Maintain adequate LATERAL separation distance from other traffic in relation to such procedures as passing, being passed, meeting oncoming vehicles, driving on freeways, entering traffic, changing lanes, and negotiating intersections.
Caution drivers that they should watch lateral separation when passing in crowded areas. Students may have hands out the windows even though they shouldn't.	1. In maintaining the appropriate lateral separation distance when PASSING, you should: a. Select the appropriate lane for the passing maneuver. (1) In general, pass on the left. (2) On a two- or three-lane roadway-- · You may pass on the right of the vehicle that is stopped for a left turn. · Use only the middle lane for passing on the left on a three-lane roadway. (3) On a four-lane roadway, you may pass moving traffic if necessary and legally permissible. (4) On six or more lanes, you may pass on the right-- · When no lane change is necessary. · When it is safe and expeditious to traffic. 2. In maintaining the appropriate lateral separation distance when BEING PASSED, you should: a. If the pass appears to be safe-- (1) Maintain position in the center of the lane, or slightly to the right,

INSTRUCTOR GUIDELINES	CONTENT
	if possible, to provide additional passing clearance. (2) Maintain or reduce speed, avoid acceleration.
Explain how to aid passing vehicles by flashing lights when it's safe for them to pull back in front of you.	b. Prepare to decelerate to provide more space if the passing vehicle cuts in front of you after passing. c. If the passing vehicle attempts to abort the pass, accelerate quickly, if there is adequate clearance ahead, to allow the passing driver to pull safely back into the driving lane. 3. In maintaining the appropriate lateral separation distance in relation to ONCOMING VEHICLES, you should: a. Keep to the right of the center line. b. Maintain maximum lane separation by-- (1) Using the right lanes whenever possible. (2) Positioning the bus in the right section of the lane whenever a move to the right lane is impossible or impractical. c. Maintain precise steering control over the bus when oncoming vehicles pass to be able to react quickly to wind gusts, road irregularities or to an oncoming vehicle crossing the center line. d. On a narrow downgrade, yield the right-of-way to the oncoming vehicles, pulling off

INSTRUCTOR GUIDELINES	CONTENT
	the road if necessary to allow the vehicle to continue. However, be cautious not to pull onto soft shoulders. 4. To maintain the appropriate lateral separation distance when CHANGING LANES, you should: a. Adjust the speed of the bus, accelerating or maintaining speed, whichever is necessary. b. Steer into the new lane, after waiting a few seconds following the signal to turn. c. Position the bus in the center of the new lane. 5. To maintain adequate lateral separation from PARKED VEHICLES, position the bus to avoid striking the vehicle door if it opens unexpectedly. 6. In maintaining adequate lateral separation distance with other traffic at INTERSECTIONS, proceed as follows: a. When turning left, in general: (1) Wait until there is a sufficient gap in traffic from both left and right to permit the turn to be made without danger. (2) Avoid pulling halfway into the intersection when it will interfere with traffic. b. If a driver in the oncoming lane suddenly makes a left turn across the path of the bus, stop or slow down to let him pass, depending on both of your speeds.

INSTRUCTOR GUIDELINES	CONTENT
	c. When turning left with no oncoming traffic, enter the appropriate lane for normal driving.
	d. When turning left with oncoming traffic approaching:
	(1) Proceed to the center of the intersection.
	(2) Remain to the right of the center line.
Explain how turning the wheels left will force the bus into oncoming traffic if the bus is hit from the rear.	(3) Keep wheels pointed straight, not turned left.
	(4) Proceed with the turn when it is safe to do so.
	e. When turning left and the oncoming vehicle also signals for a LEFT turn:
	(1) Proceed partially into the intersection and stop, leaving adequate heading to complete the turn.
	(2) Remain to the right of the center line.
	(3) Complete the left turn when assured that the oncoming vehicle will turn and conditions are otherwise safe.
	f. When turning left and the oncoming vehicle signals for a RIGHT turn:
	(1) Proceed partially into the intersection and stop until the oncoming vehicle begins his turn.
	(2) Turn left into the nearest left lane of the cross street.

INSTRUCTOR GUIDELINES	CONTENT
	g. Do not enter the intersection unless complete passage is assured.
	7. In maintaining an adequate separation distance with PEDESTRIANS AND ANIMALS, proceed as follows:
	a. Yield the right of way to pedestrians at all times.
	b. When passing pedestrians, provide the maximum possible clearance (using the passing lane if possible) and do not pass the vehicle ahead when pedestrians reduce the lane clearance.
	c. Decelerate when entering animal crossing zones or when noting animals on or alongside the roadway. Overtake animals at reduced speed and resume a normal rate after the pass has been accomplished.
Ask whether trainees have any questions. If so, discuss with class.	d. Prepare to stop or swerve if the animal enters the roadway. In this case, if swerving the bus to avoid hitting the animal would jeopardize the safety of the driver, passengers or other motorists or pedestrians, <u>do not</u> swerve the bus.
<u>Separation</u> The student must know the following: 1. Laws regarding yielding right-of-way. 2. Laws regarding bus positioning and direction of movement in the face of other traffic.	e. When in danger of striking a pedestrian or cyclist, decelerate by pumping the brake and swerve the bus gradually when an insufficient stopping distance exists. NOTES:

INSTRUCTOR GUIDELINES	CONTENT
The following exercises are provided so trainees can apply the principles in this unit to a simulated traffic situation. They should observe, make sure they are observed, and maintain adequate separation in each situation. Have trainees work each one individually. Model answers are provided. Then have each trainee present a situation to rest of class for discussion and feedback. 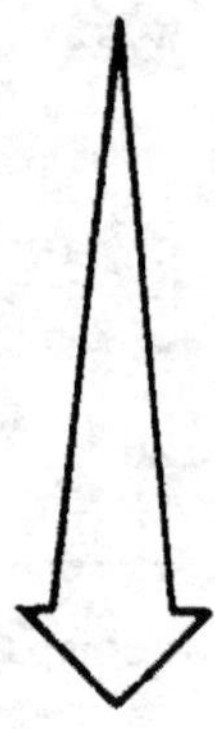	On the following pages, exercises are provided so you can apply the principles that you have just learned to simulated traffic situations. Your instructor will provide you with some guidelines. NOTES:

EXERCISE 1

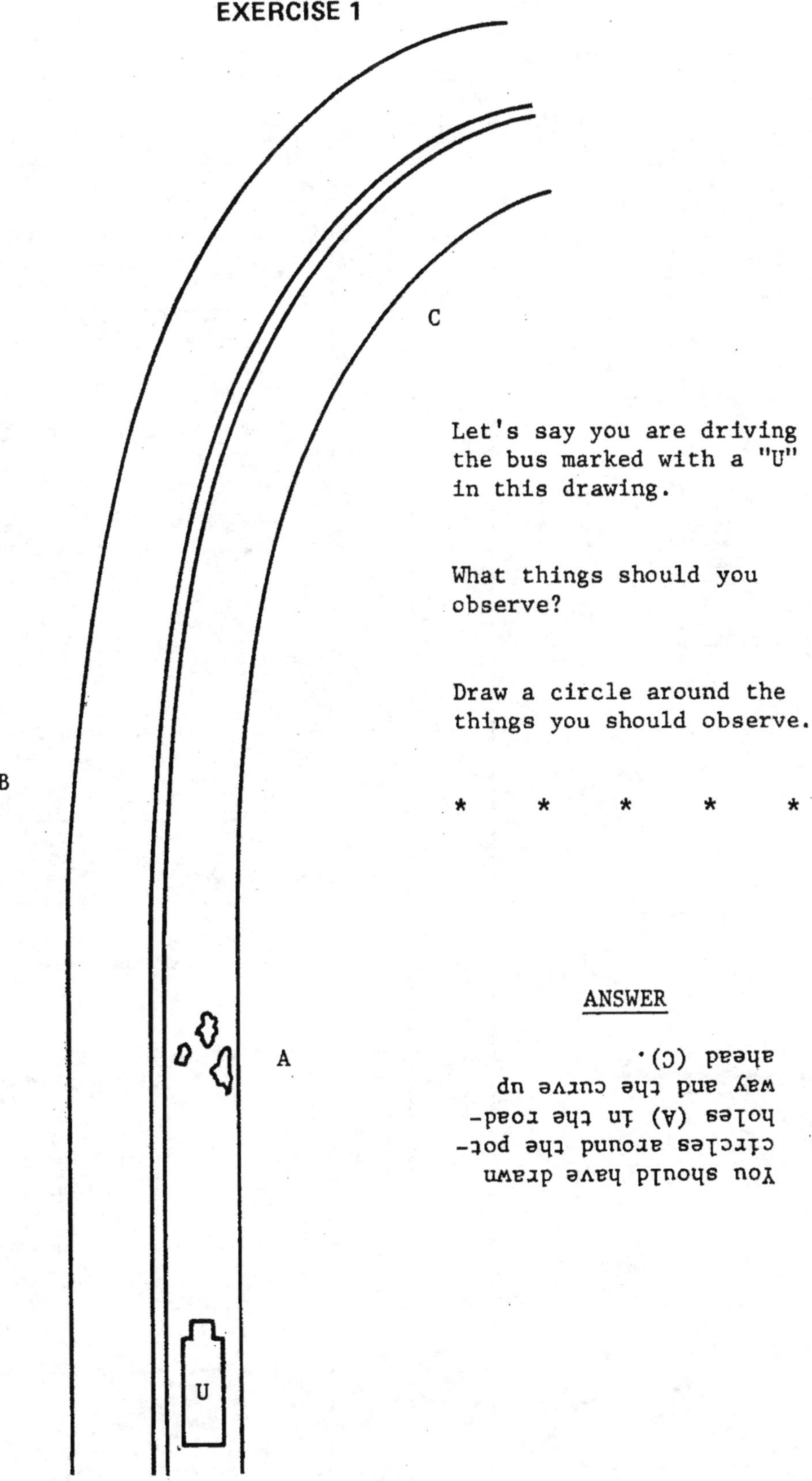

Let's say you are driving the bus marked with a "U" in this drawing.

What things should you observe?

Draw a circle around the things you should observe.

*   *   *   *   *

ANSWER

You should have drawn circles around the pot-holes (A) in the road-way and the curve up ahead (C).

EXERCISE 2

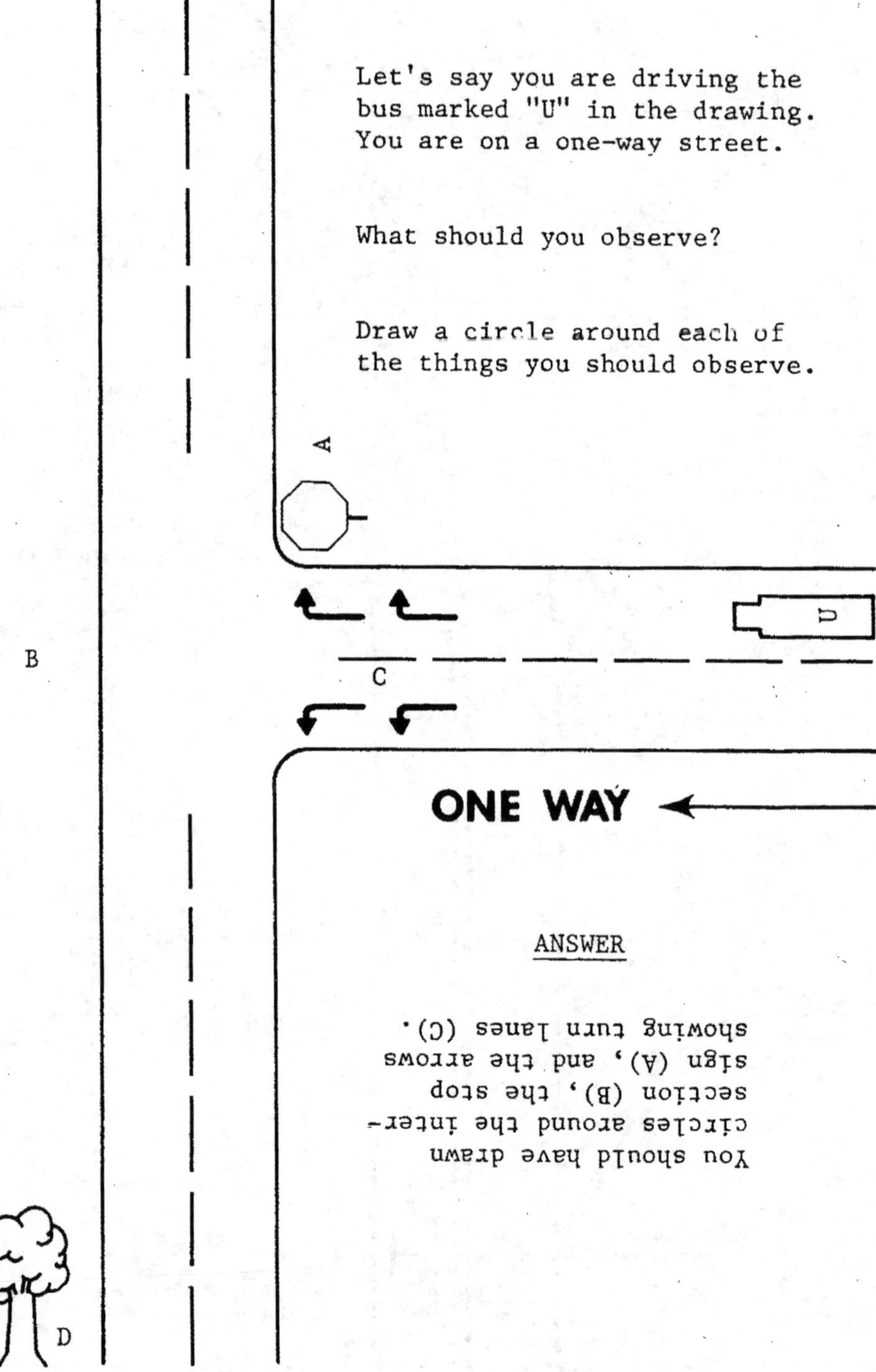

Let's say you are driving the bus marked "U" in the drawing. You are on a one-way street.

What should you observe?

Draw a circle around each of the things you should observe.

ANSWER

You should have drawn circles around the inter-section (B), the stop sign (A), and the arrows showing turn lanes (C).

EXERCISE 3

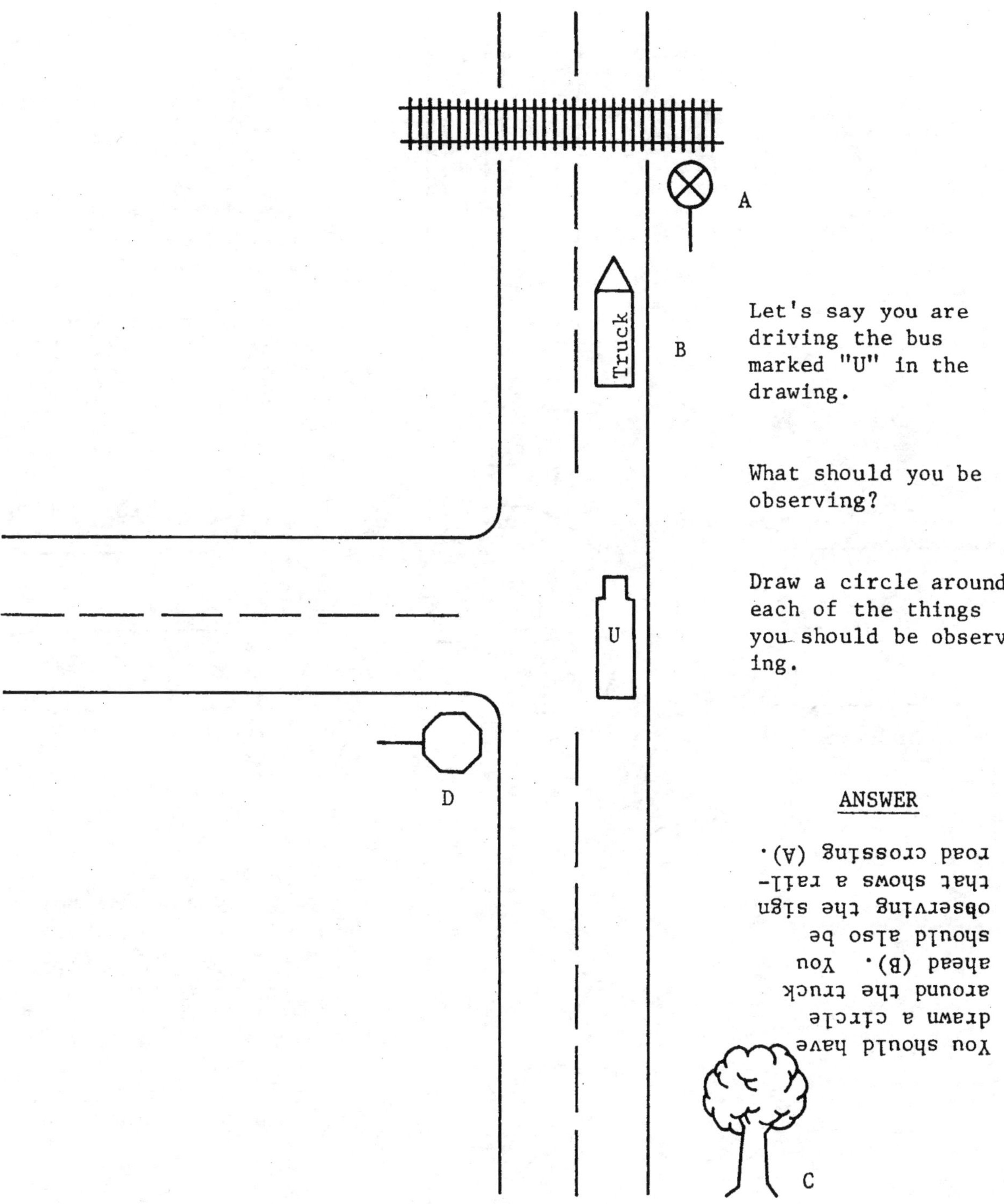

Let's say you are driving the bus marked "U" in the drawing.

What should you be observing?

Draw a circle around each of the things you should be observing.

ANSWER

You should have drawn a circle around the truck ahead (B). You should also be observing the sign that shows a rail-road crossing (A).

EXERCISE 4

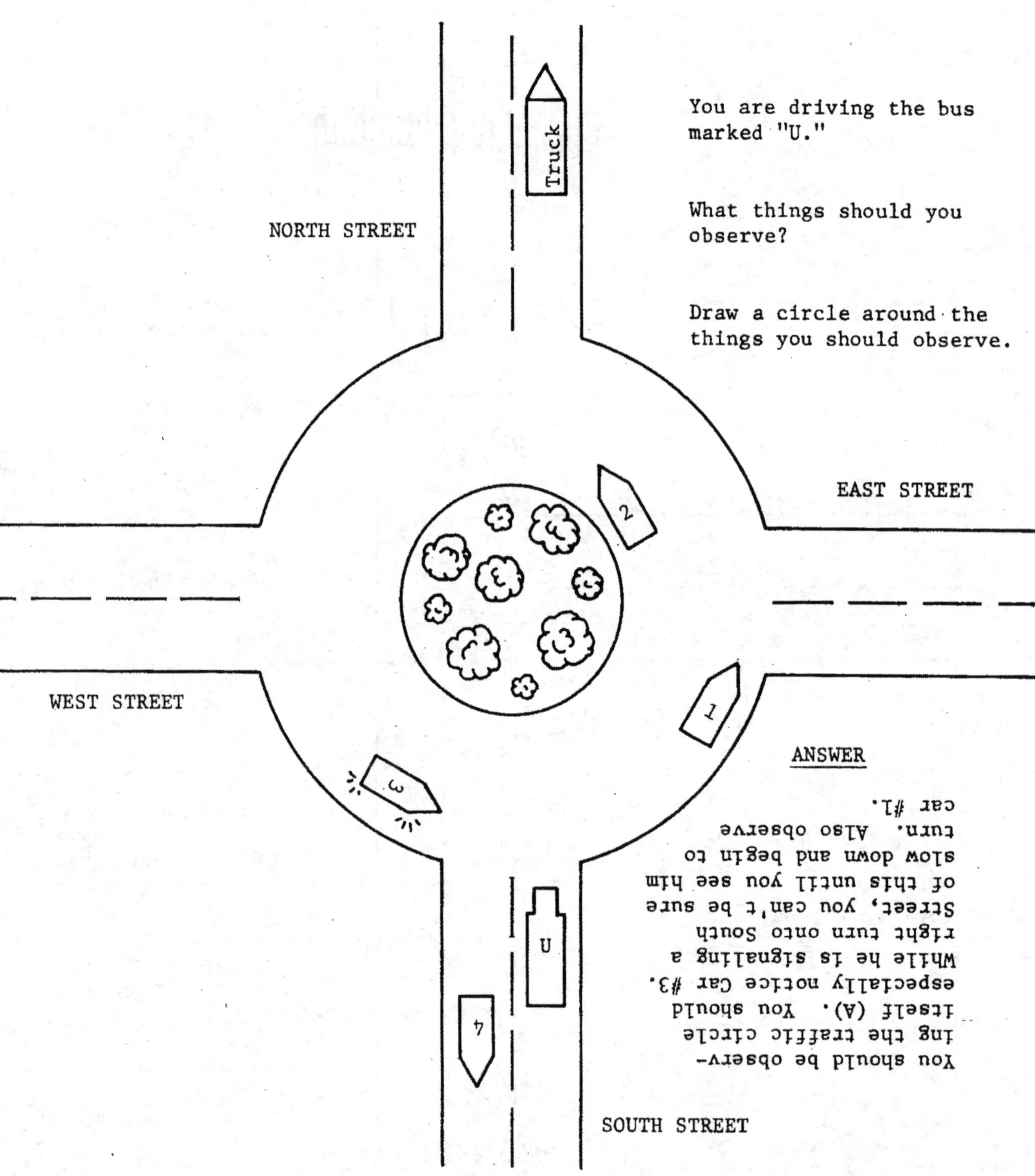

You are driving the bus marked "U."

What things should you observe?

Draw a circle around the things you should observe.

ANSWER

You should be observing the traffic circle itself (A). You should especially notice Car #3. While he is signaling a right turn onto South Street, you can't be sure of this until you see him slow down and begin to turn. Also observe car #1.

EXERCISE 5

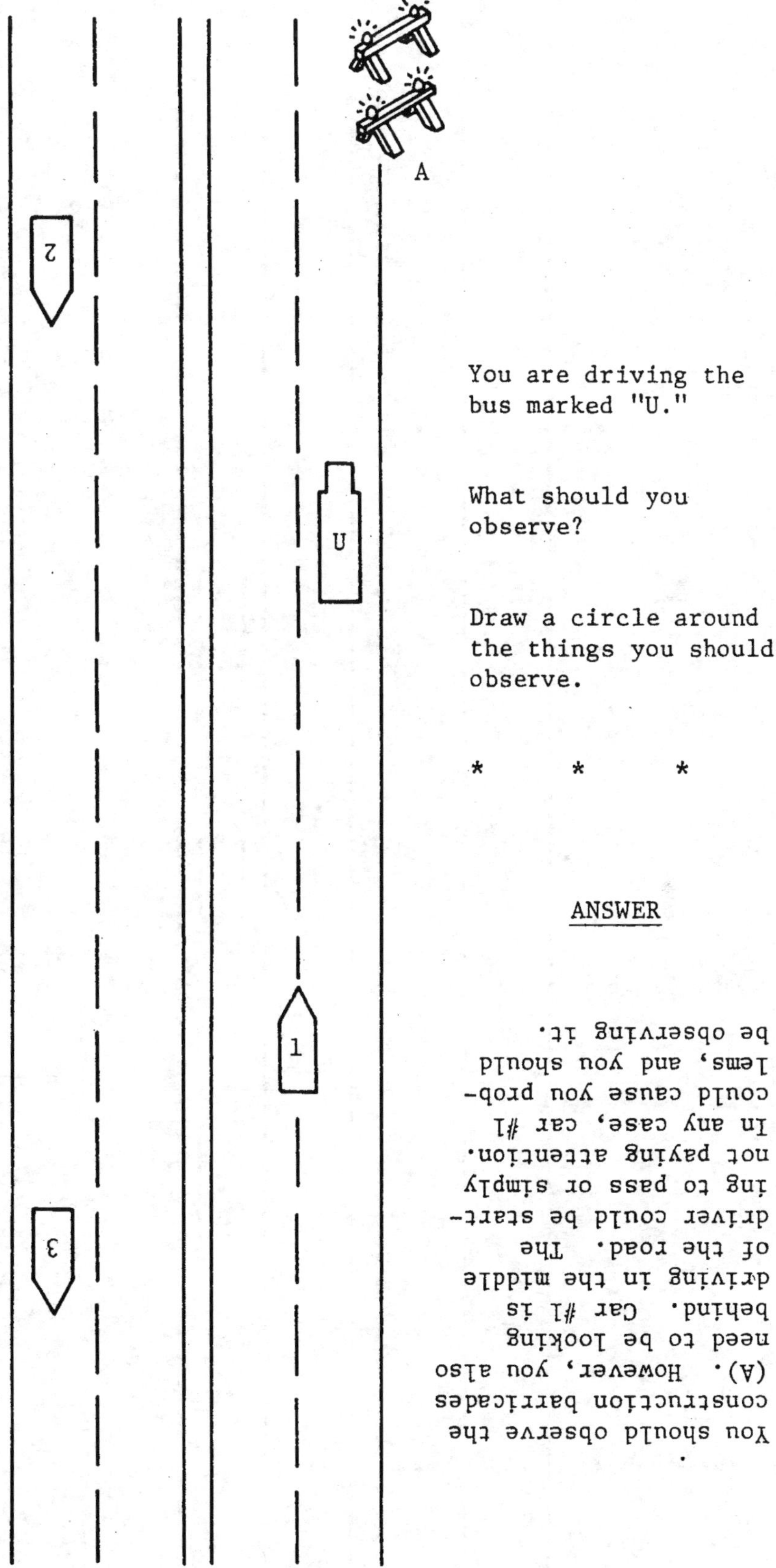

You are driving the bus marked "U."

What should you observe?

Draw a circle around the things you should observe.

* * * *

ANSWER

You should observe the construction barricades (A). However, you also need to be looking behind. Car #1 is driving in the middle of the road. The driver could be starting to pass or simply not paying attention. In any case, car #1 could cause you problems, and you should be observing it.

EXERCISE 6

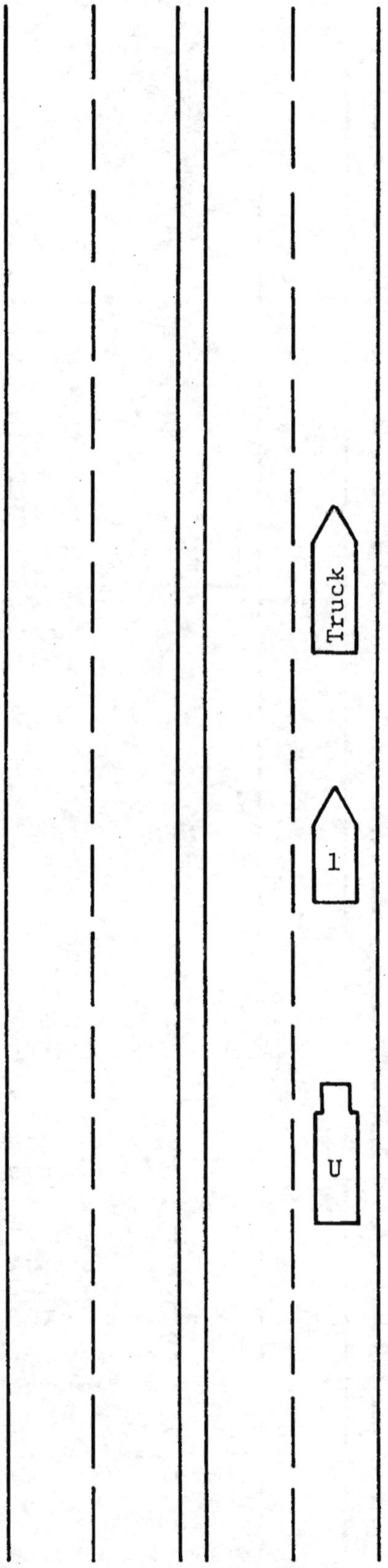

Truck

1

U

You are driving the bus marked "U." You want to pass car #1 and the truck.

In the spaces below, write three ways you should communicate what you want to do.

1. ______________________

____

____

2. ______________________

____

____

3. ______________________

____

____

ANSWERS

1. Put on your left turn signal.

2. Tap your horn.

3. Begin to move into the left lane.

EXERCISE 7

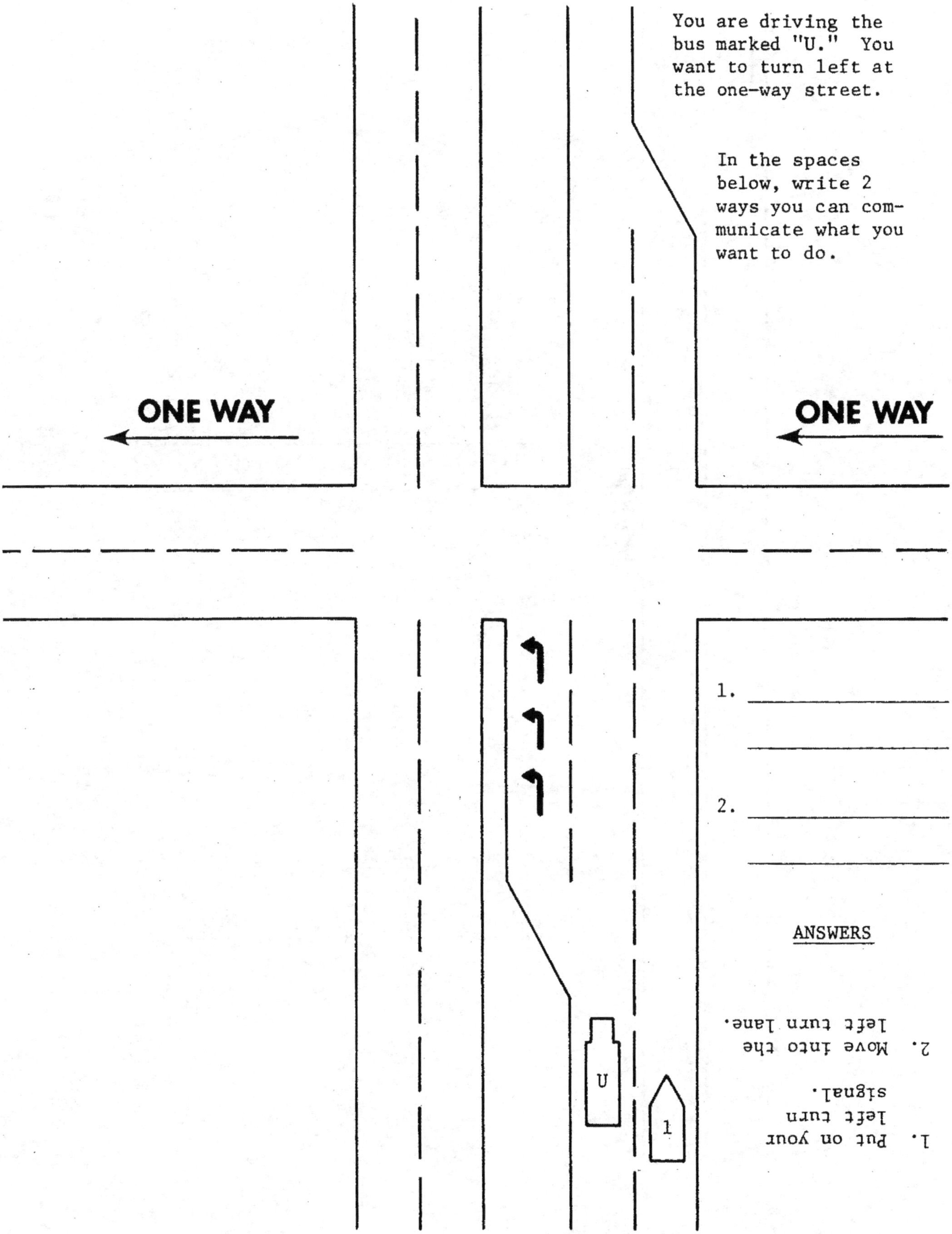

ONE WAY

ONE WAY

U

1

You are driving the bus marked "U." You want to turn left at the one-way street.

In the spaces below, write 2 ways you can communicate what you want to do.

1. ____________________

   ____

2. ____________________

   ____

ANSWERS

1. Put on your left turn signal.

2. Move into the left turn lane.

EXERCISE 8

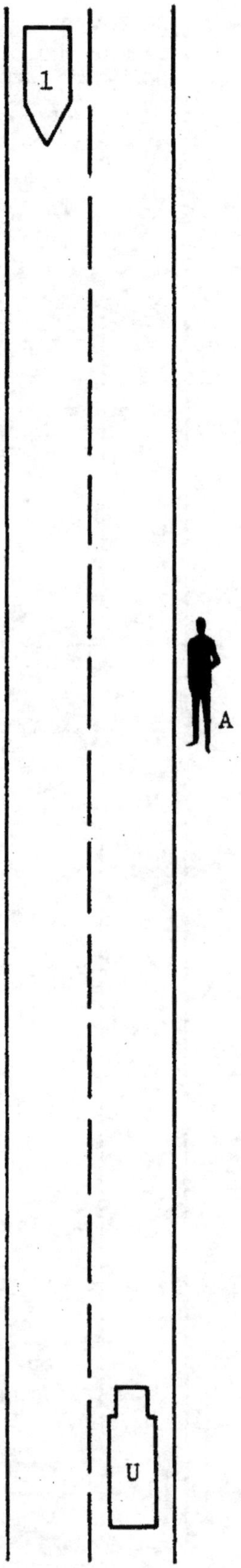

You are driving the bus marked "U."

You notice a person, walking next to the road at A.

What, if anytning, should you do to communicate? Write it here:

____

____

____

* * * * * *

<u>ANSWER</u>

Tap your horn to warn the person walking that you are approaching.

EXERCISE 9

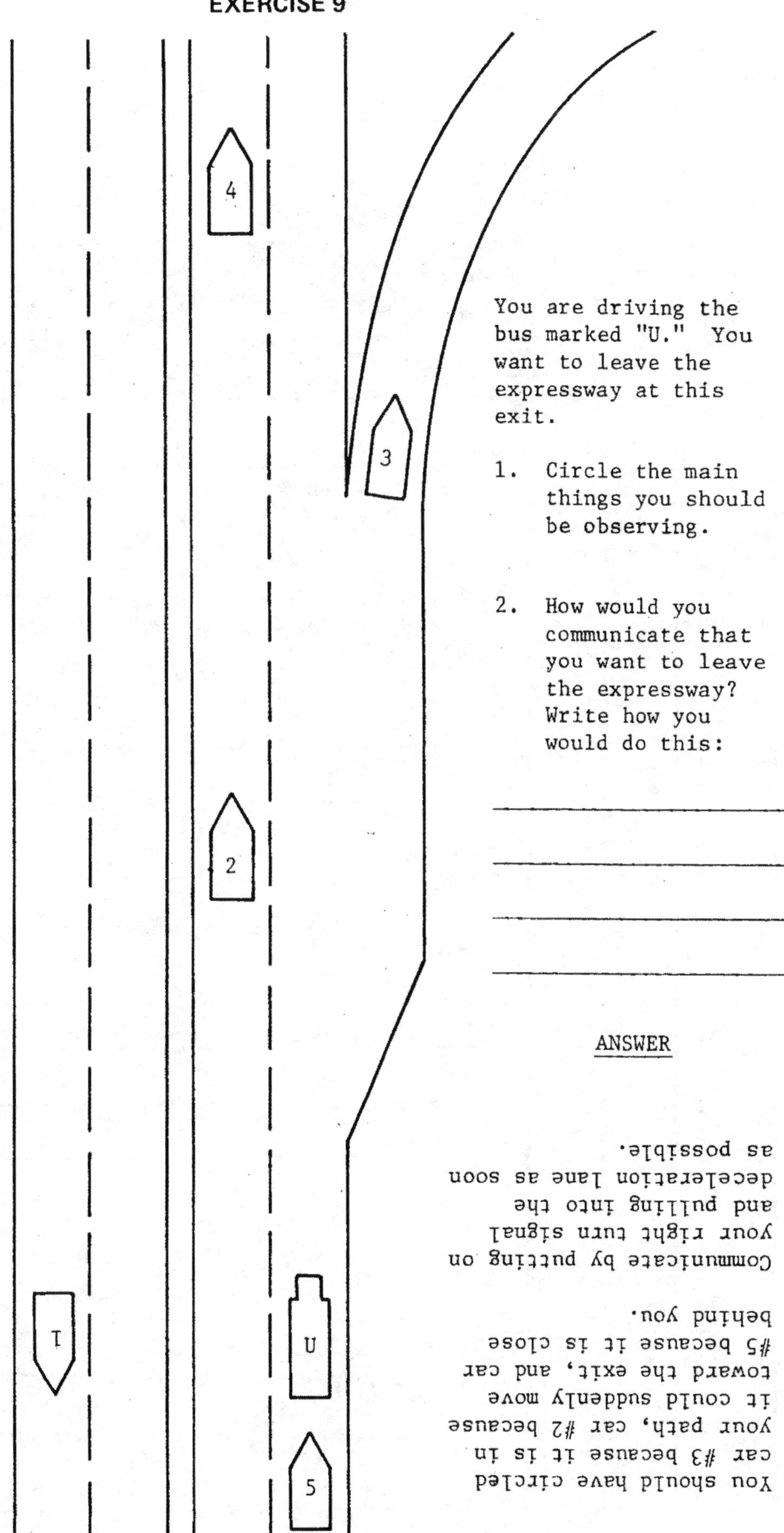

You are driving the bus marked "U." You want to leave the expressway at this exit.

1. Circle the main things you should be observing.

2. How would you communicate that you want to leave the expressway? Write how you would do this:

____

____

____

____

ANSWER

You should have circled car #3 because it is in your path, car #2 because it could suddenly move toward the exit, and car #5 because it is close behind you.

Communicate by putting on your right turn signal and pulling into the deceleration lane as soon as possible.

EXERCISE 10

(GRAVEL ROAD)

1

2

U

You are driving the bus marked "U." You have been driving on a paved highway. Now you are going to turn right on a gravel road.

What speed adjustment will you need to make on the gravel road? Write your answer here:

____

____

____

Why is this necessary? Write the answer here:

____

____

____

*   *   *   *   *

ANSWERS

You will need to reduce your speed on the gravel road.

The reason you reduce your speed is that your bus can be more difficult to control on gravel than it is on a paved highway. Your wheels have less traction. By slowing down, you increase your ability to stop or maneuver.

EXERCISE 11

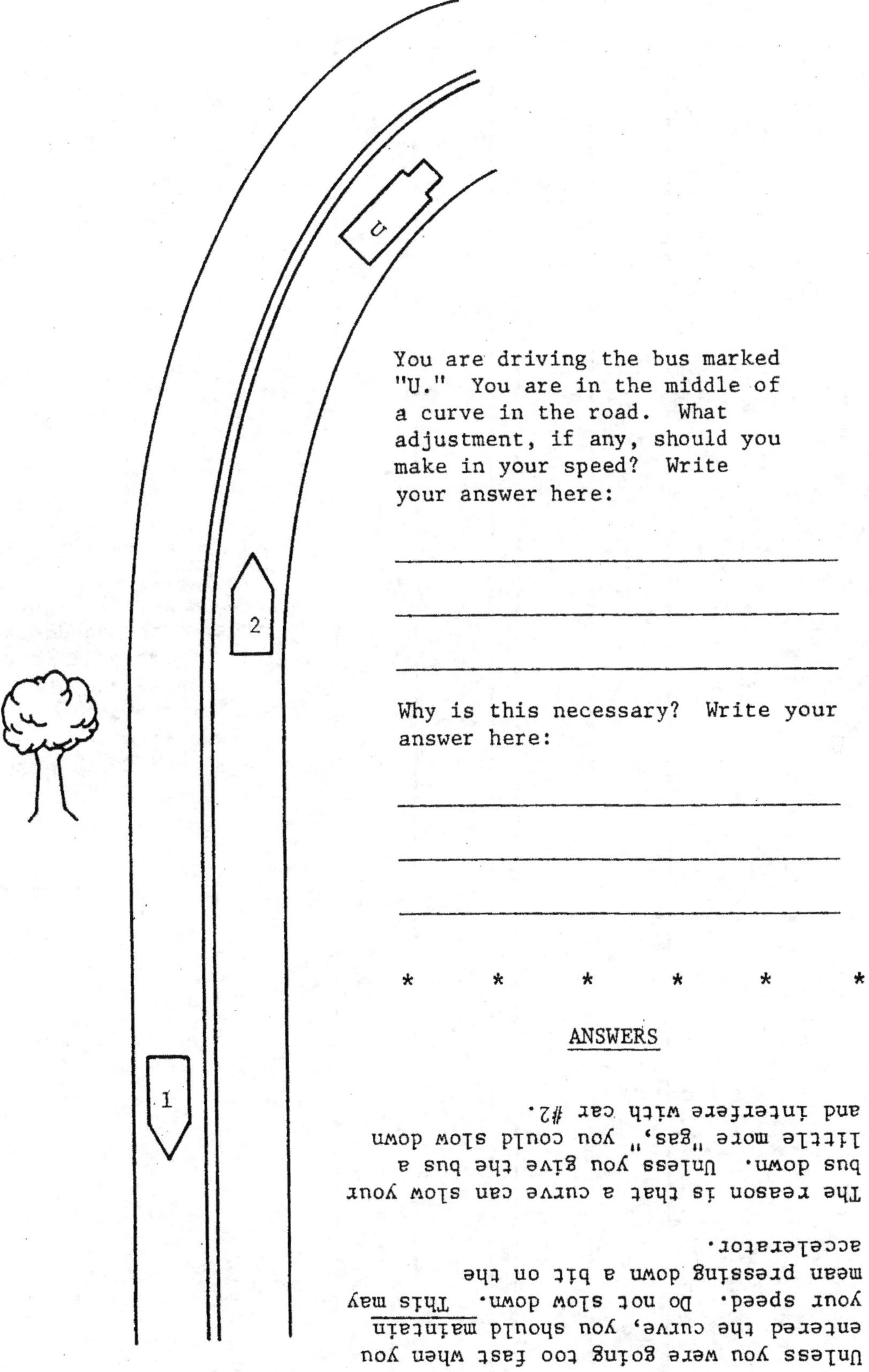

You are driving the bus marked "U." You are in the middle of a curve in the road. What adjustment, if any, should you make in your speed? Write your answer here:

____

____

____

Why is this necessary? Write your answer here:

____

____

____

* * * * * *

<u>ANSWERS</u>

Unless you were going too fast when you entered the curve, you should <u>maintain</u> your speed. Do not slow down. <u>This may</u> mean pressing down a bit on the accelerator.

The reason is that a curve can slow your bus down. Unless you give the bus a little more "gas," you could slow down and interfere with car #2.

EXERCISE 12

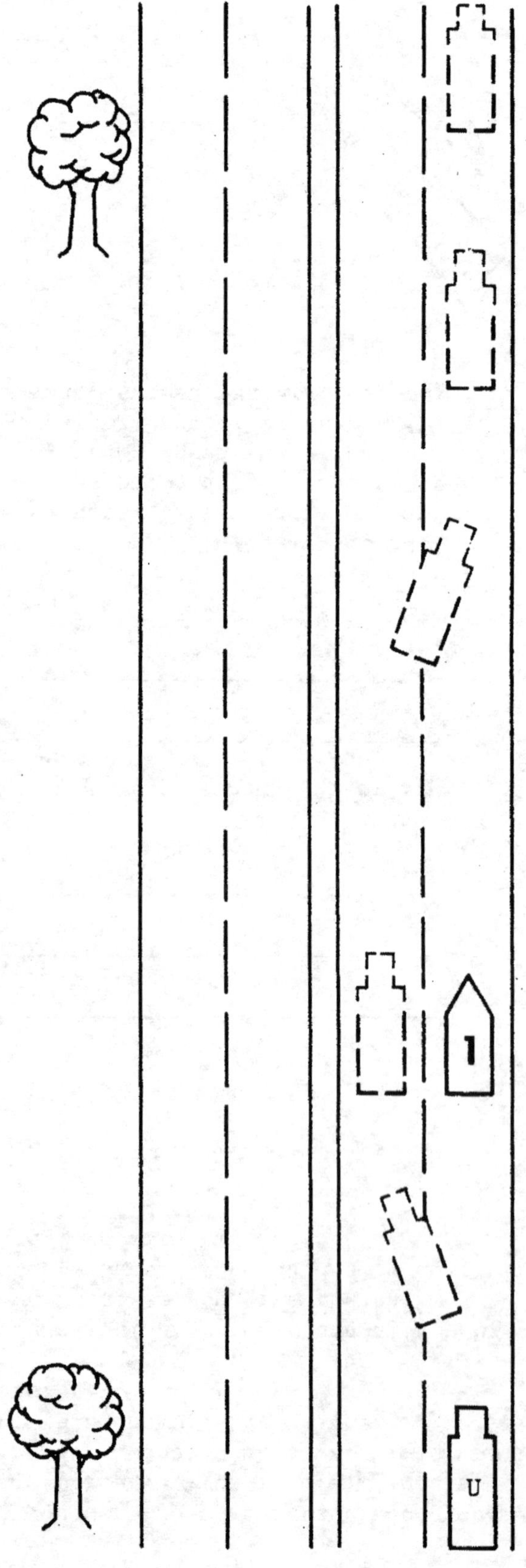

You are driving the bus marked "U." You want to pass car #1. Put either A for accelerate, or M for maintain speed, or D for decelerate in each of the unmarked buses according to what you should do in passing.

Turn the page to check your answer.

ANSWER TO EXERCISE 12

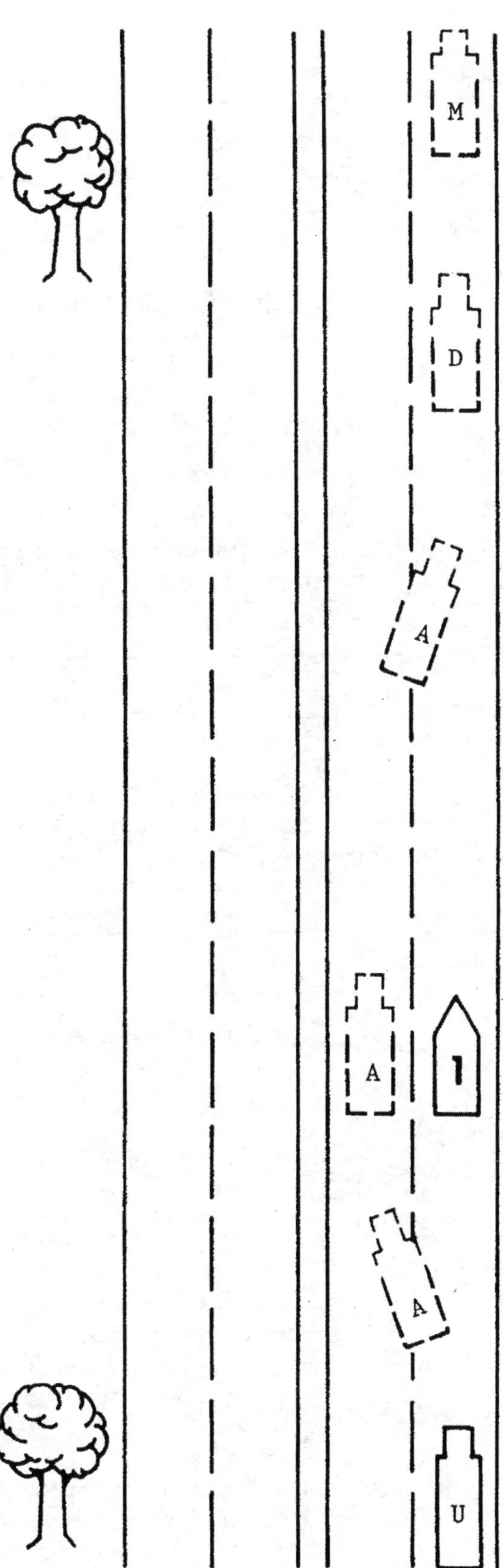

Be sure that you do not decelerate too early or too much. If you do, you could interfere with car #1

EXERCISE 13

You are driving the bus marked "U."

Draw a circle around the things you should be observing.

What, if anything, should you be doing to communicate? Write your answer here:

____

____

What, if anything, should you be doing to adjust your speed? Write your answer here:

____

____

* * * * *

ANSWERS

You should be observing the parked cars, since one might pull out, and the children playing ball, since someone could run into the street.

Unless you saw a person run toward the street, you don't need to honk to communicate. Applying your brakes will signal any traffic behind. You should slow down because of the hazards in this area.

EXERCISE 14

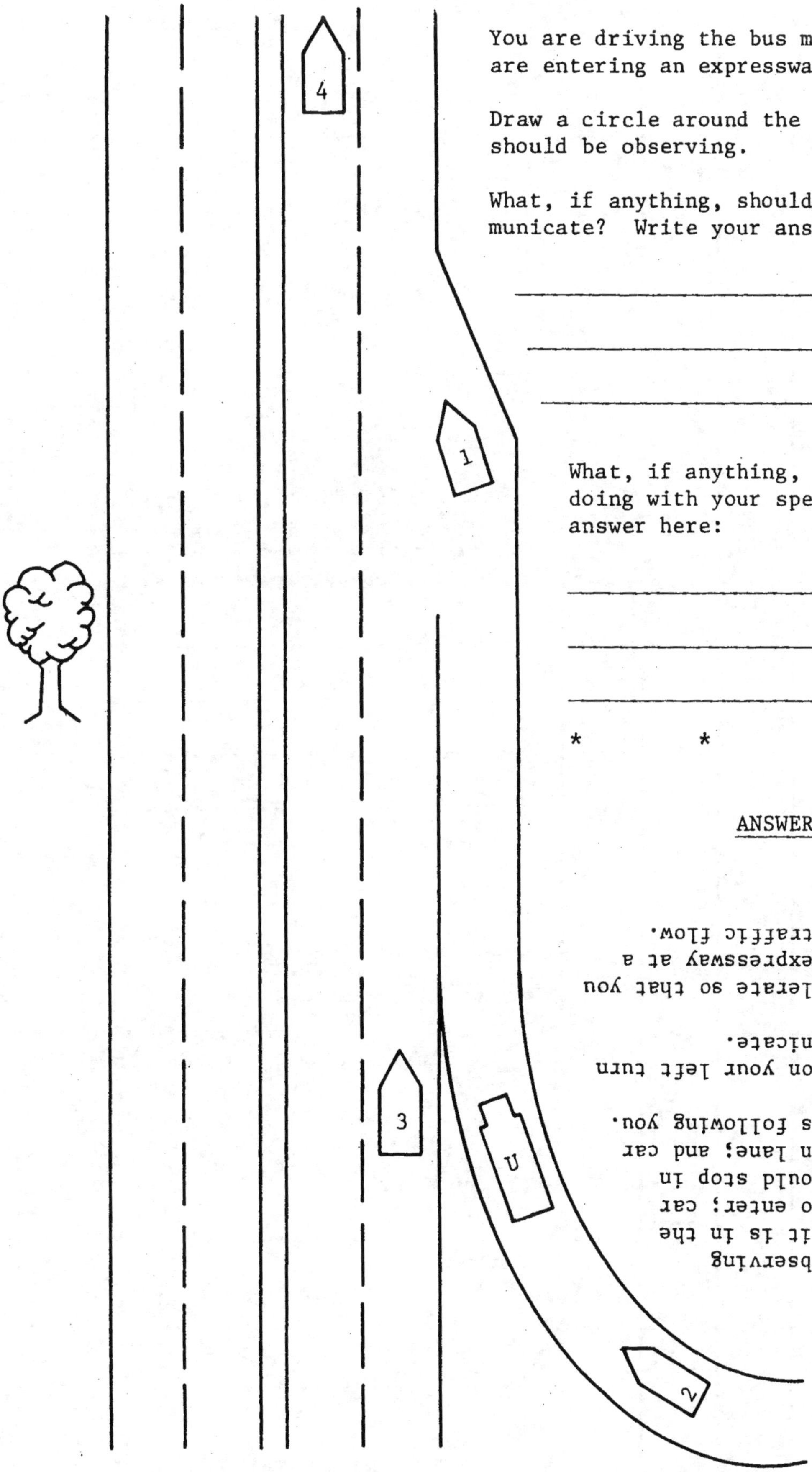

You are driving the bus marked "U." You are entering an expressway.

Draw a circle around the things you should be observing.

What, if anything, should you do to communicate? Write your answer here:

____

____

____

What, if anything, should you be doing with your speed? Write your answer here:

____

____

____

* * * *

ANSWERS

You should be observing car #3 because it is in the lane you want to enter; car #1 because it could stop in the acceleration lane; and car #2 because it is following you.

You should put on your left turn signal to communicate.

You should accelerate so that you will enter the expressway at a speed with the traffic flow.

EXERCISE 15

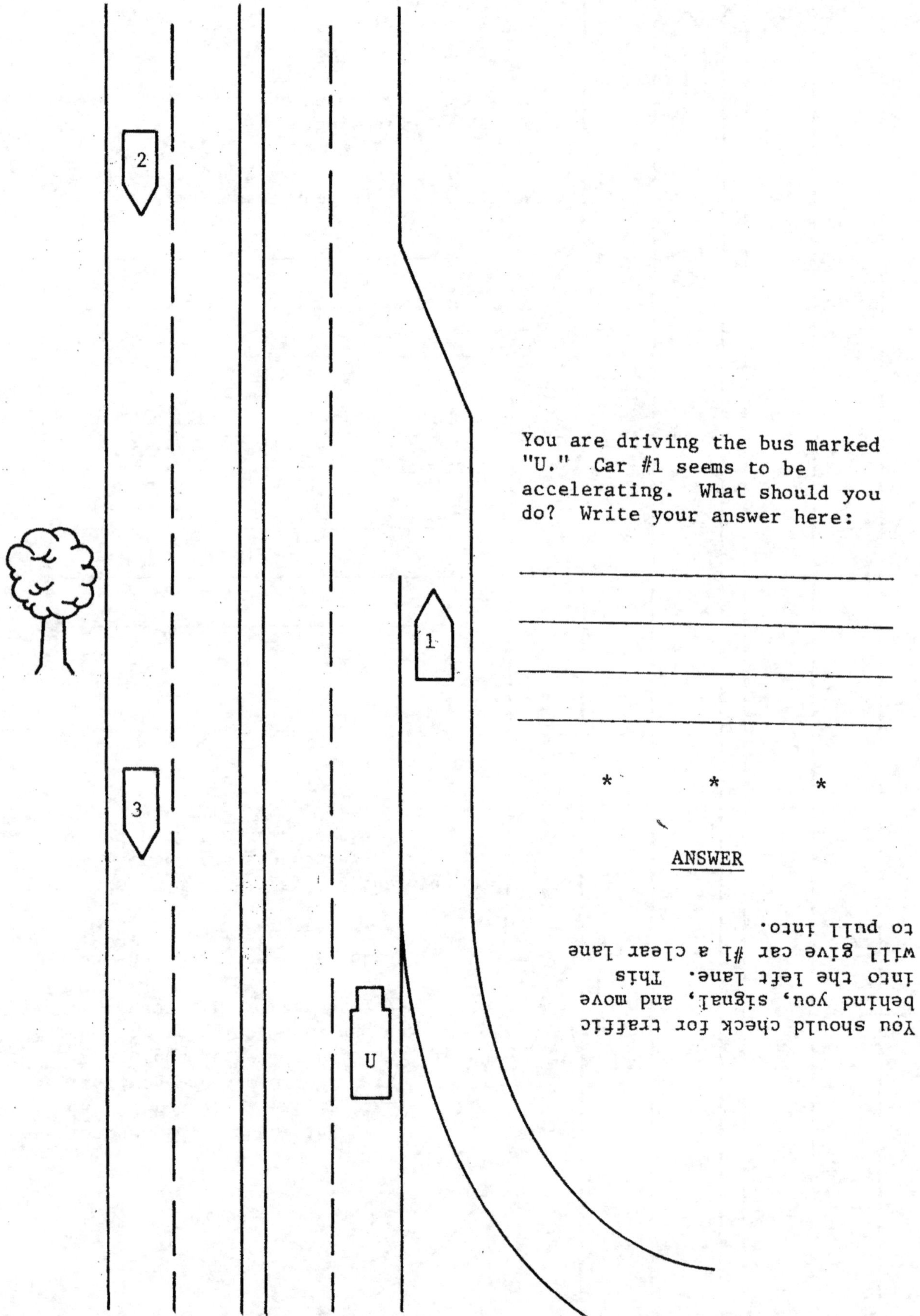

You are driving the bus marked "U." Car #1 seems to be accelerating. What should you do? Write your answer here:

____

____

____

____

* * *

ANSWER

You should check for traffic behind you, signal, and move into the left lane. This will give car #1 a clear lane to pull into.

EXERCISE 16

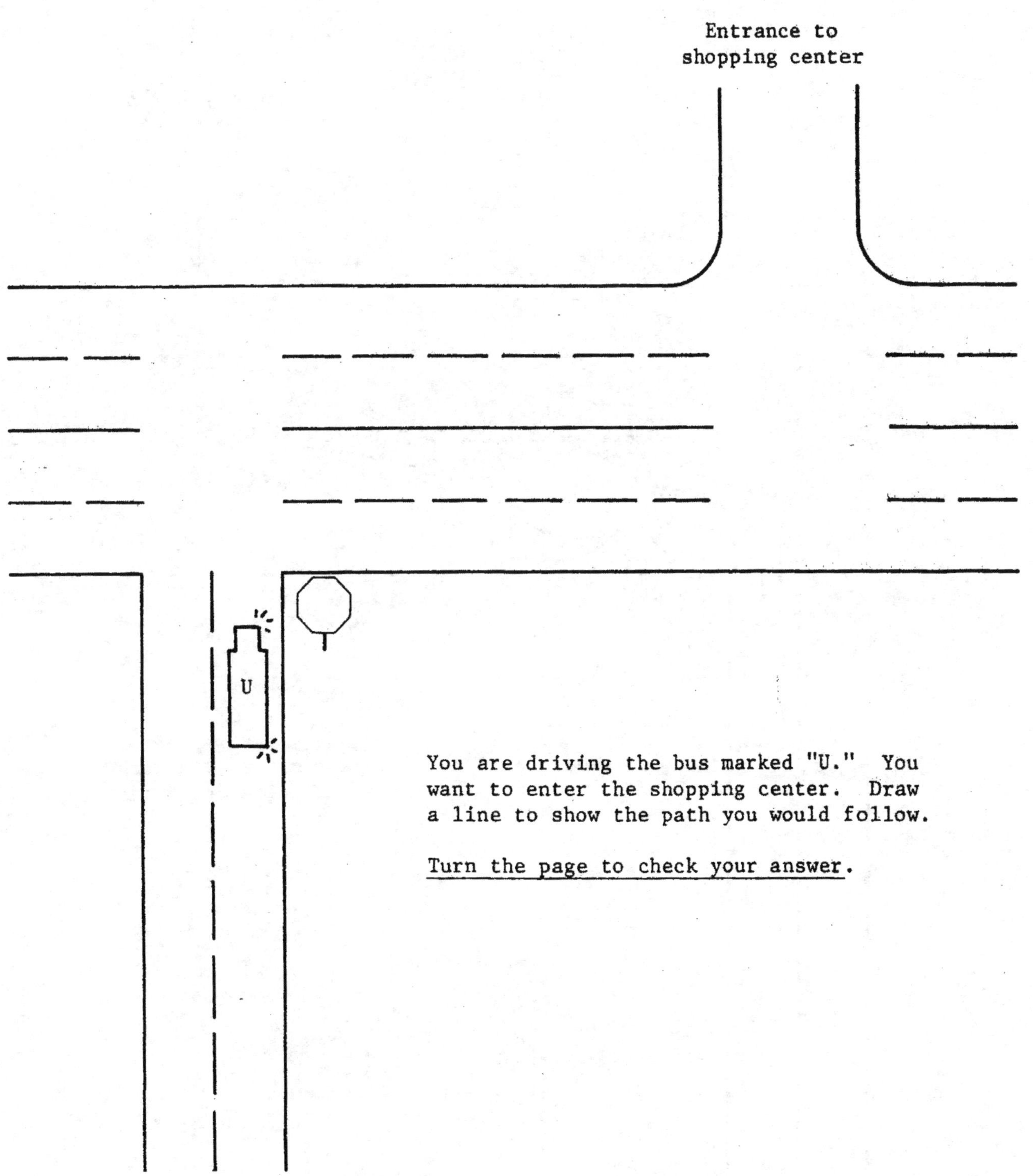

You are driving the bus marked "U." You want to enter the shopping center. Draw a line to show the path you would follow.

Turn the page to check your answer.

ANSWER TO EXERCISE 16

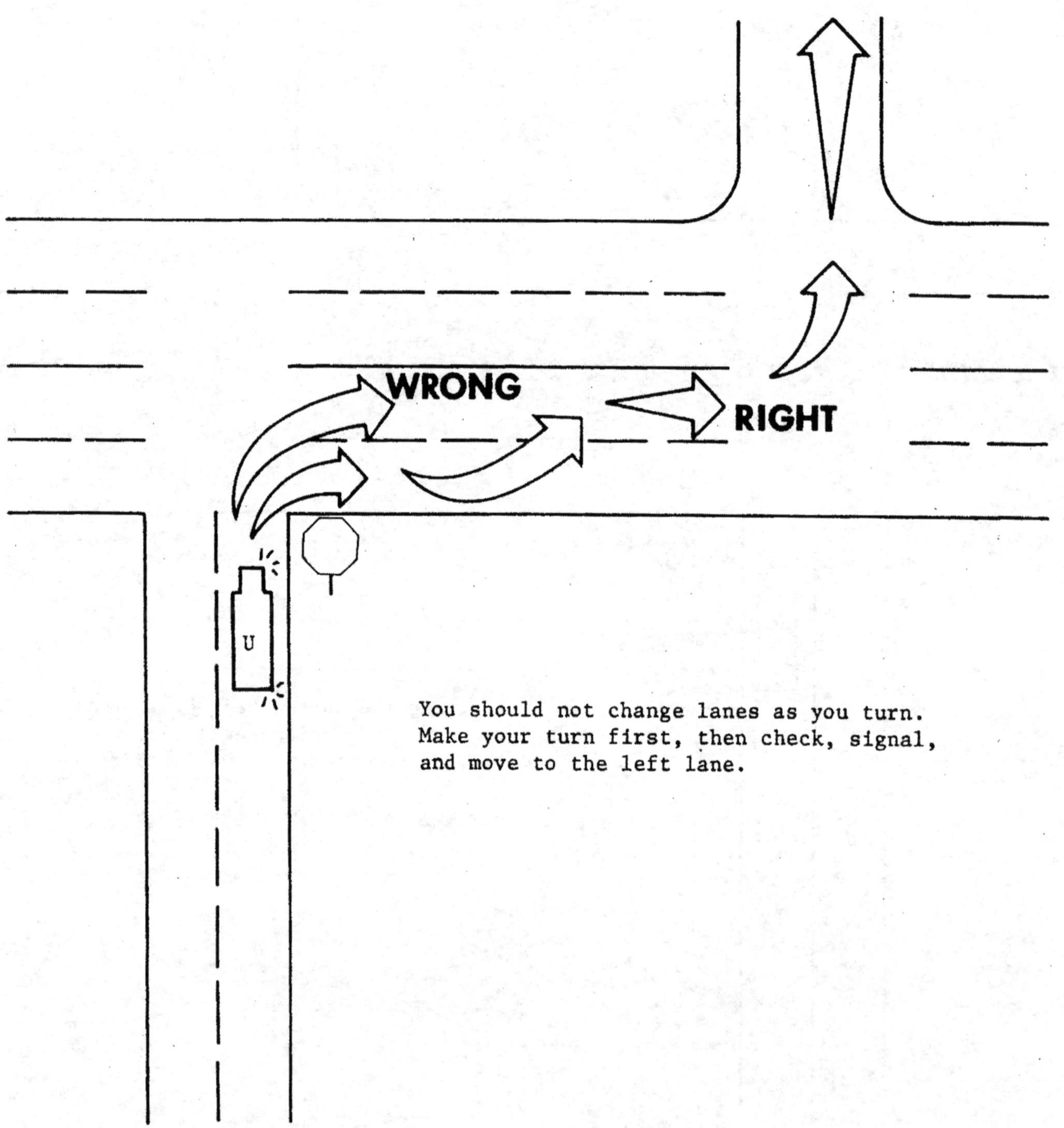

You should not change lanes as you turn. Make your turn first, then check, signal, and move to the left lane.

ON-THE-ROAD PRACTICE

INSTRUCTOR GUIDELINES	CONTENT
An on-the-road exercise should be provided for students to integrate control principles with specific driving situations. Have each trainee drive a pre-planned route. Trainees should use "Commentary Driving Techniques" to practice <u>observing</u>, <u>being observed</u>, and <u>maintaining separation</u>. Have them practice timed interval method, if you wish. You should provide feedback on performance. (See Advanced Unit E for "Commentary Driving Technique.") Situations to be included in the route are: Intersections, Traffic circles, Following another vehicle, Passing, Being passed, Leaving traffic, Changing lanes, Being followed, and Bridges/tunnels and underpass. Administer Unit Review Questions. Provide feedback. Provide additional classroom/practice sessions for any trainees who don't meet criterion.	Now you'll practice <u>observing</u>, <u>being observed</u>, and <u>maintaining separation</u> while actually driving on the road. Your instructor will describe the planned route and review the Commentary Driving Technique. NOTES:

DRIVING UNDER SPECIAL CONDITIONS

TABLE OF CONTENTS

OBJECTIVES

1. Rural and mountainous areas.

2. Urban areas.

3. Night and darkness.

4. Adverse weather conditions.

5. Expressways.

OVERVIEW

INSTRUCTOR GUIDELINES	CONTENT
The special conditions covered in this unit are ones that many bus drivers will encounter. You may de-emphasize or omit any that are not applicable to your area. Add or expand on any condition that's important in your area if you feel further coverage is necessary.	Beginning drivers too often learn to drive only under favorable driving conditions and probably with a lighter vehicle than a school bus. Then, when they have to drive a heavy bus under unfavorable road, light, traffic or weather conditions, they go right ahead with the only driving practices they have learned and they run into trouble. Special or unusual driving conditions put special responsibilities on you. They lengthen the stopping distance or danger zone. Under unfavorable conditions, you must reduce vehicle speed merely to maintain the same margin of safety that you keep under favorable conditions. You probably operate your bus over a variety of roads and under varied conditions. So, it is necessary to adapt your driving habits to the conditions under which you are driving. On poor roads, a considerable part of your attention should be devoted to getting through with the greatest degree of comfort to the passengers and without damaging the bus. On main highways, a large part of your attention should be concentrated on other traffic on the road. Know how the bus is going to respond on different types of roads and what the braking distance will be on different road surfaces--under normal conditions <u>and</u> when rain, snow, or ice is present.

DRIVING ON RURAL HIGHWAYS

INSTRUCTOR GUIDELINES	CONTENT
	Much of the school bus travel takes place on suburban or rural roads. Such highways may consist of standard-width, hard-surfaced roads, narrow hard-surfaced roads, gravel and crushed rock surfaces, and just plain dirt.
	Rural roads which are not hard-surfaced are generally quite narrow. Probably the greatest hazard on such roads is the questionable condition of the outer edges of the roadbed. During wet weather they frequently become soft and give way when the school bus gets too close to the edge. Under such conditions, the bus driver when meeting oncoming vehicles, should avoid pulling too far to the right. In many cases, it is wise to stop the bus entirely until the other car has maneuvered around it.
Provide special instructions for driving in mountainous areas, if applicable to your district. Include gear shifting and braking techniques.	Hills are another source of danger. Many motorists using these roads tend to drive toward the center of the road. Bus drivers approaching a hill, especially one with a curve, should pull over to the right as far as possible so as to minimize the possibility of a head-on collision with a motorist coming over the hill from the opposite direction.
	NOTES:

INSTRUCTOR GUIDELINES	CONTENT
One in-bus lesson should be provided in which each trainee drives on rural roads, mountainous roads, etc., that he may encounter on his job. Provide a handout describing the route the lesson will follow. The route should include rural (and mountainous, if applicable) roads of varying surfaces and widths, various types of uncontrolled intersections, poor shoulders, etc. Have trainee use "commentary driving" technique as he or she drives, and provide feedback on performance.	Many of the secondary roads, though hard-surfaced, are narrow and crooked. On such roads, the driver may permit his right wheels to run off the paved surface. When this happens, the driver should be cautious so as not to follow his instinct and attempt to pull the bus back onto the pavement immediately. He should keep going straight and allow the bus to slow down. The brakes should be applied very gently in slowing the vehicle--quick and hard application of brakes should be avoided. If conditions permit it, engine compression alone should be used to slow the bus to the desired speed. If there is sufficient space on the shoulder of the road, he should first pull further right two or three feet from the pavement after the bus has slowed down. And then, with the bus moving very slowly, turn the wheels to the left and cut back onto the pavement. Blind and uncontrolled intersections constitute an additional hazard on rural roads. All such intersections must be approached at a reduced speed and with utmost care. Where the intersection is blind to the extent that it is impossible to see down the side roads until almost at the intersection, the only safe procedure is to enter the intersection at a crawl.

URBAN DRIVING

INSTRUCTOR GUIDELINES	CONTENT
	DRIVING IN CITY TRAFFIC Regardless of the fact that the school bus will be operated most of the time on the open highway, it is important that you acquaint yourself with the sound practices that are necessary for town and city driving. Become familiar with local traffic regulations and follow the direction of officers directing traffic. One of the most common faults of school bus drivers, while driving in town, is that they do not stay in the proper lane of traffic. Many drivers feel that since they are driving a vehicle that is wider than the ordinary car, it is safer if they straddle the lane. This is an erroneous assumption and a dangerous idea; the bus is in a much safer position if it is in one lane than if it is in two. Keep the bus in the right lane, unless you are preparing to make a left turn. In this position, the bus will not interfere with other traffic to the extent that it does when occupying a portion of both lanes. If lanes are not marked off, it is up to you to imagine that the lanes exist and to operate the bus in the proper one. If you make it a habit to drive your bus in the wrong lane, or continually change from one lane to another, you demonstrate an absence of respect for other drivers and the safety of your passengers. Another factor that is important to the safe operation of a school bus in city traffic is regulating the speed of the bus in accordance with other traffic on the street. If the bus is operated at a speed that is in excess of, or greatly under, that of

INSTRUCTOR GUIDELINES	CONTENT
	other vehicles, it becomes a hazard to both the occupants of the bus and other users of the street. Be careful to maintain enough distance between the bus and other vehicles to allow room to stop without colliding with other vehicles under emergency conditions. In city traffic, the speed of the bus should be in accordance with the speed of other vehicles, so that the bus will not create a hazard and "tieup" traffic. Streets in cities, and roads leading into cities, frequently consist of four or more lanes and divided highways. If such roads are a part of the school bus route where children are picked up, consideration of the safety of the children should be paramount. The bus should be required to double back rather than to have a child cross a highway unassisted. This will permit children living on such roads to load and unload on the right side of the highway, consequently lessening the danger of accidents that have occurred at various times when students have had to cross the road to board a bus.

INTERSECTIONS IN URBAN AREAS

INSTRUCTOR GUIDELINES	CONTENT
OPTION: Show the Ford time-lapse filmstrip with accompanying record and workbooks, "Intersection Maneuvers." See AV Directory (71).	Consider these factors when you have to drive through or turn at intersections in an urban area. How will your driving be different?
	HEAVY TRAFFIC
Discuss each, emphasizing local differences. Add any not listed (e.g., trolley tracks on the streets) that are relevant for your district.	TRAFFIC OFFICERS
	TRAFFIC LIGHTS
	PEDESTRIANS
	ONE WAY STREETS
One in-bus lesson should be provided in which each trainee drives in an urban area. Provide a handout describing the route the lesson will follow. Have trainee use "Commentary Driving." Provide feedback on performance.	SAFETY ISLANDS

NIGHT DRIVING (TWILIGHT TO DAWN)

INSTRUCTOR GUIDELINES	CONTENT
	SOME THINGS YOU SHOULD KNOW • Driving at twilight is more dangerous than driving during daylight. Drivers overestimate their ability to see at twilight. Shadows increase the difficulty in judging speed and distance of other vehicles. Many drivers are also fatigued at dusk enroute home from work. One-fifth of motorists in fatal accidents were fatally injured between the hours of 5 p.m. and 8 p.m. • Distance and speed estimation for oncoming vehicles at night is almost equal to that of daytime driving in the case of standard size vehicles. However, since distance perception at night is based upon angular separation of headlights, the distance of a small foreign or compact car may be overestimated. • At 100 feet away, it is very difficult to see objects beside or beyond an approaching vehicle. Vision does not return to normal for some time after passing the vehicle. The driver actually travels effectively blind for some distance after having passed a pair of brilliant headlights. • Your visibility is affected considerably by oncoming headlights at distances even in excess of 3,000 feet. • Your high beams may blind the oncoming vehicle driver, compounding the problem of driving, especially on a wet and possibly slippery surface.

INSTRUCTOR GUIDELINES	CONTENT
	IMPROVING YOUR ABILITY TO SEE AND DRIVE DURING DARKNESS <u>Maintain the Proper Vigilance Needed to Improve Your Ability to see During Darkness</u> 1. Use the taillights of the vehicle ahead as an indication of the closing rate when driving in rural areas. 2. Watch for dark or dim objects on the roadway when driving at night. If dark objects appear, see-saw your eyes up and down, or cock your head to one side and peer out the corner of your eyes. 3. Watch beyond the headlights on and near the roadway for slow moving or unlit vehicles, curves, road obstructions or defects, pedestrians and animals. 4. Watch for pedestrians and unlit vehicles and objects on the roadway and at the curbside when driving in <u>urban</u> areas at night. 5. When approaching a pedestrian or animal at night: a. Dim the lights to low beams. b. Decelerate. c. Watch the pedestrian or animal for an indication of change in direction of movement. d. Prepare to take evasive action should the pedestrian or animal enter the roadway. 6. When approaching an animal refuge or crossing area, decelerate and watch for animals on or alongside the roadway.

INSTRUCTOR GUIDELINES	CONTENT
	Always drive more slowly than under similar circumstances during daylight. Maintain a speed that permits stopping within the distance illuminated by the headlights. ALLOW A GREATER MARGIN OF SAFETY IN PERFORMANCE OF MANEUVERS THAN DURING DAYLIGHT HOURS. If the driver of an oncoming vehicle refuses to dim his headlights: a. Decelerate. b. Maintain your headlights on low beam. c. Avoid looking directly at the vehicle's bright lights. d. Focus the eyes to the right side of the roadway, beyond the oncoming vehicle. e. Close one eye as the vehicle draws near, to save vision in that eye until the vehicle passes. f. Maintain a slower speed for a period of time after the vehicle has passed.

NIGHT DRIVING PROCEDURES

INSTRUCTOR GUIDELINES	CONTENT
Add here any legal distance as specified by your state law. If none is specified, 500 feet is the recommended distance. One night driving lesson should follow the classroom instruction. The purpose of the night lesson is to improve night driving perceptual skills and to provide the trainee with practice and instruction in handling night driving procedures and situations. During this in-bus night lesson, the trainee will perform the normal driving routines (from Core Unit E) under conditions of darkness. The night driving lesson would include exercises to improve the trainees' perceptual skills. This would involve instructing them on establishing a visual focus point, scanning, checking mirrors and instruments, using right edge of roadway as a point of reference, detecting and searching shadows for cues. Practice would also be provided for making passing and stopping distance judgments and reacting to headlight glare. Provide a handout which describes the route trainees will follow. This lesson could be given on an off-street facility. However, on-the-road practice would provide more opportunities for experiencing night time stimuli, e.g., oncoming headlights.	1. Before starting, check that all lights in the interior as well as on the exterior of the bus are in working order and that they are clean. 2. Keep headlights on low beam in cities and towns, in fog or haze, and approaching other motorists on a highway. Also put them on low beam as another vehicle passes the bus and until the vehicle is at least ____ feet in front of the bus, or until your headlights stop illuminating the back end of the vehicle that has passed. 3. Keep interior overhead lights off while driving. 4. Keep level of lights on instruments bright enough to read the instruments, but not so bright as to interfere with vision outside the bus. 5. Schedule start and return times of the trip with consideration of slower night driving time. 6. If the night driving time will require more than a one-hour stretch of driving, schedule rest stops for at least 10 minutes for each hour of driving. 7. If it is necessary to stop the bus on the shoulder of an open roadway, activate the parking lights and choose a spot which can be seen for at least 500 feet by oncoming and following traffic. NOTES:

DRIVING UNDER ADVERSE WEATHER CONDITIONS

INSTRUCTOR GUIDELINES	CONTENT
	During the course of a school year, as a bus driver you will face a variety of hazardous conditions that will demand alert and skillful action. Conditions you'll constantly face are: ice, snow, mud, and fog. A basic rule to follow is always to shift to a lower gear when it is apparent that you will encounter any of these conditions.
Discuss the proper use of sanders, if your buses have them. Drivers should drop some sand/grit <u>before</u> coming to a complete stop so that the sand/grit falls under the wheels. Then when the bus pulls out, the wheels will have better traction. They should avoid dropping too much sand as this will create a "mound" and the wheels will spin or be blocked.	A vehicle cannot be operated safely and efficiently at a high rate of speed when any of the above conditions prevail. To avoid getting stuck or spinning the wheels, try to keep the bus moving slowly and steadily forward in gear. If the wheels start to spin, let up slightly on the gas to allow the wheels to take hold. If the bus stops, do not continue to spin the wheels in hope of pulling out. In mud and soft sand, this will only serve to dig the wheels deeper. If the bus becomes stuck, first try to get it out by pointing the front wheels straight ahead, and then try "rocking" the bus by alternately putting it into reverse and into low. This can be done in a manner that the wheels do not spin, and in many cases, it will pull the bus out of a tough spot. If this fails, some material to provide friction, such as crushed rock, tree branches, pieces of timber, or burlap should be pushed down around the rear wheels to allow the bus to again get in motion.
	CONDITION OF STREETS AND HIGHWAYS
	You'll be driving over the same route twice a day all during the school year. You'll become thoroughly acquainted with the route and, after a short time,

INSTRUCTOR GUIDELINES	CONTENT
	may begin to take the road for granted. But conditions change rapidly; potholes develop overnight, the grade washes away, shoulders become soft, railroad crossing approaches change during the night or day, loose gravel appears, slick spots develop through accumulations of snow and ice or oil deposits. Each day conditions are different and you must be on the alert to detect these changes before it is too late. It is no use to say that an intersection accident happened because the road was slick. Such accidents usually happen because the driver fails to adjust his or her driving to the road condition. ADJUSTING YOUR DRIVING TO POOR ROAD CONDITIONS Rain, snow, sleet, fog, or icy pavement have never caused an accident. These conditions merely add more hazards to driving and make the normal hazards worse. Accidents are caused by drivers who do not adjust their driving to meet these conditions. Accidents blamed on skidding or bad weather conditions are classed as <u>preventable</u>. Expert drivers can drive safely on extremely slippery surfaces by reducing speed, installing chains, and using sanders when necessary. 1. Reduce speed of bus. 2. Drive well to the right hand edge of the road. 3. Watch side roads closely for entering traffic. 4. Beware of patches of wet leaves and smooth blacktop surfaces. 5. Never look directly at lights of on-coming vehicles.

INSTRUCTOR GUIDELINES	CONTENT
NOTE: Some school districts have school buses run with their headlights on at all times to increase other drivers' awareness of their presence. Provide any comments you may have that are relevant to adjusting driving practices to the condition of the road.	6. In fog, use windshield wipers and defrosters continuously. 7. In fog, haze (or rain or snow when it's overcast), drive with headlights on low beam. 8. Avoid sudden stops. Signal stops by tapping brake pedal to make the stop lights blink. NOTES:
	RAILROAD CROSSINGS--EXTRA CAUTION: WARNING DEVICES MIGHT BE AFFECTED BY WEATHER During wet, stormy, or foggy weather, before placing part of the bus on railroad tracks, you must take all extra precautions to know conclusively that the crossing can be made in safety. Any movement of warning signal or device maintained at such railroad crossings, such as ordinarily indicates the movements of trains, must be taken as an additional warning of danger. You must not accept a movement as indicating that the device is either in or out of order or not properly handled, but must always take the movement as a conclusive warning of danger. You must not cross the tracks while the warning signal is in motion until you have conclusively ascertained that, regardless of the warning signal, no train is approaching.

INSTRUCTOR GUIDELINES	CONTENT
	SNOW AND ICE*
	1. Pretrip Tasks
	a. Check that chains are securely locked with spreaders <u>on</u>.
	b. Clear lights, mirrors, and front and rear windows of precipitation.
	c. Check that door works smoothly.
	d. Place a box of sand or grit in the bus (check that sanders are full, if available).
The matter of pre-warming (e.g., keeping engines plugged into electrical circuits all night) is a matter of district or company policy.	e. "Warm up" vehicle for several minutes unless the vehicle is kept pre-warmed.
	f. Check that heater and window defroster are working.
	g. Start trip earlier than usual to compensate for slower driving time.
	2. On the Road
	a. If ice or a "wet" snow is on the ground, start up the bus in second gear for better traction.
	b. When pulling out into the roadway, allow for greater stopping time and maintain greater distance from other vehicles.
	c. Drive more slowly than is posted for dry road conditions, especially on bridges and in tunnels.
	d. When approaching intersections and stopping, pump the brakes (once or twice) so wheels do not lock on the ice.

INSTRUCTOR GUIDELINES	CONTENT
	e. To avoid a skid, disengage the clutch when the bus is almost at a standstill. f. Make turns smoothly, avoiding application of the brake. g. If a build-up of snow or ice occurs on front or rear windows, stop the bus and brush it off. 3. Posttrip Tasks a. Sweep water and snow out of bus and off steps. b. Clear excess snow from windows. RAIN 1. Pretrip Tasks a. Clear windows, lights, and mirrors of mud and other dirt. b. Check that windshield wipers are in working order. c. Start trip earlier than usual to compensate for slower driving time. 2. On the Road a. Drive more slowly than the speed posted for dry road conditions. b. Make turns slowly, avoiding use of the brake as much as possible. c. Use windshield wipers at all times. d. If rain is heavy, drive with headlights on. e. When fog occurs, drive with headlights on low beam.

INSTRUCTOR GUIDELINES	CONTENT
	3. Posttrip Tasks a. Sweep water off floor and steps of the bus. b. If mud has splashed on lights and sides of bus, clear it off.

REDUCED VISIBILITY DUE TO WEATHER

INSTRUCTOR GUIDELINES	CONTENT
Every trainee should have supervised practice in driving in adverse weather conditions. You may have to schedule in-bus practice for days when the particular conditions exist. Check PRETRIP, POSTTRIP TASKS as well as driving adjustments. Provide feedback. Many of the same adjustments required by night driving are appropriate here because the problems of reduced visibility are similar. 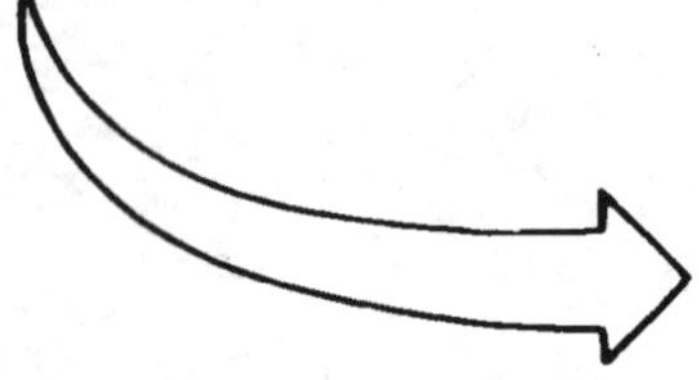	When a driver thinks of adverse weather conditions, he usually thinks of how bad the roads will be. Don't forget, rain, snow (and, of course, fog and smog) <u>also reduce visibility</u>. No matter how good your eyes are, you just can't see as well when the sun isn't shining. How should you adjust your driving under these conditions? RAIN SNOW FOG (AND SMOG) Discuss your answers with the class.

EXPRESSWAY DRIVING

INSTRUCTOR GUIDELINES	CONTENT
	Expressway driving is different from the stop-start routine you experience on city and residential roads. Expressway driving forces you to adjust your habits to high-speed travel. Experts recommend the following driving techniques which will help you take advantage of fast, convenient expressways--with safety.
Refer to Figure 1.	<u>How to Get on an Expressway</u> Slow down and look before turning into an expressway approach. 1. Survey the traffic on the main roadway when <u>entering an on-ramp</u>. a. Look briefly back over your left shoulder if entering the main roadway from the right. b. Look back over your right shoulder if you're entering the main roadway from the left 2. <u>If driving on a short entrance ramp</u>, check briefly for the main roadway approaching from the rear in selecting a gap. Specifically: a. Look briefly back over your right shoulder and look at the rearview mirror if entering the main roadway from the left. b. Look briefly back over your left shoulder and look at the side and rearview mirrors if entering the main roadway from the right.

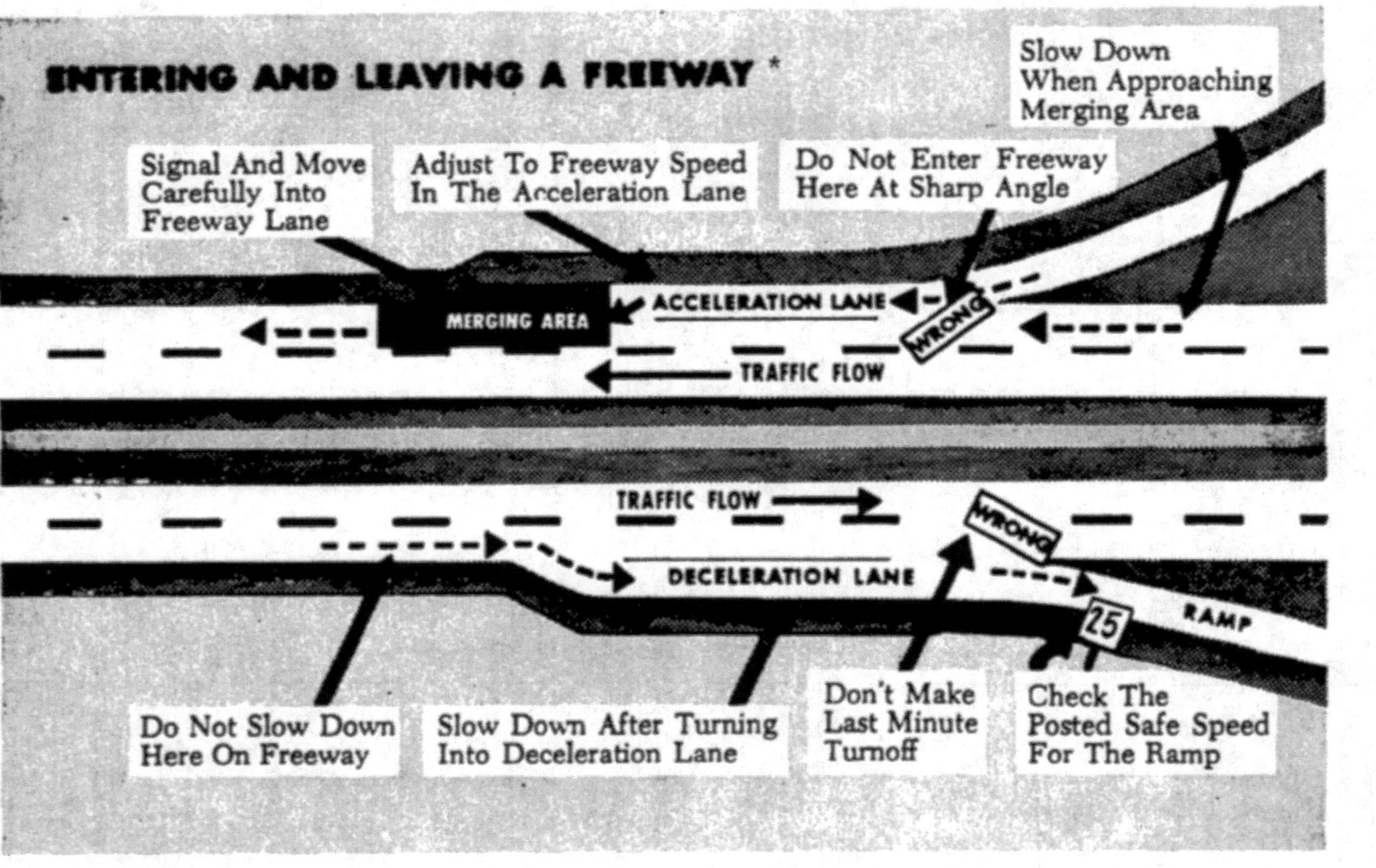

*From state of Ohio (11)

Diagram from Ontario (Canada) Department of Transport

Figure 1. Entering and Leaving a Freeway

INSTRUCTOR GUIDELINES	CONTENT
	c. Move your head from side to side in order to view the roadway through the mirrors, if necessary. d. If no gap is visible, observe the ramp ahead, periodically view the main roadway using the mirrors if possible, and stop before reaching the end of the on-ramp if it is necessary to await an acceptable gap. e. Periodically check the main roadway by quick shoulder glances or the use of mirrors, when approaching the main roadway. 3. Check the traffic on the main roadway when driving on a long entrance ramp. Specifically: a. Check the mirrors and glance briefly over your left shoulder if approaching the main roadway from the right. b. Check the rearview mirror and look briefly over your right shoulder if approaching the main roadway from the left. Wait for an opening in traffic.* Expressway drivers are traveling a lot faster than you will be at first. A car going sixty can run you down. Keep far right, preferably in an acceleration lane, while you are getting up to the average speed of traffic.

INSTRUCTOR GUIDELINES	CONTENT
	Expressways, as you know, have divided traffic streams. When you enter from a "southbound" approach you can't go north. If you make a mistake you must proceed with traffic until the next interchange. Only then can you leave the expressway and re-enter by the proper approach. NEVER attempt to cross the center strip. It's illegal--and suicidal. <u>How to Drive the "Straightway"</u> Pick your lane--and stay with it. Weaving and lane wandering are especially dangerous on a high-speed expressway. In general, keep to the right. Where slow trucks and merging traffic make this lane hazardous, move over to the next lane. Leave plenty of room between you and the car ahead. Follow no closer than one bus length for every 10 miles of speed. Signal to alert others before you pass or change lanes. Use your turn signal lights to show you are about to leave your lane. <u>How to Drive at Expressway Speeds</u> Drive smoothly at a steady speed. Give the driver behind a chance to follow or pass you safely. You're a highway hazard if you indulge in spurts of speeding and dawdling. Drive within a 25 percent range of the speed of traffic. If most cars are doing 60, you shouldn't drop below 45. If traffic is moving at 40, maintain a minimum of 30 mph. <u>Keep right</u> when you want to go slower than average.

INSTRUCTOR GUIDELINES	CONTENT
	On long drives, change your speed level every 15 to 20 minutes. Keeping the same speed dulls your reactions. A five or ten mile variation will perk you up. Watch for signs noting changes in speed limits. A 40-mile zone on a 60-mile highway signals a danger area. Drop your speed promptly and stay alert for the upcoming hazard. How to Meet a Crisis on an Expressway If you must stop, signal for a right-hand turn as you decelerate. Drive completely off the right side of the road--all four wheels and fenders. If your right wheels go off the pavement, do not brake. Stay in gear as you reduce speed to about 10 miles an hour. Look behind for a clear field. Turn left and you're back on the road again. If a car is coming at you in the wrong lane, honk your horn and blink your lights. Then take evasive action to the right. How to Get Off an Expressway Look for advance signs for your proper turn-off. Move to the correct turn-off lane. Decrease your speed. Begin signalling your intention of turning off the expressway as soon as you slow down. Read the interchange signs carefully to choose the proper turn-off lane. (If you're on a special activity trip, your pretrip plans should indicate which exits you'll take. Make sure you know these

INSTRUCTOR GUIDELINES	CONTENT
	in advance so you'll recognize the signs when you see them.)
One in-bus lesson on expressway driving should be provided. Provide a handout describing the local expressway you choose for the practice route. Include diagrams of on-ramps/off-ramps (or other entrance/exits) and other pertinent local landmarks. Have each trainee drive through the expressway practice.	Drive slowly, or stop if necessary, before you enter traffic on the cross highway. And remember--you're back in slow-driving territory, with side streets, traffic lights and pedestrians.
	Defensive Driving Tactics for Expressways
	Look ahead for signs of trouble. A knot of cars in the distance means reduce your speed now. Prepare for slow moving traffic or a complete stop.
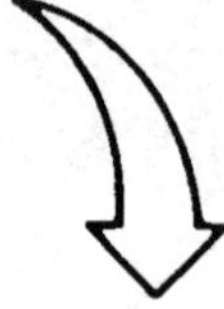	Look behind for signs of trouble. Your rearview mirror will forewarn you of a speeder, a passer, a car out of control.
	Watch the pavement for signs of trouble. A rough patch that would cause mild bumping at moderate speed can throw your bus off the road at high speed.
	Expressways at Night
	Drive at least 10 miles an hour slower than you do in daylight.
	Don't trust oncoming headlights as road guides. The traffic streams may be widely separated.
Administer Unit Review Questions. Provide feedback. For any trainees who don't meet criterion, provide additional classroom/practice sessions.	Dim your lights for oncoming cars.

PREVENTIVE MAINTENANCE OF THE BUS

TABLE OF CONTENTS

OBJECTIVES

1. Use their senses to detect symptoms of possible trouble.

2. Describe basic bus components.

3. Identify driving actions which avoid undue wear on the bus.

OVERVIEW

INSTRUCTOR GUIDELINES	CONTENT
	Preventive maintenance is the scientific care of a vehicle that will guarantee the dependability and maximum life from the various parts. It is a carefully organized system of inspections made at regular mileage and/or time intervals, combined with immediate attention to all reported defects. These inspections are made up of a series of well-balanced checking procedures combined with the process of cleaning, tightening, lubricating, and adjusting of parts and units. It is the best known, simplest, and most economical means of protecting the original investment in a fleet of motor vehicles.
Refer to Figures 1 and 2 for sample inspection forms. Substitute your own forms if more appropriate. Explain why and how forms are filled out. Provide an example form filled out.	A regular periodic inspection program is the key to a good preventive maintenance program. (For sample inspection forms refer to Figures 1 and 2.) You have a responsibility in this field, in addition to the inspection program carried out by a trained mechanic. You are on the road with the bus for a number of hours each day. You and you alone are in a position to observe its performance under all
Provide examples of symptoms they can detect through their senses. For example, <u>smelling</u> burning insulation, <u>feeling</u> a shimmy in the steering, <u>hearing</u> a knock or rattle, <u>seeing</u> a loose wire or connection, etc. Ask them for other suggestions of defects they might detect. Provide feedback.	conditions. You should learn to recognize defects and immediately report the symptoms to the maintenance department. Don't attempt to diagnose the trouble but report anything unusual that you HEAR, SEE, SMELL, and FEEL. <u>Remember, defects cannot be repaired if they are not reported</u>. 1. <u>Listening for trouble.</u> a. Sharp knock when picking up speed. b. Light knock when engine is running at idle speed. c. Dull regular knock.

SCHOOL BUS MONTHLY OR 1000 MILE INSPECTION REPORT

Bus. No. _____ Driver ______________ Inspection Date ________________

Speedometer Reading _____________

BODY		ENGINE	
1 Check all instrument panel gauges		27 Inspect motor supports: front, rear	
2. Check all lights, signals, and wiring		28 Check oil and air filters	
3 Check horn; first aid kit		29 Check muffler, manifold and exhaust line	
4 Check flares; fusees; flags; axe		30 Inspect fan belt	
5 Inspect heater and defroster equipment		31 Inspect generator and distributor	
6 Inspect fire extinguisher		32 Check battery and starter	
7 Inspect windshield wipers		33 Check cooling system	
8 Check and adjust rear view mirrors		34 Check carburetor and fuel line	
9 Check cleanliness: Interior; Exterior		35 Others	
10 Inspect windows; windshield; door glass			
11 Check seats and upholstery (seats must be tight to floor)			
12 Inspect emergency door, latches, warning signal			
13 Inspect service door, controls, steps			
14 Check stop arm			
TIRES			
15 Check for cuts, bruises, uneven wear, air pressure			
FRONT END			
16 Check spindles; wheel alignment; tie rods; drag links			
17 Check springs; clamps; shackles			
18 Check steering mechanism			
REAR AXLE			
19 Check springs; clamps; shackles			
CLUTCH			
20 Check pedal clearance & adjustment			
21 Check clutch for slipping or dragging			
TRANSMISSION			
22 Check shifting for noise			
23 Check for leaks and cracks			
BRAKES			
24 Check pedal clearance and pressure			
25 Check fluid			
26 Check emergency brake			

I certify that I have completed the inspection of this bus as indicated above.

__________ Date ____________________ Mechanic

NOTE: Place a check mark (✓) in the column when each item is completed. If an item is unsatisfactory, leave column blank until repairs are made. If there is more than one item on a line, circle the ones that are unsatisfactory. A check mark in the column will indicate that the circled items have been completed.

Figure 1. Sample School Bus Monthly or 1000 Mile Inspection Report

SCHOOL BUS ANNUAL INSPECTION SHEET

Bus Number _____ Make __________ Year Model _____ Driver ______________

Date of Inspection ______________ Speedometer Reading ______________

MOTOR

1 Inspect for oil or grease leaks and any unusual noises
2 Tighten cyclinder head bolts
3 Tighten manifolds--stop leaks
4 Inspect muffler and exhaust line
5 Inspect and adjust fan belt
6 Tighten engine block to base
7 Tighten engine support bolts
8 Tighten lower crankcase bolts
9 Adjust valves and tappets
10 Inspect ignition cables
11 Check battery:clean, tighten, refill
12 Clean and adjust distributor points
13 Inspect and adjust carburetor
14 Check and clean generator and starter
15 Oil generator and starting motor
16 Check voltage regulator, connections and charging rate
17 Clean fuel pump; air cleaner
18 Clean or replace oil filter
19 Clean and adjust spark plug gaps

COOLING SYSTEM

20 Drain and flush radiator
21 Inspect & tighten hose connections
22 Inspect water pump & cooling system
23 Tighten radiator stay rods and hold-down bolts

STEERING AND FRONT END

24 Check wheel bearings, knuckle pins bushings, spindles, steering arms, tie rod ends, drag link; align front wheels
25 Tighten steering housing to frame
26 Tighten pitman arm
27 Adjust play in steering post
28 Inspect springs for faulty leaves
29 Tighten spring clips & U-bolts
30 Tighten spring shackles & hangers

CLUTCH

31 Check pedal clearance & adjustment
32 Check clutch for slipping or dragging

TRANSMISSION

33 Check shifting and for noise
34 Check for leaks and cracks

REAR END

35 Inspect differential for leaks
36 Inspect differential pinion for play
37 Tighten differential housing bolts
38 Tighten rear axle flange bolts
39 Tighten spring clips & U-bolts
40 Tighten spring shackles & hangers

BRAKES

41 Remove wheels, inspect lining, linkage, drums, wheel bearings, hydraulic cylinders and lines
42 Inspect booster and hoses
43 Check air compressor, governor, gauge
44 Check emergency relay valve
45 Check chambers, travel & adjustment
46 Inspect emergency brake lining, ratchet and pawl

CHASSIS

47 Check all wheels for trueness
48 Tighten rim lugs, check studs
49 Tighten body bolts and clips
50 Tighten fenders, bumpers
51 Inspect universal joints and flanges; tighten all bolts
52 Check propeller shaft center bearing
53 Check & adjust radius rods

BODY

54 Inspect windshield wipers; test horn
55 Check seats and upholstery (seats must be tight to floor)
56 Inspect and adjust rearview mirrors
57 Inspect heater & defroster equipment
58 Inspect fire extinguishers
59 Inspect windshield, windows, glass
60 Inspect emergency door, latches, hinges, warning signal
61 Inspect service door, controls, rubber
62 Check stop arm
63 Check all instrument panel gauges
64 Flares, fusees, flags, first aid kit, axe (replace when necessary)
65 Check floor covering, safety shield
66 Inspect body mounting sills & bolsters
67 Tighten tank support bands
68 Check visibility of all signs and lettering
69 Check all lights, signals, wiring

TIRES

70 Check for cuts, bruises, uneven wear
71 Check tread (replace if smooth)

CHANGE OIL AND GREASE

LUBRICATE ACCORDING TO CHART

I certify that I have completed the annual inspection of this bus as indicated above.

NOTE: Place a check mark (✔) in column when each item is completed.

__________ Date ______________ Mechanic

Figure 2. Sample School Bus Annual Inspection Sheet

INSTRUCTOR GUIDELINES	CONTENT
	d. Clicking or tapping noises.
Emphasize:	e. Continuous or intermittent squeal or squeak.
<u>listening</u>	f. Loud exhaust noise.
	g. Engine backfiring, missing, popping, spitting, or overheating.
	h. Steaming or hissing.
	2. <u>Feeling for trouble</u>.
	a. Excessive vibration.
<u>feeling</u>	(1) Engine compartment
	(2) Steering wheel
	(3) Drive line
	b. Low speed or high speed shimmy.
	c. Hard steering and steering wander.
	3. <u>Looking for trouble</u>.
	a. Sudden drop in oil pressure.
<u>looking</u>	b. Low oil pressure.
	c. No oil pressure.
	NOTE: If any of the above exist, the vehicle shall not be driven until corrected.
	d. Excessive oil consumption.
	e. Smoke coming from under dash.
	f. Smoke coming from under hood.
	g. Scuffed tires or spotty wear.
	4. <u>Smelling trouble</u>.
<u>smelling</u>	a. Odor of gasoline.
	b. Odor of burning rubber.

INSTRUCTOR GUIDELINES	CONTENT
	c. Odor of burning oil. d. Odor of burning rags. e. Exhaust fumes.
Stress that anything they notice that is out of the ordinary should be reported. There is a danger of thinking that an unusual noise, etc., is nothing to worry about, especially if a driver has mechanical experience. It's better to report any unusual condition and have it be something minor, than not to report it; it could be a very costly and even dangerous defect. Stress that they don't need to know what is wrong before they report something "suspicious."	Any other unusual conditions should be reported immediately to the proper authority.

BUS COMPONENTS

INSTRUCTOR GUIDELINES	CONTENT
	You should have a basic knowledge of the school bus components to know generally how these will affect the bus' operation. There will be times when this knowledge will be useful to you in adjusting your driving performance and in detecting trouble while on the route. Proper driving habits will increase the efficiency and economy of the bus operation.
	Brief explanations of the basic bus components are provided on the next few pages.
Discuss each component briefly. Avoid long technical explanations. Complete comprehension of mechanical operation is <u>not</u> the purpose here. Provide line drawings of each part and show the flow of the process from ignition to bus motion.	Bus components included are: · Braking System · Engine · Transmission and Driveshaft · Clutch · Steering · Electrical System · Suspension
	Your instructor will discuss how each bus component works.

INSTRUCTOR GUIDELINES	CONTENT	
	BUS COMPONENT	HOW IT WORKS
	BRAKING SYSTEM · Hydraulic · Vacuum-Hydraulic · Air	Pressing on brake pedal causes fluid or air to flow into brake cylinder. Cylinder moves brake shoes outward against brake drum (inner surface of metal wheel). This pressure of shoes against drum causes wheel to slow and stop.
	ENGINE · Carburetor · Combustion Chambers · Pistons · Crankshaft	Takes fuel in gas tank, mixes it with air in carburetor. Mixture is fed into combustion chamber where it's ignited by spark plugs. The exploding mixture causes pistons to move. The motion of the pistons causes the crankshaft to turn. The rotating crankshaft connects the final power from the engine to the transmission The power is then carried to the driveshaft, the differential, the rear axles, and the rear wheels.
	TRANSMISSION AND DRIVESHAFT	A system of gears which allows you to change the ratio of number of engine revolutions to number of wheel revolutions For example, in low gear, engine might turn 100 times for one wheel turn. In a

INSTRUCTOR GUIDELINES	CONTENT	
		higher gear, the engine might turn 10 times for one wheel turn. Driveshaft connects transmission to rear wheels, making them turn.
	CLUTCH	When depressed, disconnects engine from transmission so you can change transmission gears.
	STEERING	Steering wheel and column connects to gears and linkage mechanism which changes direction of front wheels.
	ELECTRICAL SYSTEM	Supplies power for primary engine functions and auxiliary functions: <u>Primary Engine Functions</u> · Power generation and storage (battery, generator/alternator, and voltage regulator) · Power distribution (engine wiring) · Timing (distributor) · Spark generation (spark plugs and coil) <u>Auxiliary Functions</u> · Inside/outside lighting (headlights, amber/red flashing warning lights, turn

INSTRUCTOR GUIDELINES	CONTENT
	signals, instrument panel lights, etc.) · Air/heat circulation (heater, defroster, blowers) · Horn
	SUSPENSION — Springs and shock absorbers which enable driver to handle bus properly on rough terrain and sharp curves, etc.
Have trainees volunteer answers to the questions. Provide feedback. Correct answers are:	Answer these questions:
1. Transmission	1. Which bus component is made up of a system of gears?
2. Suspension	2. Which component is responsible for the way the bus handles and rides on rough terrain and sharp curves?
3. Brakes	3. Which bus component works on fluid or air pressure?
4. Clutch	4. Which component disconnects the engine from the transmission so you can change gears?
Answer any questions trainees ask. Lead discussion.	Your instructor will answer any questions you may have on how the bus works.

PREVENTING MAJOR PROBLEMS BY DETECTING EARLY SIGNS OF TROUBLE

INSTRUCTOR GUIDELINES	CONTENT
OPTION: You may want to have one of your bus mechanics on hand to answer questions. The intent here is a basic knowledge of the operations so trainees can spot troubles early. Do not lead them to believe they are being trained to be mechanics.	1. BRAKING SYSTEM--EARLY SIGNS OF TROUBLE a. Air pressure drop (air brakes only) b. Brake pedal low (hydraulic or vacuum-hydraulic brakes) c. Pedal spongy (hydraulic or vacuum-hydraulic brakes) d. Smell or see brake fluid (hydraulic or vacuum-hydraulic brakes) e. Brake drum very hot (all types) f. Bus swerves when brakes are applied (all types) 2. ENGINE--EARLY SIGNS OF TROUBLE a. Engine miss at low speed b. Engine miss at high speed c. Ping when accelerating d. Dull "clunk" at idle e. Sharp loud knocking. <u>SHUT OFF ENGINE IMMEDIATELY</u> f. Heat gauge indicates temperature rising higher than normal g. Oil pressure dropping below normal. <u>SHUT OFF ENGINE IMMEDIATELY</u> h. Engine stalls or runs sluggish on cold damp morning

INSTRUCTOR GUIDELINES	CONTENT
	3. TRANSMISSION AND DRIVESHAFT--EARLY SIGNS OF TROUBLE a. Hard shifting b. Slipping out of gear c. Clunk or jerk when power is applied or released d. Unusual sounds when power is applied 4. CLUTCH--EARLY SIGNS OF TROUBLE a. Motor revving with clutch engaged and vehicle moving and in gear b. Odor of burning clutch lining c. Gear clash d. Squealing sound when clutch pedal is depressed, with engine running e. Clutch "chattering" 5. STEERING--EARLY SIGNS OF TROUBLE a. Steering very difficult b. Wheels shimmy c. Bus veers one way or the other d. Bus wanders on roadway 6. ELECTRICAL SYSTEM--EARLY SIGNS OF TROUBLE a. Ammeter indicates a discharge. WATCH OUT FOR FIRE b. Smoke appearing around wires, switches, etc. DISCONNECT BATTERY IMMEDIATELY c. Ammeter indicates heavy charging d. Lights dim

INSTRUCTOR GUIDELINES	CONTENT
	7. SUSPENSION--EARLY SIGNS OF TROUBLE a. Bus bounces or rolls from side to side easily b. Bus out of alignment as it travels along road c. Bus "bottoms" on bumps
Describe in detail your local procedures for reporting any of these symptoms. Provide your own forms that drivers are to use. Explain how to fill them out.	NOTES:

WHAT YOU SHOULD DO TO PROLONG THE LIFE OF THE BUS

INSTRUCTOR GUIDELINES	CONTENT
Explain the reasons for "WHAT YOU SHOULD DO." Avoid long, technical explanations. For example, you might describe the wearing action on the discs when a driver "slips the clutch."	You can develop good driving habits that will avoid undue wear on each specific bus component.
OPTION: If you have access to actual worn brake shoes, clutch plates, etc., pass them around for examination by the class.	BRAKES • Do not jam brakes on hard. Apply them smoothly and steadily. • Do not depress clutch until engine stall speed is reached so engine can assist in stopping the bus. • Do not drive with your foot resting on the brake pedal. • Drain water out of air reservoir on buses equipped with air brakes. (If board policy permits.) • Pump the brakes (once or twice) on long hard stops and on hills to aid heat dissipation and reduce brake fade.
	ENGINE • Don't race engine during warm-up. • Don't over-speed engine at any time.
Explain what is meant by "lugging"--e.g., trying to go up a hill in too high a gear which causes a strain on the engine.	• Don't lug engine; this causes engine and drive-line damage.
	• Don't allow engine to operate beyond established oil change and maintenance intervals. • Don't accelerate harshly; this causes extreme stress during periods when oil pressure is low; therefore, excessive wear.

INSTRUCTOR GUIDELINES	CONTENT
	• Don't attempt to operate engine when oil pressure is low, temperature is high, or ammeter indicates a continuous discharge. • Do not add water to over-heated engine. • Use caution when removing radiator cap on a hot engine.
	TRANSMISSION AND DRIVE SHAFT . Usually you shouldn't skip gears when upshifting or downshifting. • Do not lug the engine. • Do not speed in any gear. • Do not release the clutch quickly. • Transmit power smoothly (coordination). • Shift smoothly. • Avoid fast acceleration on rough surfaces. • Avoid jerky movements of any kind.
	CLUTCH
Explain what "riding the clutch" means, e.g., keeping foot on clutch pedal and leaving pedal part way depressed when not shifting gears.	• Don't "ride" the clutch, it partially disengages the clutch causing excess heat or wear.
	• Don't upshift at low engine speed. Permit engine to speed up enough in one gear so that when the shift is made to the next gear, the engine won't lug. • Usually, you shouldn't skip gears when upshifting or downshifting; this causes undue engine lugging and shock-loading of clutch and driveline. • Don't speed.

INSTRUCTOR GUIDELINES	CONTENT
	· Usually, you shouldn't skip gears when down-shifting, this causes the clutch components to turn at very high speeds.
	· Don't coast with the clutch disengaged; the asbestos clutch disc will spin at a very high speed and may disintegrate.
Explain what is meant by "slipping the clutch," e.g., keeping the clutch partially engaged with the accelerator also partially depressed to the point where the bus can hold on the hill without the use of the brake pedal.	· Don't hold the bus on a hill by slipping the clutch. Nothing wears out a clutch faster. Adjust shifting speeds to accommodate load and terrain.
	STEERING
	· Avoid potholes--slow up! (Drive around if possible.)
	· Have mechanic inspect steering if you hit a bad bump or pothole.
	ELECTRICAL SYSTEM
	· Don't drive when ammeter indicates discharge.
	· Don't start engine when lights and/or heaters are on.
	· Don't forget to check belt tension and battery water level.
	· Don't allow heaters and lights to remain in operation when bus is not moving or engine is stopped for an extended period.
	· Make sure polarity is correct when using jumper cables (+ to +, - to -).
	SUSPENSION
	· Don't travel fast on rough roads.

INSTRUCTOR GUIDELINES	CONTENT
Administer Unit Review Questions. Provide feedback. Provide review discussion for any trainee who does not meet criterion.	• Don't cross rough areas at an excessive rate of speed. • Avoid "potholes" when possible (but don't turn out of your lane. It's better to slow down.) • Don't accelerate harshly on rough surfaces. • Check wheel alignment of bus that is on a rough road frequently.